W9-BLW-138

JAMES DEAN

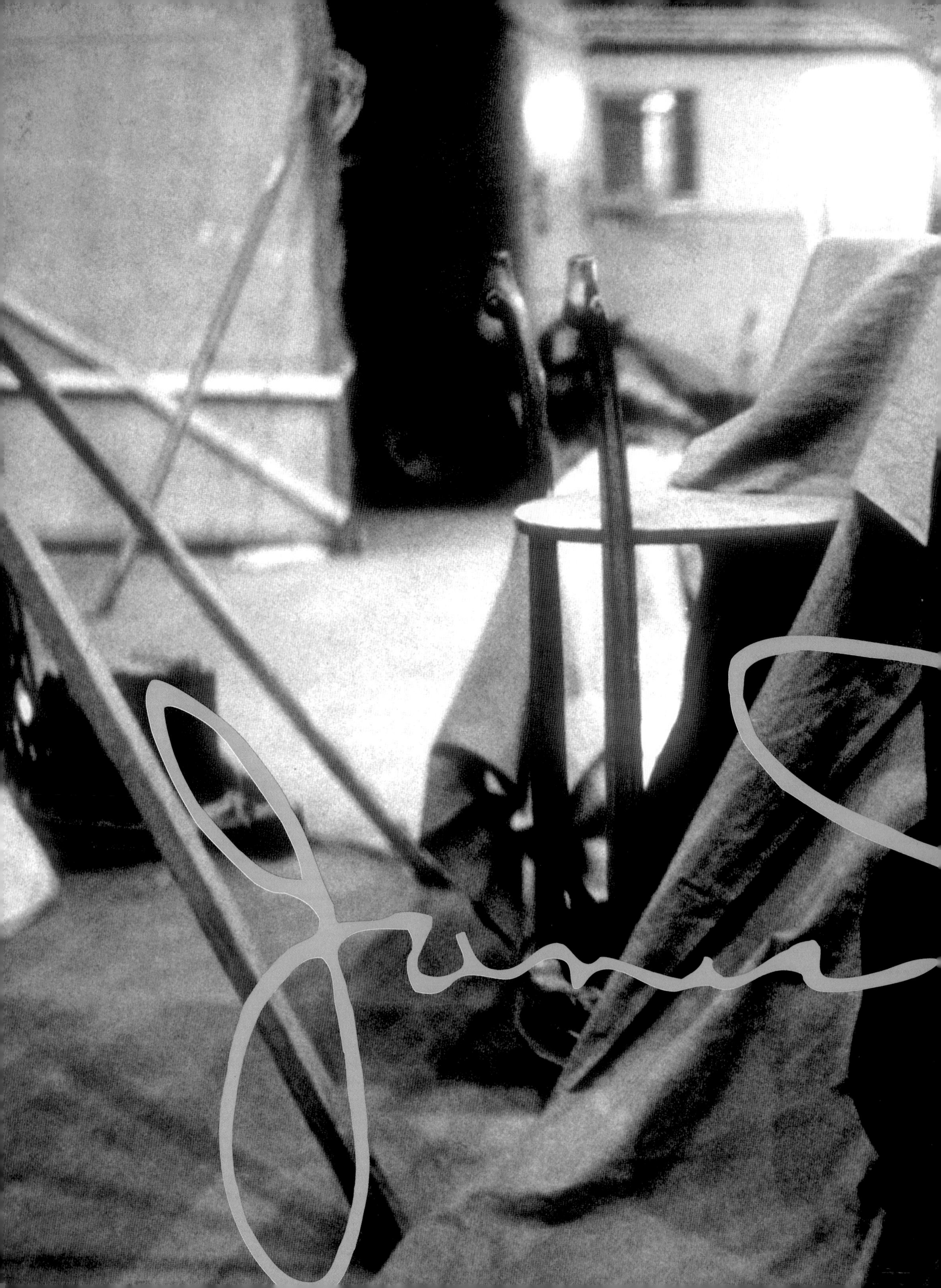

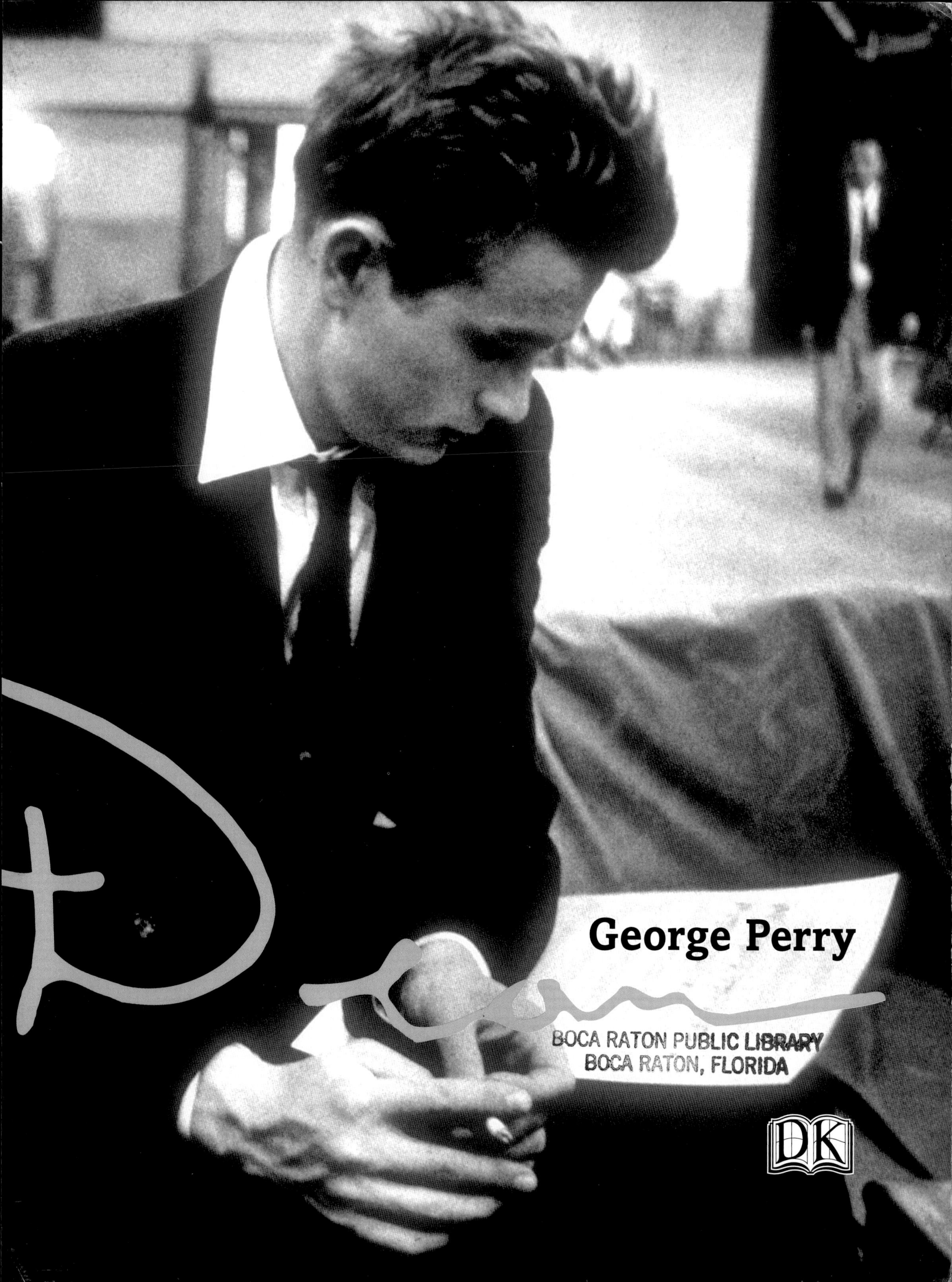

Dean
George Perry

DK

LONDON, NEW YORK, MUNICH,
MELBOURNE AND DELHI

Category Publisher Stephanie Jackson
Art Director Peter Luff
Publishing Manager Adèle Hayward

Managing Editor Julie Oughton
Managing Art Editor Heather McCarry
Senior Editor Dawn Henderson
DTP Designer Adam Walker
Production Controller Luca Frassinetti

Produced for Dorling Kindersley by
PALAZZO EDITIONS LIMITED
15 Gay Street, Bath, BA1 2PH

Managing Director Colin Webb
Art Director David Costa
Archivist David Loehr
Designers Sian Rance and Nadine Levy
Managing Editor Sonya Newland
Researcher Kip Brown

First published in the United States in 2005
by DK Publishing, Inc.
375 Hudson Street, New York, New York, 10014

First published in Great Britain in 2005
by Dorling Kindersley Limited
80 Strand, London, WC2R 0RL

A Penguin Company

2 4 6 8 10 9 7 5 3 1

A CIP catalogue record for this book is available from the British Library.
Cataloging-in-Publication data is available from the Library of Congress.

US ISBN 0 7566 0934 8
UK ISBN 1 4053 0525 8

Reproduced by Media Development Printing Ltd., UK
Printed and bound in Hong Kong by L.Rex

Discover more at
www.dk.com

Contents

Prologue 8

CHAPTER ONE: **The Early Years** 16

CHAPTER TWO: **The Apprenticeship** 54

CHAPTER THREE: **The Star** 98

CHAPTER FOUR: **The Legacy** 190

Timeline 223

Stage and Television Appearances 229

Filmographies 231

Select Bibliography 234

Index 235

Acknowledgments 239

James Dean The Legend

"James Dean was the perfect embodiment of an eternal struggle. It might be innocence struggling with experience, youth with age, or man with his image. But in every aspect his struggle was a mirror to a generation of rebels without a cause."

ANDY WARHOL

"... an intelligent young actor who seemed to live only for his work. He was completely dedicated...." RONALD REAGAN

"... there was a saying that Marlon Brando changed the way actors acted, James Dean changed the way people lived. I believe that." MARTIN SHEEN

"He was sensitive and there were elements of surprise in his personality. He wasn't volcanic or dynamic, but he had a subtle energy and an intangible injured quality." MARLON BRANDO

"He did his number, and he did it better than anyone in the world."

SAMMY DAVIS JNR.

"Had he lived long enough, I feel he would have made some incredible films. He had sensitivity and a capacity to express emotion."

GARY COOPER

"I liken it to a kind of star or comet that fell through the sky and everybody still talks about it. They say, 'Ah, remember the night when you saw that shooting star?' "

JULIE HARRIS

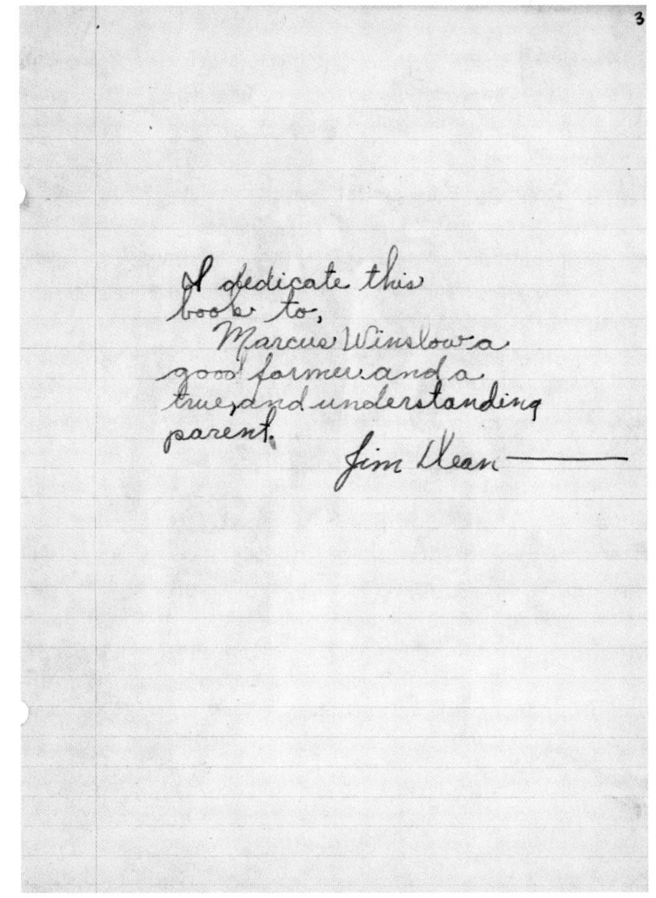

3

I dedicate this
book to,
Marcus Winslow a
good farmer and a
true and understanding
parent.
Jim Dean

▶ **DEDICATION:** In a school exercise book, Dean dedicates an essay on his chosen career to his uncle, Marcus Winslow.

130

Prologue

"Dream as if you'll live forever. Live as if you'll die today." JAMES DEAN

In the mid-1950s Patsy D'Amore's Villa Capri restaurant on North McCadden Place was a popular rendezvous for Hollywood's hot new stars, and James Dean dined there often. At the end of September 1955 he had just completed *Giant*, his third film, and was in a celebratory mood. **He had arrived at the Villa Capri in his latest high-speed acquisition – a new Porsche 550 Spyder, bought in the flush of his recent success**. Among the guests was Alec Guinness, the British actor who had just triumphed in

The Ladykillers, and was soon to star in *The Bridge on the River Kwai*. Jimmy enthusiastically showed him his tiny racer parked at the curbside. Guinness later recalled in his autobiography: **"I heard myself saying in a voice I could hardly recognize as my own 'Please, never get in it.'** I looked at my watch. 'It is now ten o'clock, Friday the 23rd of September, 1955. If you get in that car you will be found dead in it this time next week.'"

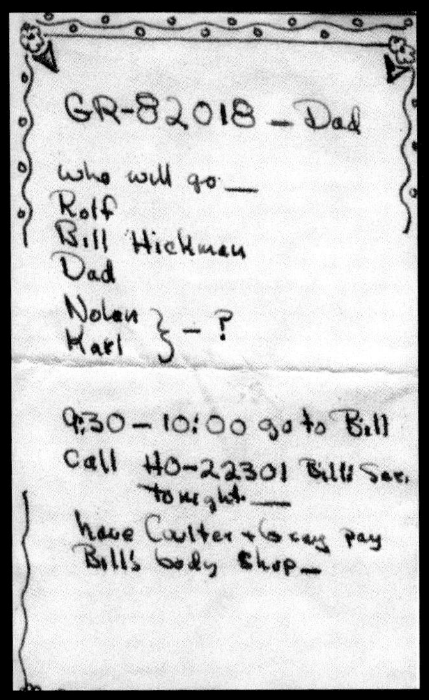

GR-82018 – Dad
who will go –
Rolf
Bill Hickman
Dad
Nolan
Karl } – ?
9:30 – 10:00 go to Bill
Call HO-22301 Bill Sat. tonight –
have Coulter + [illegible] pay
Bill's body shop –

▲ **WHO WILL GO:** A day or two before departing for Salinas, Jimmy jotted down names of those who might also go, including his father. Rolf Weutherich would accompany him in the Spyder, with Bill Hickman and the photographer Sanford Roth traveling behind.

◄ **FUEL STOP:** Jimmy stopped off at a gas station on Ventura Boulevard. His Ford station wagon and flat-bed trailer are behind the Porsche.

A week later to the day, on September 30, 24-year-old Jimmy was on his way eastward from Los Angeles to Salinas to race his silver bullet, which he called "Little Bastard." Motor racing had become for him as much of a passion as acting, and at the end of an arduous movie schedule, testing his new car and his racing skills on the track at Salinas was a liberating prospect.

He was accompanied on the 300-mile journey by Rolf Weutherich, a 28-year-old Porsche mechanic who as a teenager had flown for the wartime Luftwaffe. Weutherich was on an attachment from the company headquarters in Germany to Competition Motors at 1219 North Vine Street in Hollywood, the west-coast dealership for these high-performance cars. Following them a short distance behind, in a 1955 Ford station wagon also owned by Jimmy, were Bill Hickman, a stunt driver who had taught him much about cars, and Sanford Roth, a photographer who had been shooting a photo-essay on the star for *Colliers*, then a leading national weekly magazine.

Around 170 miles from Los Angeles, two highways met at Cholame – Highway 466 westbound from Bakersfield to Paso Robles, and Highway 41, joining from Fresno in the northeast – the routes forming the prongs of a Y fork. Today the realigned and renumbered Highway 46 is protected at this intersection by a cantilevered, flashing yellow signal indicating the need for caution, and the junction layout was changed in 1959, allowing traffic from the north to merge with the westbound flow. It is still hazardous, especially as vehicles leaving 46 have to execute a 90-degree turn across oncoming traffic, and for years there has been talk of an overpass.

Jimmy was renowned as a fast driver, and the Spyder was theoretically capable of 130mph. Already that afternoon, near Wheeler Ridge south of Bakersfield, he had been stopped by a highway patrolman, Otie V. Hunter, and ticketed for driving at over 65mph in a 55mph zone. Hunter had been unaware that he was booking a famous movie star, even when Jimmy gave his place of work as "Warner Brothers." No doubt relieved that his infringement was not going to be immediately passed on to the news wire services, Jimmy signed his citation with the last autograph he was ever to give.

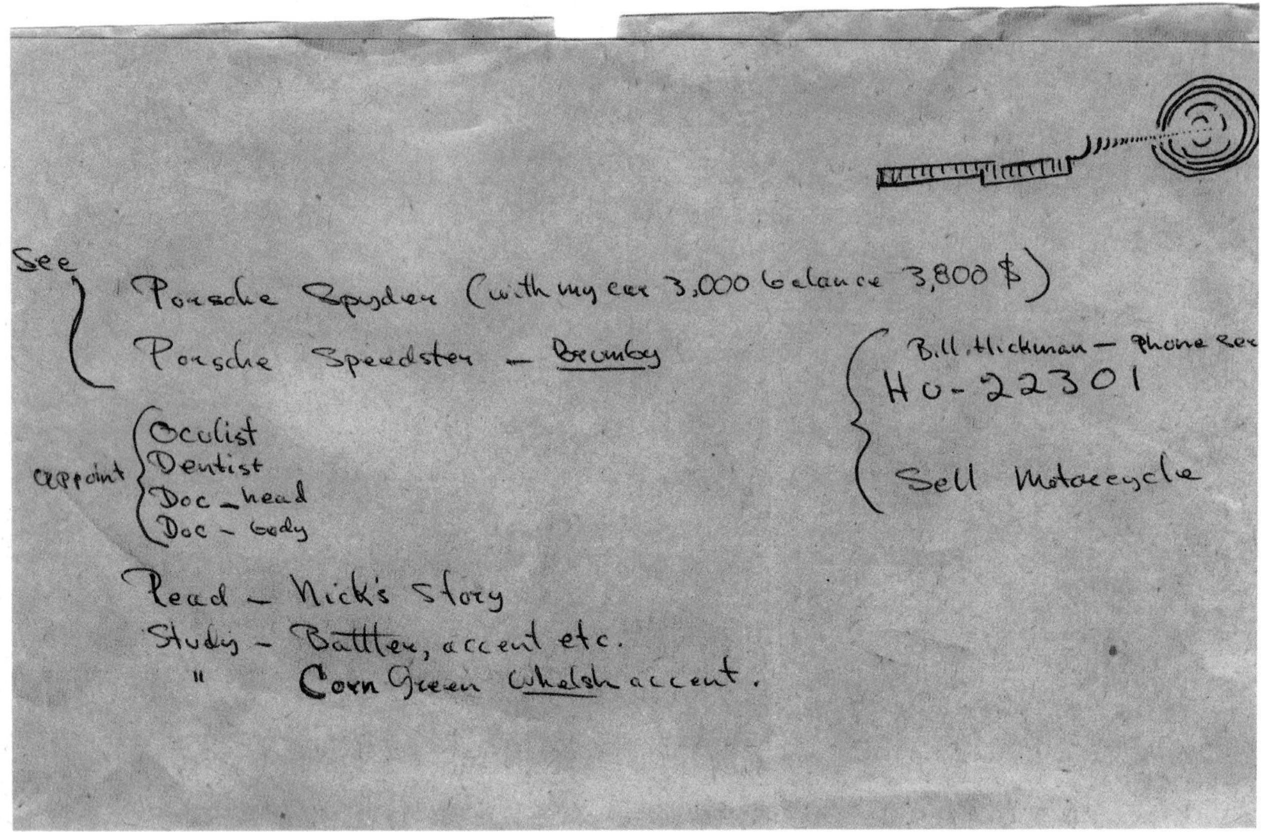

See
Porsche Spyder (with my car 3,000 balance 3,800 $)
Porsche Speedster — Bromby

appoint
Oculist
Dentist
Doc – head
Doc – body

Read – Nick's story
Study – Battler, accent etc.
" Corn Green Welsh accent.

Bill Hickman – Phone rec
HO-22301
Sell Motorcycle

▲ **THINGS TO DO:** Another of Jimmy's notes refers to appointments he has to make, a script of Nicholas Ray's to read, and the TV production of *The Corn is Green.*

▼ **CITATION:** The speeding ticket issued to Jimmy, bearing his last autograph.

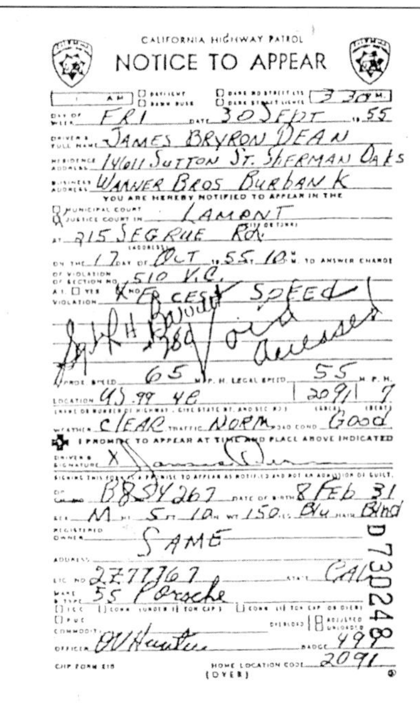

CALIFORNIA HIGHWAY PATROL
NOTICE TO APPEAR

FRI 30 SEPT 55
JAMES BRYRON DEAN
14611 SUTTON ST. SHERMAN OAKS
WARNER BROS BURBANK
YOU ARE HEREBY NOTIFIED TO APPEAR IN THE
LAMONT
215 SEGRUE RD.
17 OCT 55 10:
510 V.C.
EXCESS SPEED
65 55
CLEAR NORM. Good
I PROMISE TO APPEAR AT TIME AND PLACE ABOVE INDICATED
B854267 8 FEB 31
M 5 10 150 Blu Blnd
SAME
277767 CAL
55 Porsche
2091
D730248

Late that afternoon, 27 miles east of Cholame at a fuel stop known as Blackwell's Corner, he spotted the gull-wing Mercedes 300 SL belonging to Lance Reventlow, the 21-year-old son of the Woolworth heiress Barbara Hutton. After a few minutes' discussion on the relative performance of their cars they agreed to meet for dinner at Paso Robles.

The shadows were beginning to lengthen and the sun sank lower ahead as Jimmy drove onward. For several miles the road was straight, but as it ascended the Cholame Hills it began to twist. He passed several slower cars on his way westward, and at one point misjudged his maneuver so badly that an oncoming Pontiac was forced on to the hard shoulder to avoid a head-on collision. He continued around a bend, and then down the following slope toward the point where 41 joined from the right.

Coming from the opposite direction on 466 was a 1950 Ford Tudor coupe, painted black and white in the popular 1950s two-tone style, giving it an appearance similar to a police cruiser. Donald Turnupseed, a 23-year-old ex-sailor, and a freshman at the California Polytechnic Institute, San Luis Obispo, was on his way home to Tulare for the weekend; he needed to turn on to 41, so he made his way to the center line in readiness. Jimmy was approaching in his Spyder down the hill toward him. Turnupseed accelerated to turn quickly, braked, skidded, stopped, started again, skidded.

Cholame

As a place, Cholame (pronounced "shoal-lamb") barely exists, and it is possible to pass through without even noticing it.

All that stands on the main highway is a diner, the Jack Ranch Cafe, a parking lot, a US Post Office rural collection point, and under a tree, a simple Japanese memorial to James Dean, with his name and "1931Feb8-1955Sep30pm5:59" inscribed on an aluminum beam which, from a certain angle, reflects the accident scene half a mile away. There used to be a gas station, but that has long gone.

Officially the 2000 census gave Cholame a population of 65, taking in various farms along the valley of Cholame Creek, but the highway marker claims 116, and an elevation of 1,160 feet above sea level. The only reason that the place appears on the map at all is because of the traffic junction where the road to the east divides for Fresno along Highway 41 and Bakersfield along Highway 46.

▼ **CRASH LOCALE:** In the distance, down the hill, is the intersection where Jimmy crashed and died in 1955.

His hesitance made an accident inevitable – it was impossible to interpret his intentions. The Spyder smashed into the driver's side of the solidly built Ford, and bounced across the road, ending up by a telephone pole. The Ford's interior remained intact, but a fender had been torn off, and the engine compartment was badly damaged. The flimsy aluminum skin of Jimmy's Spyder had crumpled so violently that, in an instant, it had become a tangled, shapeless mess.

Turnupseed's steering wheel had impacted his chest, his nose was streaming blood, and his left shoulder was causing him severe pain. He was able to get out of his car. Other cars stopped, and a driver took off to find the nearest phone to alert the police. Weutherich had been flung out at the moment of impact and lay badly injured on the highway. Jimmy was trapped in the remains of the Spyder, 15 feet from the pavement, his white tee-shirt soaked with blood. A woman who had nursing experience discerned a faint pulse, but noted that his neck was broken and respiration seemed to have stopped. Death appeared to have been instantaneous.

▼ **HITTING THE ROAD:** Rolf, the Porsche mechanic, and Jimmy leave Los Angeles in "Little Bastard."

► **JIMMY'S END:** Sanford Roth took the last picture of James Dean alive from the following Ford as they headed north. At Cholame his body was wheeled to the Buick ambulance past Turnupseed's battered Ford.

Almost 15 minutes after the crash an ambulance arrived, later followed by two patrol cars. Soon Hickman and Roth in the station wagon arrived at the scene of the accident. Hickman had been aware of the flashing police lights and a knot of vehicles ahead as he rounded the bend. He immediately suspected that Jimmy had crashed. He stopped and ran over to the wreck. He could see the lifeless body. Jimmy's foot was trapped by the clutch and brake pedals, and the ambulance crew had trouble cutting him free. His body was placed on a gurney and wheeled to the rear door of the big Buick ambulance. Weutherich, on another gurney, was lifted in alongside Jimmy, and the vehicle departed for Paso Robles and the War Memorial Hospital, 28 miles west of the scene.

A call was put through from the hospital to Warner Brothers' studio in Burbank. The working day had ended, and a studio policeman was the first to hear that James Dean, their most important new young star, was dead. The officer immediately alerted Henry Ginsberg, the producer of *Giant*, who, in shock, passed the word on. The news was beginning to be heard on the radio. Within hours it would be banner headlines around the world.

The death certificate – issued on October 3, the Monday after the crash – gave as cause of death a broken neck, accompanied by injuries to the jaw, arms, and internal organs. A few weeks earlier Jimmy had appeared in a short promotional film on road safety, in which the actor Gig Young interviewed him on the subject of fast driving. Asked if he had any special advice for young people, Jimmy, with a cool shrug, had replied:

"Take it easy driving. The life you save – may be mine."

The Early Years

In 1948 Roland DuBois, the new principal of Fairmount High School, asked his students to write short autobiographical essays in order to help his psychological evaluation of them. **One of them, headed "My Case Study" read:**

"I, James Byron Dean, was born February 8, 1931, Marion, Indiana. My parents, Winton Dean and Mildred Dean, formerly Mildred Wilson, and myself existed in the state of Indiana until I was six years of age. Dad's work with the government caused a change so Dad, a dental mechanic, was transferred to California. There we lived until fourth year. Mom became ill and passed out of my life at the age of nine. **I never knew the reason for Mom's death, in fact it still preys on my mind.** I had always lived such a talented life. I studied violin, played in concerts, tap danced on theatre stages but most of all I like art, to mold and create things with my hands. **I came back to Indiana to live with my uncle. I lost the dancing and violin but not the art.**

◀ **HOMECOMING:** Jimmy aged nine in front of the Winslow farmhouse, his home from 1940 to 1949. His uncle's Chevrolet is parked under the porch.

I think my life will be devoted to art and dramatics. And there are so many different fields of art it would be hard to foul up, and if I did there are so many different things to do – farm, sports, science, geology, coaching, teaching, music. I got it and I know if I better myself then there will be no match. A fellow must have confidence.

When living in California my young eyes experienced many things. It was also my luck to make three visiting trips to Indiana, going and coming a different route each time. I have been in almost every state west of Indiana. I remember all. My hobby, or what I do in my spare

"She never wanted to die and leave Jimmy." ORTENSE WINSLOW, RECALLING MILDRED DEAN

time, is motor cycle. I know a lot about them mechanically and I love to ride. I have been in a few races and I have done well. I own a small cycle myself. When I'm not doing that I'm usually engaged in athletics, the heartbeat of every American boy. As one strives to make a goal in a game there should be a goal in this crazy world for each of us. I hope I know what mine is – anyway, I'm after it.

I don't mind telling you, Mr. Dubois, this is the hardest subject to write about, considering the information one knows of himself, I ever attempted."

▲ **LOVING COUPLE:** Jimmy's mother Mildred and father Winton married in Marion in 1930.

▶ **ARRIVAL:** Jimmy was born in 1931, on February 8, although the birth certificate says it was at 2am, rather than the more civilized 9am that was given on the announcement card (inset).

▶ **LITTLE CHARMER:** An studio portrait of Jimmy (opposite) shows that even as a baby he already had the look that would eventually captivate the world.

Mr. DuBois could not have realized at the time that this document, with its confident, earnest, teenage handwriting, would be the testament of the school's most famous alumnus. It is preserved, and displayed in the Fairmount Historical Museum in rural Indiana. James Dean emerged from that American heartland to become a key iconographic figure of the 20th century – his immortality secured by early death. His background was not one of poverty and deprivation that defined those two other icons of popular culture, Marilyn Monroe and Elvis Presley. His late childhood and adolescence were spent in the secure, sheltered, and comfortable environment of a Midwestern farm.

Marion, Indiana, a small city with a population of just over 31,000, is 70 miles northeast of Indianapolis. Winton Dean, a dental technician in the local veterans' administration hospital, and Mildred Wilson, who worked in a drugstore, were married there on July 26, 1930. Marion owed its existence to the gas and oil deposits, still recognized in the quaint name of Gas City, the nearby town where Mildred was raised, the daughter of a sometime farmhand and factory worker. By then the wells had run dry and the nationwide Depression was causing other companies to put up the shutters.

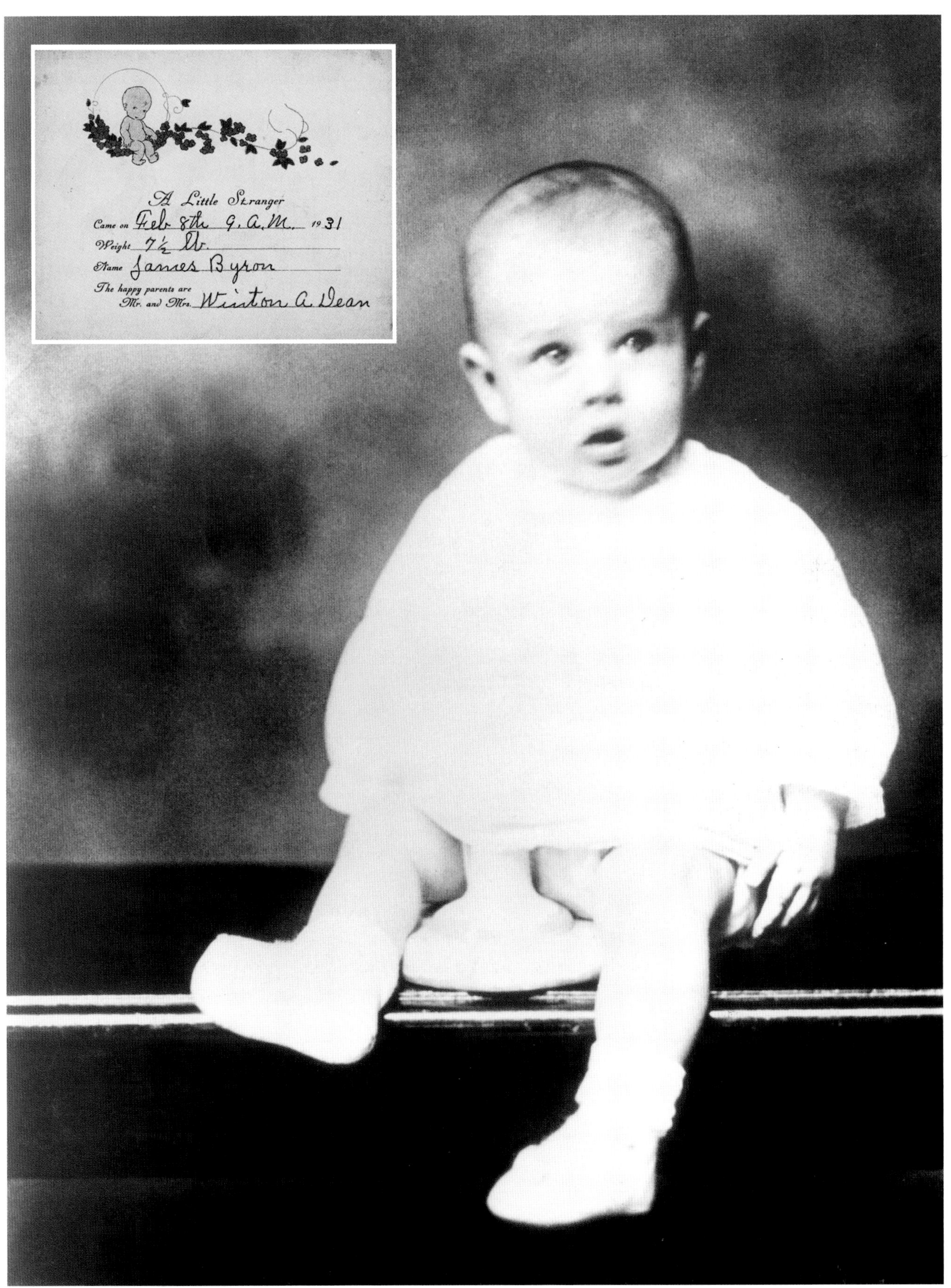

A Little Stranger
Came on Feb 8th 9. A.M. 1931
Weight 7½ lb.
Name James Byron
The happy parents are
Mr. and Mrs. Winton A. Dean

"He was a pretty boy ... fair-skinned, rosy cheeked, lips, and his mother dressed him cute." ORTENSE WINSLOW

Indiana

Indiana was admitted as the 19th state of the Union in 1816. Nearly 36,000 square miles in extent, it lies to the southeast of Chicago and Lake Michigan. Flanked by Ohio to the east and Illinois to the west, it extends south nearly 300 miles to where the Ohio River separates it from Kentucky. Indianapolis, the state capital and largest city, is roughly at its center.

Today, it is a prosperous state, its industrial prominence achieved largely following the discovery of extensive natural gas fields in the 1860s, and it was the pioneering producer of automobiles before Michigan's more relaxed labor laws led to Detroit assuming supremacy over a century ago. The Indianapolis 500, the world-famous Memorial Day motor-racing event held each May, is the last reminder of Indiana's former eminence in the automotive field. The northern part of the state, drained by the Wabash, is a rich, arable plateau, with extensive dairy farming and staple crops.

Indiana is heartland America, with a rich and varied literary heritage: Theodore Dreiser, Booth Tarkington, James Whitcomb Riley, Lew Wallace, and Kurt Vonnegut are among its writers. The countryside is peaceful, gently undulating, with woods and meadows divided by long, straight roads, and punctuated by small, sleepy towns where nothing much happens. This is the land of the "Hoosiers," the nickname for its residents. Nobody knows for certain how the name derived, but its first use dates back to the 1830s. One of dozens of explanations is that it is a dialect word for "big," thus "big man, mountaineer" describing the Kentucky mountain men, who were among the first settlers. Others suggest that it is an archaism imported from Cumberland, England, where "hoozer" meant "large" or "high," or that they were named after a contractor named Hoosier, who built the Louisville and Portland Canal. Then there is the version from James Whitcomb Riley, the whimsical, popular state poet. James Dean was a loyal reader and reciter of his local bard, often bringing him to the attention of those whose sophisticated educations had not extended so far. Riley's explanation of "Hoosier" alleged that early Indianans, a rambunctious lot, engaged in such vicious tavern affrays that noses and ears would sometimes be torn off. If an ear was found lying in the sawdust the following day, a drinker might inquire "whose ear?"

In some respects the state is like a finger of the South stretching up through the Middle West toward the Great Lakes. The reason for this is that 19th-century migrants tended to come from that direction rather than from the eastern states, gently steered by the geography that drew them toward the heartland's metropolis, Chicago, lying just across the state line in Illinois, and acting as the focal point for the highways and railroads of the plains. Before the Civil War, the invisible "underground railroad" flowed through Indiana and became the conduit to freedom in Canada for thousands of slaves, as they fled their shackles in the South. Aptly, the state motto is "The Crossroads of America." Fairmount, Indiana, childhood home of James Dean, was a station on the route and his ancestors had an honorable record in assisting its fugitive travelers.

Yet, politically conservative, Indiana is usually seen as a traditional bastion of the Republican Party. There is also a dark side, not just from 18th-century battles with the British and 19th-century massacres of the Indians, who gave the state its name. Indiana, in spite of its placid rural appearance has been a hotbed of crime. In the 19th century there were some infamous cases of bloody serial killing. John Dillinger, the notorious Public Enemy No. 1 gunned down by the FBI after seeing *Manhattan Melodrama* at the Biograph Theater on Lincoln Avenue, Chicago in 1934, was a native of Indiana. There was also the Brady Gang, which terrorized eastern America all the way from Indianapolis to Bangor, Maine, where its members were finished off in 1937 by J. Edgar Hoover's G-men.

Violence was a feature of life in the interwar years. When the Ku Klux Klan had its revival in the 1920s, its northern bastion was Indiana, where attitudes were every bit as oppressive as they might have been in Alabama or Mississippi. Lynching was commonplace, and black males were regularly taken off and killed, often for only mildly insulting behavior, especially if this was directed toward white women. There is a famous image of a double lynching, with two broken-necked black bodies hanging from branches of the same tree, the camera's flashlight revealing an excited crowd of whites of both sexes. The gruesome scene was photographed not in the Deep South, but in Marion, Indiana in 1930, after some hotheads in a mob of 10,000 had sledge-hammered their way into the county jail and carried off their victims, who were being held for the alleged rape of a white girl.

That sinister picture was taken in the same year and place in which James Dean's parents married, and where, the following year, he was born.

▲ **HOOSIER STATE:** Landmarks of Indianapolis, the state capitol building and Lake Michigan, are on this early postcard.

▲ **BABY JIMMY:** The infant on his father's knee, as a youngster on the running board of a 1933 Chevrolet with his father, and with his mother Mildred in his first year.

When Mildred's widowed father decided to remarry, the 19-year-old girl felt that it was time to leave home and go to live in Marion where, a month later, in April 1930, she met Winton – then just 23 – as she sat on a park bench by the Mississinewa River. The Deans were an old-established family who claimed a lineage extending back to the Mayflower Pilgrims, and who had settled in that part of Indiana after migrating from Lexington, Kentucky in 1815.

Although considered handsome, with blond hair and blue eyes, Winton Dean was known to be taciturn and modest. That someone so relatively unassuming could have turned the head of an attractive and outgoing girl is surprising, but, as a newcomer to the town,

> "Jimmy was a cute little boy." ORTENSE WINSLOW

she may have felt lonely and vulnerable. Winton, secure in what was, in Depression America, a sound job, may well have seemed like a rock to which she could anchor and feel safe. Soon after that first meeting they were married, and Mildred was pregnant.

They had a difference of faith. Mildred had been raised a Methodist (possibly a conversion because James Dean later claimed that her family was part Indian) and Winton was a Quaker. It was a Methodist minister, the Reverend Zeno Doan, who performed the marriage ceremony, in the afternoon of the same day in which the couple had obtained their license. As the pregnancy advanced, they took a room at the Seven Gables apartment house, 320 East 4th Street where, according to the birth certificate, at 2am on February 8, 1931, a son was born. He was named James, after Dr. James Amick, a colleague at the veterans' hospital, and Byron, supposedly after another friend, Byron Feist. In later years, James Byron Dean said that his mother had really been thinking of the English romantic poet Lord Byron. The baby weighed 8lb 10oz, and the doctor exacted a delivery fee of $15.

The city authorities allowed the old, rambling building on the corner of 4th and McClure Streets to be torn down in the 1970s, and later regretted it. The only commemorative indications for visiting Dean fans are a plaque, and a star set in the sidewalk marking the site of his birth and bearing the words: "James Dean, Movie Actor. 1931–1955. A Legend in His Lifetime."

Within a year the young family had moved from Seven Gables, and went on to live in a number of houses and apartments in Jonesboro and Fairmount, the town ten miles south of Marion that was the place of Winton's origin and where his family had first settled. The extrovert Mildred would sing, play phonograph records, and read stories to her appreciative, somewhat sickly child, who would respond by acting out the parts with enthusiasm. Winton preferred his son to be outdoors, learning to catch a ball like a regular American boy. That he lacked aptitude for catching sounded alarm bells, and he was taken to the medical center for an eye check. He was found to be so nearsighted that he would have to wear eyeglasses full-time.

In infancy a pattern emerged. Little Jimmie (as his diminutive was usually spelled by the family, although the world would later favor "Jimmy") was very close to his mother, who freely gave him her time and devotion. His working father knew him far less well, and in common with most men thought he could mold the boy to match his expectations. At the age of three Jimmy was signed up by his mother for tap lessons at the Marion College of Dance and Theatrical Arts, and soon impressed the instructors with his quickness of step.

As a child, Jimmy's health was far from robust. Apart from myopia, he suffered from inexplicable rashes, vomiting, diarrhea, nosebleeds, and listlessness. He was also diagnosed as seriously anemic. The cause of these maladies is unknown, but Mildred's decorating of every new apartment with paint containing toxins may have been a contributing factor.

Jimmy's health improved when he and his parents went to live in a cottage abutting Back Creek, on the Winslow farm along the Jonesboro road, two miles north of Fairmount. Winton's sister Ortense, who was seven years older than him, had married Marcus Winslow in 1924 and had turned the farmhouse into an attractive family home. Marcus grew oats, corn, soyabeans, and wheat in the rich, black soil, and tended the herds of dairy cattle that grazed on the 180 acres of farmland. Six-year-old Joan, their daughter,

▼ **BOUNCING BABY:** Jimmy is dandled on the knee of his grandmother, Emma Dean, with his cousin Joan flanking them.

Santa Monica

Santa Monica, a separate municipality from Los Angeles, is an attractive, bustling ocean-side resort city, facing Santa Monica Bay and its renowned sunsets.

To the north, just beyond the point at Pacific Palisades where Sunset Boulevard ends its lengthy, twisting 27-mile journey from near the Union Station in downtown Los Angeles, are the Santa Monica Mountains, which separate the main part of the Californian megalopolis from the San Fernando Valley, the scene of a massive population explosion after World War II.

As they swoop down to the ocean by the desirable beach village of Malibu, the mountains frame the vista enjoyed from Santa Monica's palm-lined Ocean Drive, a handsome thoroughfare along the cliff top, with luxurious hotels and apartments on the landside, and the grassy strip of Palisades Park on the other. The park's tree-shaded walkway is popular with joggers and walkers because of its magnificent views of the Pacific, the inbound breezes mitigating any discomfort from the hot summer sun.

As the wedge between the ocean, Hollywood, and Beverly Hills, Santa Monica has always been popular with movie people. Mack Sennett made much use of the precipitous cliffs in his *Keystone Kops* silent comedies, and at shore level William Randolph Hearst built the world's most sumptuous beach house for Marion Davies, his star protégée and mistress.

The more popular attractions include the Santa Monica Pier, with its Ferris wheel, roller coaster, and carousel, and the miles of sandy beaches. At weekends in the 1930s, when Santa Monica was within easy reach of Los Angeles by way of the big red trolley cars of the Pacific Electric Railroad, the beach around the pier would be crowded with families, bathers, and sun worshipers enjoying their day by the ocean.

The South Beach boardwalk was punctuated by ice-cream, hot-dog, candy, and salt-water taffy stands, as well as other stalls selling beach balls, mattresses, water wings, and swimming rings. On the sand the bronzed, toned torsos of gymnasts somersaulted from vaulting horses, swung and spun from dangling ropes, and formed human pyramids in a special area reserved for their acrobatics, designated in the 1930s as "Muscle Beach." Today it has relocated southward, to Venice.

▲ **BEACH BOY:** Santa Monica in the 1930s was the ocean playground for the city dwellers of nearby Los Angeles, and big beach hotels entertained vacationers. For Jimmy the safe, sandy beaches were a wonderful new playground.

who was already a competitor in dance classes, was a lively new playmate for Jimmy.

Jimmy was only five when the first big upheaval of his life took place. Answering a call from the government for dental technicians needed in California, Winton had decided to accept a posting at the West Los Angeles Veterans' Administration Center in Westwood, often known to its residents as the Sawtelle "Old Soldiers Home," the name bestowed when it first opened in 1888 for disabled Civil War veterans. Mildred immediately embraced the move as an opportunity to escape her restricted background. Until then she had never been out of the state, and here was a chance to live by the Pacific Ocean in the agreeable, balmy climate of southern California. She was also sure that the sunshine would be of great benefit to Jimmy, and no doubt felt that her whole life would undergo revitalization with the adjustment to a new and exciting environment.

After Fairmount, southern California must have seemed a place of wonder and delight to the Dean family. The first home in Santa Monica was at 1215-A 26th Street, but later the family moved into a rented stucco bungalow at 1422 23rd Street. It had two bedrooms, a parlor, a backyard, and a palm tree on the front lawn. Jimmy first attended the Brentwood School, but transferred shortly afterward to the McKinley Elementary School, progressing there from grades one through three. Meanwhile Mildred continued to encourage his tap dancing and arranged violin lessons for him. Her constant protective presence helped to shield him from the taunts of other children, who thought his Indiana accent and manner unusual.

▲ **CHILDHOOD IN CALIFORNIA:** Young Jimmy poses in the overalls that were the typical outfit for youngsters in the 1930s.

"He had a lot of pep. And he was always just doing things." ORTENSE WINSLOW

The new life did not last long. In 1938 Mildred unexpectedly became ill with acute stomach pains. She began to lose weight at an alarming rate, and X-rays revealed uterine cancer, a condition that was rarely mentioned in those days. She spent the last few months of her life fading away. Her bewildered son was not told that her illness was terminal; he was only aware that his mother was no longer her usual self, but had become a wasted, bedridden invalid. As Mildred's condition worsened, Emma Dean, Jimmy's grandmother, known in the family as Grandma Dean, was summoned from Fairmount. Two days before Mildred's death on July 14, Winton finally told Jimmy that the time left was short. The boy said little. "He never liked to talk about his hurts," said his father many years later.

▲ **SNAPPY DRESSER:** Mildred liked her son to look neat and tidy, even to the point of wearing an adult-style fedora.

▲ **WITH HIS GRANDMOTHER:** Returned to Indiana, Jimmy faces a commercial portrait photographer with his grandmother, Emma Dean, who brought him back from California after his mother Mildred's death.

Jimmy and his grandmother were at the hospital the day Jimmy was told. The following morning Mildred was allowed to go home, but in the early afternoon of the next day she died. She was only 29.

Winton had already sold his car to meet the medical bills and was having to move into cheaper accommodation. He could not even afford to travel to his wife's funeral in Marion. With Grandma Dean's encouragement, he made the brave decision that, for the sake of Jimmy's future, his nine-year-old son should go back to Indiana, where Ortense and her husband Marcus were fully prepared to raise him as their own, with their daughter Joan becoming his surrogate big sister. Winton reasoned that it would be a far more satisfactory environment for a bereaved child, where he could be with his family who loved him. So Jimmy made the long journey in the company of his grandmother, with his mother's coffin in a box car on the same train. That Winton did not scrape together or borrow the train fare to make the journey himself has often been unjustly cited as an example of his indifference toward his son.

Marcus Winslow Jr., Dean's cousin who, as "little Markie," was more like his kid brother, has always been dismayed by the perception of Winton as a callous, unfeeling man. "Jimmy's dad really didn't want to give him up, but he realized that, at least for the time being, that was going to be the best thing for him. The problem was that he had sold his car and done everything he could to raise money for doctor bills and he was pretty much out there by himself, so he decided, at least for the time being, it would be best to have Jimmy come back here and live until he could get things straightened out and get on his feet. Of course, in 1941, America got involved in World War II and Winton was drafted,

Jimmy's Sad Return

▲ **CONSOLING GRANDPARENTS:** Nine-year-old Jimmy, with Charles and Emma Dean soon after his return.

The train, *The Challenger*, made the 2,000-mile journey from California to Indiana. Legend has it that whenever it stopped at stations en route Jimmy would run along to the box car and make sure that his mother's coffin was still aboard.

As the destination approached, a kindly conductor presented him with a cup and saucer bearing the train's logo as a memento of the journey.

Awaiting them at the railroad station in Marion were the Winslows, as well as other relations and close family friends, gathered en masse to greet the new member of the household.

A few days later, Mildred Dean was buried at the Grant Memorial Park Cemetery. Jimmy's loss was profound, and in many respects defined the rest of his life. Mildred had been his mentor, his motivator, his confidante, his closest friend, and had tragically left him at a crucial point in his development.

▲ **BACK IN INDIANA:** At the Marion train station Jimmy and his grandmother are photographed after their long journey. Inset is the cup and saucer that the conductor gave Jimmy as a souvenir.

▲ **CARING FAMILY:** Jimmy with cousin Joan and uncle and aunt Marcus and Ortense.

and he was in the service until 1945 or 1946. So something would have had to have been done. Uncle Winton said he never ever really thought when he lost his wife he would also lose his son."

As he grew older, Jimmy's pain at losing his mother was compounded by the immense geographical gulf between father and son. Winton believed that Ortense and Marcus's task would be made easier if he receded into the background, and silently and privately bore the pain of losing his son, knowing that he would be safe and cared for in a good, loving home. Jimmy was not outwardly demonstrative in his grief, but instead retreated into himself, putting on a brave face to the world as he set about adjusting to a new home and very different circumstances.

The Winslow farmhouse, a solid 14-room, white-painted structure with a generously proportioned porch, stands on the Jonesboro road, known locally as "the Sand Pike," on a gently sloping rise overlooking the placid green meadows abutting Back Creek. The handsome farmstead was built in 1904 for Ansel and Ida Winslow. Their family, like the Deans, had a long-term presence in Fairmount. Walker Winslow had run the stagecoach concession in the pre-railroad years of the 19th century. Another Winslow, Levi, had owned and operated a local boarding house. The earliest Back Creek Friends' meetings had been held in Joseph Winslow's cabin in 1829. Fairmount history reveals that he was one of the initial settlers, having moved up from North Carolina to get away from living in a state that supported slavery. In 1831 he helped to build a log meeting house on his land, the first of several Quaker establishments in the county. The present church, a short walk away from the Winslow farm, was built in 1899. The Winslows had weathered the Depression, holding on to their 180-acre farm when many others had failed; by 1940 a feeling that the corner had been fully turned was in the air and the acreage was beginning to hum with activity. Jimmy's foster parents were good, decent people, and lavished love and care on the boy, indulging him when he was sad, humoring him when he was ill-tempered. No matter how provocative his behavior, he was never spanked. They even yielded their bedroom furniture to him because he liked the texture of the maplewood. Young Jimmy soon grew used to the habits of farm life: the early rising and the myriad new tasks such as sweeping the barn, feeding the chickens, collecting the eggs, milking, planting, and reaping. He was not a natural farm boy, having spent his recent childhood by the Pacific Ocean in Santa Monica, but he was soon absorbed by the new environment. The anemia from which he had suffered rapidly disappeared as he took on new activities.

"Everybody just bent over backward for him."

ORTENSE WINSLOW

▲ **JIMMY'S CHILDHOOD HOME:** The Winslow farmhouse still looks much as it did in Marcus and Ortense's time.

► **INDUCTED:** Winton in army uniform visits Jimmy in wartime. His son is both proud of his father's service and glad to be with him.

Joan, then aged 14, remembers the time vividly and recalls how Jimmy was quickly brought into the family fold. She was happy to let him learn to ride her bicycle around the farmyard and she soon noted his approach to new interests. "He was always taking things up and getting completely absorbed for a while," she recalls, "and then he

▲ **TALL IN THE SADDLE:** The Winslow farm gave Jimmy plenty of opportunities to get to know animals, and ride a favorite pony.

would suddenly drop whatever it was and move on to something else." It was a recurring pattern throughout his life.

On December 7, 1941, the day President Roosevelt called a "date that will live in infamy," the United States entered World War II. The following year, news came from California that Winton had been drafted, and had gone to serve in the Army Medical Corps. By now Ortense and Marcus were "Mom and Mark." Jimmy was 12 when their son Marcus Jr. was born in 1943, and shortly afterward Joan married Myron Peacock, a farmer, and moved to the east of Fairmount. The arrival of the baby made no difference to the love Marcus and Ortense lavished on Jimmy. Ortense was a stalwart of the Women's Christian Temperance Union, an organization that supported basic Christian beliefs and strict prohibition of alcohol, and this, combined with Marcus's devout adherence to Quakerism, meant that Jimmy was raised in a home in which traditional values were revered.

The Winslow farm offered countless opportunities for adventures. A tree in the yard provided the perfect site for a swing, and Marcus installed it for him. Jimmy fished for carp in the creek and rode a pony in the fields. He had a friend in his cousin Markie's little dog Tuck, who followed him everywhere except to school. A basketball net on the barn was also a big attraction. The pond was a great place for summer swimming, and in the winter there was ice skating, one of the occasions when other children in the neighborhood would come over and share the fun. Marcus slung light bulbs on a wire over the ice so that the boys could play hockey even after darkness had fallen. Indiana winters can be severe and the creek and ponds would often freeze solid.

Violin lessons and tap dancing gave way to healthy outdoor activities. The gift of a new bicycle sharpened Jimmy's interest in things mechanical and he reveled in undoing all its nuts, dismantling, and then reconstructing it. As he grew older, Marcus taught Jimmy to drive a tractor, years before he could have a driver's license to take a car on the road. But innocent childhood pleasures occasionally had their dangers. Keen to emulate a circus aerialist, Jimmy had persuaded Marcus to create a trapeze for him in the barn, accessed by a rope to be climbed hand-over-hand. He fell off, knocking out his front teeth. He had to be fitted with a dental bridge. Thereafter, one of Jimmy's running jokes through to adulthood was to remove the bridge simply to upset people, who might suddenly find his teeth at the bottom of their drinking glasses.

Initially, Jimmy went into the fourth grade at West Ward Elementary School, in the former Fairmount Academy building. He was an unsure new boy. One teacher, India Nose, recalled how he would often seem far away, wrapped in a world of his own. She discovered the reason one day when he burst into tears before the whole class and declared: "I miss my mother." The children, who had been poking fun at him, backed off after that, recognizing that his grief was a private matter.

Both the school and the church offered opportunities for Jimmy to use his talents for mimicry. In the age of radio he often listened to

Fairmount

Fairmount is a small farm town in Grant County, and is little more than a crossroads on the straight stretch of the Indiana highway 26, running east from Lafayette.

The little main street in Fairmount happily lacks McDonald's, Burger King, Taco Bell, and all the other emblems of a homogenized America, and the town diner wears an air of timelessness, with its unpretentious decor, welcoming service, and tasty daily specials. The maple-shaded Main Street, running north, lined with comfortable Victorian houses, looks magnificent in the fall, as the leaves burst into an array of blazing colors. Inevitably, the work of the artist Norman Rockwell springs to mind. This is a surviving fragment of the Americana he celebrated in his covers for *The Saturday Evening Post.*

Fairmount is on a byway off route 9 to Marion, ten miles north, which is where the shopping malls, highway hotels, fast-food outlets, and gas stations can be found, rendering it indistinguishable from everywhere else. A short distance to the east of Fairmount the federal superhighway I-69 passes, connecting Indianapolis to Fort Wayne. The Fairmount exit is numbered 55, in accordance with the custom of designating them after their mileage along the freeway – a coincidence in that '55 happens to be the year of James Dean's death.

In the 1940s the center of the town – the intersection of Main and Washington, then controlled by a traffic light mounted on a yellow pole, which is now preserved outside the Fairmount Historical Museum – may have been livelier than today. The southeast corner was occupied by a long-vanished Rexall drugstore, then an institution throughout America, with its chrome-heavy soda fountain acting as a social focus for the young population. Officially, Fairmount has over 3,000 inhabitants, but it is normally so quiet and traffic-free that it is hard to imagine where they all can be. As though in recognition of its quintessential American character, the first name given by the US Post Office was A1, which was actually based on its map coordinates. Other pioneer designations included Kingston and Pucker. In 1850 it received its present name, after a park in Philadelphia.

Remarkably, for such a small a place in a vast country, James Dean is not its only world-famous local boy. Jim Davis, the creator of the *Garfield* comic strip, was born in 1945 and raised on a farm close by. Fairmount also lays a claim to having thought of the hamburger many years before it was supposed to have made its official debut in 1904 at the St. Louis World's Fair, although quite a few small towns in other states also have a case. A similar claim is made by Fairmount in respect of another St. Louis innovation, the ice-cream cone. Fairmount remembers James Dean on its welcome sign with the slogan "Where cool was born."

▼ **HOMETOWN USA:** Fairmount bustled in the 1940s, as this postwar view of Main Street shows.

▲ **SCHOOL GROUP:** Jimmy (third from right, front row) soon integrated with other kids his age. His slender build did not deter him from physical activity.

plays and entertainment shows starring great comedians such as Jack Benny and Bob Hope, and he loved to imitate the voices he heard. The family declared that this talent was inherited from Grandma Dean, who had dabbled in amateur theatricals, and also from his mother, who had been an excellent mimic. He saw the plays that were put on by students at Fairmount High, where the drama coach Adeline Nall (who became Adeline Brookshire when she remarried in 1943) was a renowned teacher. She would later be a key figure in the recognition and development of Jimmy's acting skill. She had arrived at the school in 1940, and had quickly instituted a drama program that included the staging of plays during the year. The elementary-school children were allowed to attend the dress rehearsals, although they were expected to pay a dime each for the privilege.

> "There was a genius quality about that boy."
>
> ADELINE BROOKSHIRE

▲ **INSPIRING TEACHER:** Adeline Brookshire quickly recognized Jimmy's gift, and did all she could to nurture and encourage it.

► **TESTIMONY:** Jimmy chooses a career in farming – perhaps trying to please his teachers.

Jimmy's earliest experiences of acting in public, outside the family and school, came about through Ortense's involvement with the Women's Christian Temperance Union, which encouraged dramatic recitations on the evils of the demon drink, and the ruin that imbibers faced if they were unable to shake off the pernicious habit. Jimmy spiced up his performances so effectively that his audiences were clearly shaken.

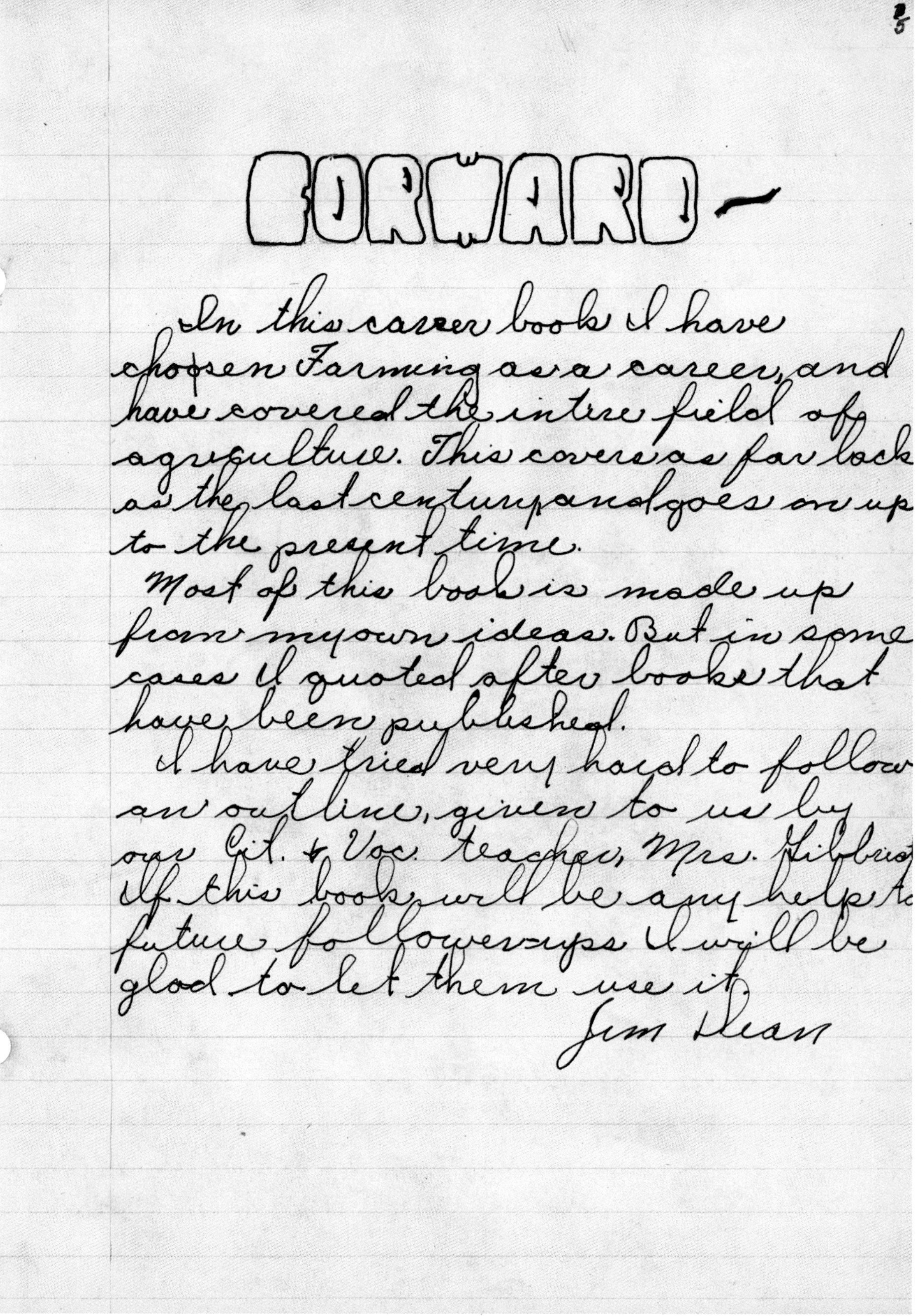

25

FORWARD —

In this career book I have choosen Farming as a career, and have covered the intire field of agruculture. This covers as far back as the last centurys and goes on up to the present time.

Most of this book is made up from my own ideas. But in some cases I quoted after books that have been published.

I have tried very hard to follow an outline, given to us by our Cit. & Voc. teacher, Mrs. Gilbrath. If this book will be any help to future followers-ups I will be glad to let them use it.

Jim Dean

He later delivered even more heartrending monologues, winning prizes and medals. The Back Creek Friends Church also staged plays, which were rudimentary and amateurish in nature, but which gave opportunities for his talents. In a Christmas piece he played a blind boy who regained his sight, an event conveyed by his recognition of a star in the night sky. Jimmy's affecting performance was long remembered by some members of the audience.

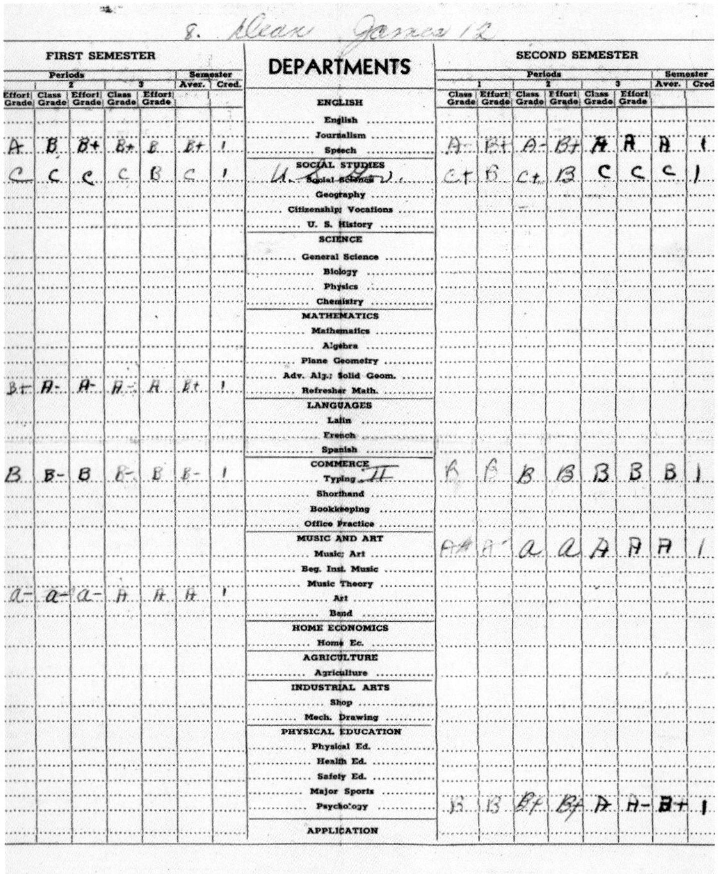

8. Dean James 12

FIRST SEMESTER Periods 1 Effort Grade	2 Class Grade	2 Effort Grade	3 Class Grade	3 Effort Grade	Semester Aver.	Semester Cred.	DEPARTMENTS	SECOND SEMESTER Periods 1 Class Grade	1 Effort Grade	2 Class Grade	2 Effort Grade	3 Class Grade	3 Effort Grade	Semester Aver.	Semester Cred.
							ENGLISH								
							English								
							Journalism								
A	B	B+	B+	B	B+	1	Speech	A-	B+	A-	B+	A	A	A	1
							SOCIAL STUDIES								
C	C	C	C	B	C	1	U. S. Gov. Social Science	C+	B	C+	B	C	C	C	1
							Geography								
							Citizenship; Vocations								
							U. S. History								
							SCIENCE								
							General Science								
							Biology								
							Physics								
							Chemistry								
							MATHEMATICS								
							Mathematics								
							Algebra								
							Plane Geometry								
							Adv. Alg.; Solid Geom.								
B+	A-	A-	A-	A	B+	1	Refresher Math.								
							LANGUAGES								
							Latin								
							French								
							Spanish								
							COMMERCE								
B	B-	B	B-	B	B-	1	Typing II	B	B	B	B	B	B	B	1
							Shorthand								
							Bookkeeping								
							Office Practice								
							MUSIC AND ART								
							Music; Art	AA	A	a	a	A	A	A	1
							Beg. Inst. Music								
							Music Theory								
a-	a-	a-	A	A	A	1	Art								
							Band								
							HOME ECONOMICS								
							Home Ec.								
							AGRICULTURE								
							Agriculture								
							INDUSTRIAL ARTS								
							Shop								
							Mech. Drawing								
							PHYSICAL EDUCATION								
							Physical Ed.								
							Health Ed.								
							Safety Ed.								
							Major Sports								
							Psychology	B	B	B+	B+	A	A-	B+	1
							APPLICATION								

▲ **REPORT CARD:** An academic assessment of Jimmy reveals him to have been an average student in most areas, with few "A"s.

Adeline Brookshire began to guide him in how to deliver his words, and he set out to win the WCTU's most coveted recitation trophy, the Pearl Medal. The material delivered for this award was a sentimental exercise in Victorian temperance propaganda called *Bars*, a title with a double meaning, in which a drunk kills a man and then regrets it in an interminable, self-pitying monologue from prison. Adeline coached him carefully, and in rehearsals she allowed him to incorporate into the performance the chair on which he would be sitting, even though the rules forbade props. The chair gave him something to work with, and he first used the inverted seat as a bar counter, then spun it around to peer through the rungs of the seat back as though they were the bars of a prison cell. His ingenuity offered the tired recitation exercise a spark of life.

The night of the performance was a strained occasion. The date and time had coincided with a junior-high track meet, giving Jimmy's conscience a jolt because the team had expected him there. Then, just as he was due to begin his presentation, the judges decreed that he could not use the chair after all, as they held that it constituted a prop. Jimmy took up center stage and everyone waited for him to begin. And waited. And waited. All he did was stand in silence, scowling at the onlookers. Eventually he was persuaded to withdraw, and the next competitor took his place. Instead of receiving an explanation from him, Adeline endured a stormy tirade as her pupil exploded in a rage, claiming that she had brought about his downfall and stolen the prize from him. His tantrum lasted for weeks. The lesson to be taken from it, she concluded, was that "You couldn't make Jimmy Dean do things he didn't want to do."

What is revealed by this incident is that, by employing the chair as the focus of his projection, long before he had heard of Stanislavsky or the Method, or even the Actors Studio, he was already unconsciously using similar techniques of acting by reacting. The committee had unwittingly deprived him of the root of his performance by denying him the prop, and his refusal to deliver may not have been merely willful, but due in part to a genuine inability to perform. His talent was instinctive rather than nurtured by tuition.

Shortly before the arrival of little Markie, Jimmy had moved into the seventh grade, which meant that he now transferred to Fairmount High School, a substantial institution that first opened its doors in 1898.

It was in his sophomore year that Adeline Brookshire became a major influence in his life. He already knew her well from his WCTU recitations,

▲ **SCHOOL PLAY:** The ensemble cast of *You Can't Take It With You* is photographed in rehearsal on the high-school stage. Jimmy is right foreground.

JUNIOR CLASS
OF
FAIRMOUNT HIGH SCHOOL
PRESENTS
"Our Hearts Were Young and Gay"

THREE ACT COMEDY
DIRECTED BY
ADELINE NALL BROOKSHIRE

High School Auditorium
Thursday and Friday, October 16 and 17

▲ **SIGNED PROGRAM:** Juniors' signatures, including Jimmy's, adorn the school play program. Jimmy played the distinguished real-life American actor Otis Skinner.

but now she had officially become his drama and speech teacher. A native of Marion, she was born in 1906, had taken a degree in English and French at Marion College, and later taught in Chicago. Drama was in her blood, but, realizing that however good she was as an amateur, her professional aspirations would come to nothing, she decided that it was better to teach the subject, and thus joined the faculty at Fairmount, where she also ran Spanish and French classes.

She noted shrewdly a number of character traits that informed Jimmy's approach to work. One was his predisposition to shock, and his satisfaction when he got a reaction, evidenced by the time he offered his teacher a cigarette in front of his classmates, an offense that, had it been committed by others, would have warranted a rapid application of the dreaded paddle, then still in use in Indiana schools and inflicted without favor on misbehaving girls as well as boys. Adeline also saw how sensitive Jimmy was to criticism, and he would engage his teacher's time to an inordinate degree discussing his involvement in a play. He was, she later reflected, one of the most manipulative students she had ever taught, with a studied charm that ensured things would go his way, often without others noticing how he had tricked them.

In the first of his school plays, a dismal one-act drama called *Mooncalf Mugford* by Brainard Duffield, he played a crazed, elderly man, and managed to engage the audience with a convincing performance. His teacher's next choice was considerably more light-hearted – *Our Hearts Were Young and Gay*. Set in the 1920s, this was the dramatized version of a popular autobiography by Cornelia Otis Skinner and Emily Kimbrough, which told the story of two well-connected but naive college girls from Indiana who set off for Europe,

▲ **MONSTER TIME:** Cleverly designing his own prosthetics, Jimmy scared the girls as Frankenstein's monster in the school's Halloween spoof.

pursued by Harvard boys, and their engagement in screwball adventures. Jimmy (or Jim as he liked to be known at school) played Otis Skinner, a distinguished stage actor and the father of one of the girls, and he took to the heavy makeup and the histrionic delivery of his lines with such relish that he stole the show. In *The Monkey's Paw*, a melodramatic supernatural thriller adapted by Louis N. Parker from the 1904 short story by the English writer W.W. Jacobs, he played a young man who meets a nasty end in an industrial accident.

When Halloween 1948 came, the students mounted a lighthearted fundraising revue, *Goon with the Wind*. Indulging in his newfound interest in extreme caricature, Jimmy once again stole the show, first as a mustachioed, caped villain, and then, at the climactic moment, as Frankenstein's

"He was nobody's tragic hero." ADELINE BROOKSHIRE

monster in a hideous makeshift prosthetic mask based on Boris Karloff's definitive portrayal on screen. He had spent hours perfecting his costume and makeup, and the fact that the girls cringed in terror as he stomped around the stage gave him a considerable thrill. Getting dramatic reactions from females was one of his lifelong pleasures.

A disappointment followed. The school drama production in spring 1949 was the famous George S. Kaufman & Moss Hart comedy *You Can't Take It With You*, and Adeline Brookshire felt that Jimmy's commitments were too heavy for him to take on a leading role as

Grandpa Vanderhof. Instead she assigned him the relatively small part of the mad Russian ballet master Kolenkhov. Bearded, and speaking in a thick, barely comprehensible accent, he leapt and bounced around the stage with unbridled energy, even managing a spirited burst of Russian-style dancing. His teacher knew that no one else could put so much into the relatively short performance.

Jimmy had also tried debating, and as a senior he became a member of the school team. Along with another student, Barbara Leach, a transplanted New Yorker, he was chosen to represent the school in a debate against Marion High School, which was aired on the Sunday night "Voice of Youth" program on WBAT, a Marion radio station. The motion that they proposed and seconded was "The United States President should be elected by a direct vote of the people." So well did they argue the proposition that they carried the day, but were disappointed when the moderator declared it a draw because the standard of argument was so high on both sides. They suspected that the Marion team did not want the stigma of being defeated by opponents from a little place like Fairmount, and had secured the cooperation of the radio station, but they were mollified a few months later when they received the award for their feat and found that it had been inscribed "winner."

▲ **SCHOOL FRIENDS:** Jimmy (right) with high-school friends. His interest in girls was completely normal. "He wasn't reckless," said Adeline Brookshire.

Jimmy was a fluent, persuasive speaker, which may seem surprising when he was later stereotyped as a member of the new, mumbling, inarticulate faction of professional actors. Adeline Brookshire, in bafflement over his screen mumbling, said: "I don't know where he got it. Was it his natural way of speaking? Heavens, no. Well, just listen to me. I articulate like crazy, and he knew how to articulate."

However, when debating he was adept at "winging it," pretending convincingly to cite seemingly authentic sources that he had written out on cards to refer to during his speech, when he had actually made them up. His debating partner would cringe in embarrassment and fear that his deception should be found out. On one occasion it was, but he shrugged off the attempt to lay disgrace on his shoulders. To him it was just another kind of performance, and his interest in politics was actually very superficial.

He accepted the lesser part in *You Can't Take It With You* because he was working closely with Adeline Brookshire on the preparation of a piece for the National Forensic League, which had taken weeks of effort. In the early stages, trying it on classmates, he had become so angry by the lack of respect shown by another student that he broke off, although seemingly still in character, and chased the offender out of the hall, down a flight of stairs, then tried to throttle him in the stairwell. He was only deterred when the principal and other teachers intervened. His violence earned him a three-day suspension, causing him to miss a key basketball game against another school, which

Fairmount managed to win by a single point. He had to undergo the added humiliation of being refused entry because the rules required him to stay away from the school during his three days of suspension. To compound the consequences of his infraction even further, missing the game meant that he lost his position as the top scorer of his year because his rivals had played one more game than he had.

The violence of his reaction to his heckler suggested more than just a short temper. It could also be interpreted as the response of a born actor goaded into defending the sanctity of his craft by a nonbeliever. "I bequeath my temper to Dave Fox" (the victim), he wrote in the school yearbook, showing that he bore no grudges.

Jimmy's selected piece for the National Forensic League was *A Madman's Manuscript*, a document produced by an old clergyman in Chapter 11 of Charles Dickens' *The Pickwick Papers*. It is a macabre horror story of a man who kills his wife after driving her insane, his capture after a manhunt, and his incarceration in a lunatic asylum, from which he delivers his blood-curdling account in between bouts of acute dementia. Jimmy had worked hard to memorize the dialog and to imitate the behavior of a madman. His coach remembered how he chilled the audience by speaking plausibly and rationally one moment and then breaking into the frenetic, uncontrolled derangement of somebody devoid of reason the next.

His final presentation was slightly marred by a touch of hubris. He had been warned by his coach Adeline Brookshire that his piece as timed was two minutes over the required length. He remonstrated with her that it could not be cut without destroying its integrity, and argued that every moment was absolutely necessary to make it work. Having grown

◀ **JIMMY AT 18:** Neatly scrubbed for a formal photograph, Jimmy epitomizes the clean-cut look of a model student in his last school year.

THE FAIRMOUNT NEWS

Volume LXXIV — Fairmount, Grant County, Indiana, Thursday, April 14, 1949 — Number 12

F.H.S. Students Win State Meets

DAVID NALL AWARDED FIRST PLACE HONORS IN F. F. A. CONTEST

Board Gets Water Works Report

JAMES DEAN FIRST PLACE WINNER IN DRAMATIC SPEAKING

Summitville Students Win Recognition In Geometry Contests

DISTRIBUTION SYSTEM WHOLLY INADEQUATE TO SERVE FAIRMOUNT

Bring Honors to Fairmount High

39 STUDENTS NAMED ON HONOR ROLL AT THE HIGH SCHOOL

Churches to Present Easter Programs

RALPH W. PACK WAS

▲ **FRONT-PAGE NEWS:** Jimmy's first-place success in the state National Forensic League contest was signaled by a banner headline in the local paper.

used to his stubborn streak she let it go, hoping that the judges would be tolerant. On this occasion they were. He was so impressive in the two-day state contest, held in the nearby town of Peru, that he was awarded first place, an achievement heralded by headlines in *The Fairmount News*. It meant that he was now eligible to take part in the national competition, due to be held in Longmont, Colorado. It was a huge honor for his school, and a fund was launched to get him there.

Jimmy and Adeline were given an ecstatic send-off as they departed for Colorado, with the school band and the cheerleader squad turning out to perform as a procession of cars drove them the ten miles to the railroad depot at Marion. From there, Jimmy joined other Indiana contestants on a train for Chicago. After two or three hours looking around the city they boarded the Burlington flagship express, the gleaming, stainless-steel *Denver Zephyr*, which had smartly uniformed hostesses known as Zephyrettes and Vista Dome cars offering panoramic views from a raised deck. It was one of the finest of

"I have to get there fast, Mrs. Nall." JAMES DEAN

American journeys in the twilight of the golden age of rail. Adeline, pretending to retire to the powder room, would go discreetly to the club car and smoke in order not to offend her charge; he, in her absence, would also light up without her knowledge.

In Denver they had to transfer to a local train for the short ride up to Longmont. Jimmy was now well over 1,000 miles from home, and just one of 125 competitors from 24 states. As he waited, he fussed over his performance. He intended to appear before the judges in an open shirt and jeans, while the other contestants were sporting neat suits and ties. A fellow competitor, Jim McCarthy from LaSalle Academy, New York City, tried hard to persuade him to smarten up, and even offered to lend him a spare shirt, tie, and suit from his own overstocked wardrobe. It was to no avail. Jimmy argued: "How the heck can I go crazy in a shirt and tie?" In spite of his sartorial indifference, he was given a good rating in the first round and went on to the next. He was, however, issued with a warning that his piece was too long, and that he could be penalized in a tight contest, as preference would be given to an entrant who adhered more closely to the rules. Once again Adeline tried to persuade him to cut the piece, and once again he refused.

The consequences were only to be expected. In spite of thunderous applause when he had finished, he was awarded sixth place out of 22, a ranking too low for him to go on to the final round. Distraught, he disappeared for hours, and when his teacher finally found him, huddled in solitude on the bleachers of an empty gymnasium, she had trouble coaxing him to talk. Finally he rounded on her for not supporting him in explaining to the judges that the timing was essential to the integrity of the piece. She was flabbergasted. In spite of the personal rebuff, she knew that he had given an outstanding performance, but he had been floored by the zealous application of rules which, given that other competitors were involved, was necessary for the sake of fairness. Self-discipline, she tried to press on him, was part of an actor's armor. He returned to Fairmount not so much chastened as bitter that once more he had been compromised by authority. It was an outcome that would rankle for the rest of his life. Later, in interviews given during his Hollywood career, he even denied going on to Colorado after he had won the state contest.

At least the school had given him plenty of scope to exercise his abilities on stage and platform, and in his time he was the dominant student actor, whose performances were hailed for the way they towered over those of his contemporaries. Local audiences packed out the plays that the school put on in the third-floor auditorium, and so early on Jimmy had the exhilarating experience of never playing to anything less than a full house.

Alongside his fascination for stagecraft ran his other passion – sports. In spite of his poor sight

► **HOOPS STAR:** In spite of lack of inches and poor eyesight, Jimmy excelled in school basketball.

necessitating the need for glasses, even when playing basketball, he hurled himself into track and field pursuits. Marcus Winslow made him a special rubber strap to keep his glasses on his head, but they were always vulnerable, and Marcus estimated that he must have used up 15 pairs while engaged in athletics: "He broke them as fast as I could get them."

Interestingly, in spite of his prowess at basketball – almost a religion in Indiana – Jimmy was not tall. When he had stopped growing he was a wiry 5ft 8in and weighed only 140lbs. Yet he had been a formidable player even at his junior high school, and was

"All in all I'd say James Dean was pretty normal." JERRY GARNER, CLASSMATE

often top scorer for the Fairmount High team, the Quakers, as effective at close range as from a distance. He usually played guard. His aggressive attack attracted the attention of sports writers, who commented on his quickness and agility, and he became Fairmount's star player. In 1948 *The Fairmount News* described him as "an outstanding threat on the high-school team" after he accumulated 40 points in three games. "Jim is our regular basketball guy, and when you're around him time will fly" commented the Fairmount High Yearbook in the caption to his picture.

▲ **FOOLING AROUND:** Seniors' high jinks are captured by the camera lens with Jimmy as part of a human pyramid (second row on the left).

He had achieved his letter in baseball in the 1946–47 school year, and began his track career in 1947–48. He also became Grant County's champion pole-vaulter. Privately he worked out by lifting weights, exercising strenuously, and constantly shooting at the basketball hoop on the Winslow barn. The drive to excel was, in part, the throwing-off of his earlier frailty, but was also due to his desire to be seen as a regular member of the crowd. Nobody dared to criticize or sneer at him for caring about play-acting, poetry, and storytelling, activities that without the counterweight of a powerful sports reputation would be regarded as soft and unmanly.

He was not, however, a paragon as an athlete. The sensitivity to criticism extended to the way he reacted to adverse decisions on the court, and if he was pulled up for a contravention he was as likely as not to go into a sulk. Coaches had to be careful not to show him up in front of others. This was sometimes difficult in an intensive team game, but they knew that embarrassment was likely to affect his play. His short temper occasionally landed him in trouble. Paul Weaver, Jimmy's basketball coach at the time, said: "He wasn't too coachable. You had to be careful about not changing his style."

▲ **HIS FIRST MOTORCYCLE:** Jimmy and his Czech, the basic machine that even flat-out could only reach 50mph. What it lacked in speed it made up for in noise. He is on Main Street, Fairmount.

► **WINTON'S NEW WIFE:** Jimmy's father remarried, and he brought Ethel to Indiana to meet Jimmy soon after the war's end and his demobilization.

He was, however, a popular student. Scholastically he was average in most classes except speech and drama, in which he excelled. He was also impressive in art class, and many of his adolescent drawings and paintings survive in the Fairmount Historical Museum. He was adept at sketching landscapes and still-lifes, and used color with a sensitive, confident eye. His knowledge of mechanics was represented by the intricate drawings of machinery that he made as he endeavored to understand how things worked.

When Jimmy was around 15, Marcus presented him with a simple, cheap motorcycle, a low-powered import from Czechoslovakia which, even when ridden flat-out, could only attain 50mph. Near the farm, on the road into Fairmount, was Marvin Carter's Indian motorcycle shop, a gathering-point at weekends for all the young enthusiasts in the area. Jimmy spent much of his free time here, hanging out and learning the technicalities by tinkering. Marvin taught him how to strip down his machine and tune it for maximum performance, and the townsfolk of Fairmount quickly became used to the roar of the Czech C/Z along Main Street, its throaty sound suggesting a speed considerably greater than the moderate pace at which the 1.5hp machine was actually traveling. Even though its performance was modest, Jimmy liked to push it as hard as possible, and to perform stunts such as lying flat over the saddle at top speed. The bike helped promote his "cool" image, which he was already carefully cultivating. The Czech was the beginning of a passion for the motorcycle that would endure until his death. Jimmy later told Hedda Hopper, the Hollywood columnist, that back home he had herded cattle on his bike, and that he would chase them across the meadow, their udders swinging so vigorously that each must have lost a quart of milk.

A profile in the school newspaper referred to his Californian childhood without mentioning his mother's death, and cited banana salad as his favorite food. His "peeves" included women (a "fact" that sparked subsequent ill-informed speculation) and the "New Look," the notorious fashion of the period that had been invented by Christian Dior in Paris, France, which gave women wasp waists and full skirts reaching down to their ankles, thus depriving leg-watchers of their interest. He gave as his hobbies art, drama, ice skating, and motorcycles. He could have added 4-H, the Head, Heart, Hands, and Health organization that flourishes throughout rural America, which he had probably joined to please Marcus. Throughout the school year it had a rolling program of field trips and visits to places of interest, which he enjoyed as a break from school surroundings, even if only to see various agricultural processes. He had raised chicks, made a garden, and learned the rudiments of cattle husbandry. He won a 4-H blue ribbon for his work on a soil project, which had been inspired by the sight of a drill-rig crew working on a gas well near the Winslow farm.

"Whatever abilities I may have, crystallized there in high school, when I was trying to prove something to myself – that I could do it, I suppose." JAMES DEAN

He assiduously collected soil samples from various levels and presented them in a specially constructed wooden box. As there was no category for soil samples, the ribbon he was given was actually for "Champion Bull." But having won his award, 4-H became another forgotten enthusiasm.

Other than Adeline Brookshire, another influential figure in Jimmy's adolescence was Fairmount's charismatic Wesleyan Methodist minister, the Reverend James DeWeerd. His church, in the midst of a Quaker community, was the next in importance, and a Wesleyan summer camp was located on the outskirts of Fairmount. DeWeerd was an unusual figure in the context of a staid, small, country town, although he had been born and raised there. His sermons were noted for their impassioned oratory and spellbinding

"At about 12 or 13 I found out what I really was useful for – to live." JAMES DEAN

histrionics, and he made no effort to conceal his contempt for the parochialism of Fairmount's values. Then in his early thirties, he had plenty of experience of the world beyond. He had studied in California, traveled widely, lived in Europe, and taken a postgraduate course at the University of Cambridge, England. During the war he had been an army chaplain, and had served in France after D-Day, winning a Silver Star for gallantry, and a Purple Heart with Oak Leaf Cluster for wounds sustained rescuing men under fire. He was a cultured man with a surprisingly broad range of tastes, from classical music to motor racing. He was also known for his tolerance and was aware that America would eventually have to face up to a multi-ethnic society long before such views were generally accepted. He was magnetic, genial, a good host, and a compelling speaker, although he spiced up his conversation with quotations, maxims, and aphorisms in the manner of an old-time evangelist.

DeWeerd lived in a house he shared with his mother, in what to farm folk would have seemed splendor more appropriate to a big city – with linen napery and silver on the dinner table, and imported wine to accompany the evening meal. Jimmy was fascinated by DeWeerd, as he opened a window on the life that lay beyond the immediate surroundings of family, high school, and the close-knit community of Fairmount. In fact, DeWeerd had a following among many of the Fairmount boys, and hosted convivial evenings listening to classical records and watching home movies of the pastor's exotic vacations in places such as Mexico. It was through DeWeerd that Jimmy developed his interest in bullfighting, bongo drums, yoga, Tchaikovsky, and Shakespeare. He was also taken by him to the Indy 500, where he was introduced to some of the drivers, including the legendary ace of the day "Cannon Ball" Baker, and it was clearly DeWeerd who sparked Jimmy's lifelong passion for motor racing. A good friendship developed between them; they often discussed poetry and philosophy, and the emotional problems that beset a youth who, at an early age, had lost the mother to whom he had been devoted. By this time Winton, having returned to California as a veteran of the Army Medical Corps, had remarried. His second wife was Ethel Nuckells.

Shortly after his 18th birthday, in accordance with prevailing law, James Dean had registered with the local draft board, or Selective Service System (SSS). Some biographers have stated that he told the board he was homosexual, which would have exempted him from the draft, and this has become part of the Dean mythology. It was not unknown for youths to use this declaration as a ruse to escape military service, whether it was the truth or not. However, neither Jimmy's papers nor his draft card substantiate the claim, leading to the conclusion that it was never made. The board's records were public documents, available to all interested parties, and such a statement could not have been concealed from the school or the people of Fairmount. Small-town America was gripped by a paranoid fear of "perverts" at this time: even a mildly leftwing stance could generate "reds under the bed" fantasies and draw the attentions of the FBI. In any case, Dean needed no such excuse: his bad eyesight would undoubtedly have made him ineligible to serve.

Although he was not the school's most ardent pursuer of girls, he certainly had a few perfectly normal adolescent infatuations with members of the opposite sex. Rules were strict then in a Quaker community, with dating largely confined to weekends. On schooldays curfew was 9pm, even on light summer evenings, and 10pm at weekends. Jimmy seems to have had a considerable regard for

▼ **CLASS TRIP TO D.C.:** In 1949 Fairmount seniors went to Washington, saw the sights and posed as a group on Capitol Hill. Jimmy is in the back row.

▲ **HECTIC VISIT:** Jimmy poses with classmates, a button missing from his 49er sweater. During his Washington trip he made a solo pilgrimage to Ford's Theatre.

older girls. Even some teachers would be totally entranced by his charms – to the extent of improving his grades on occasion. Adeline Brookshire confessed: "Jim knew how to play people. He could work me around his little finger." He was extremely attracted to the young teacher Elizabeth McPherson, who ran physical education classes for the girls and who was also an art student. They even had a liaison of sorts – enough for Jimmy to climb up and carve his name in the rafters of the church where she worked on her art. There was, however, an age difference of seven or eight years, which eventually appeared to worry her rather more than him.

He spent so much of his schooldays engaged in a multitude of activities that dating girls was not high on his agenda. Many of those who knew him then have said the same thing. He was eager to take up anything new that came his way, and after a few frenetic weeks, or merely days – in which his life would seem subsumed as he mastered the skills required to become expertly adept – he would suddenly lose interest and move on to yet another fad of the moment, until that in turn bored him. The same attitude prevailed with people.

The seniors' school trip to Washington, D.C. was a very exciting and relatively unusual venture. The students had used money raised from their Halloween show to part-finance it. They had also staged other events throughout the school year, such as buffet suppers in which each participant paid a cent for the privilege of attending. In 1949 a penny still held a certain value. Having amassed the then-impressive sum of $1,765, the party of 47 students (only one or two of the senior class did not participate) and chaperones – the art instructor Elizabeth McPherson, and Fairmount school's superintendent F. Stanton Galey and his wife – traveled by long-distance bus to spend two nights in the nation's capital, residing at a modestly priced boarding establishment called the Roosevelt Apartments. In spite of the sexes being segregated on separate floors, the lusty 18-year-olds soon found opportunities to break the rules, and on the second night, having managed to obtain a case of beer, the students engaged in a bout of mayhem that led to censure.

"If a man can bridge the gap between life and death, I mean, if he can live on after he's dead, then maybe he was a great man." JAMES DEAN

The ringleader, it seems, was Jimmy Dean, but no serious penalty was imposed and by the standards of today their mild fling seems relatively unremarkable.

The visit embraced the usual sightseeing attractions, such as the Lincoln Memorial, the Smithsonian, and a riverboat cruise along the Potomac. The students stood and gazed at the White House, hoping that the incumbent, President Harry S. Truman, might temporarily forgo affairs of state and step outside for a moment to wave to them, and then later they posed for a picturesque and decorative class photograph in late-spring sunshine on a lawn in front of the defining Washington emblem, the Capitol dome. Jimmy was clad like several others in the group – in his '49 sweater, casually fastened by a single button. He also, in a rare, spare moment, broke away from the party to make a personal pilgrimage to Ford's Theatre on 10th Street, and looked in wonder at the box in which Abraham Lincoln had been shot by John Wilkes Booth on that infamous night in 1865. It was

"I'm gonna show you! I'm gonna be great."
JAMES DEAN

something he had been urged to do by Adeline Brookshire, and he was looking forward to reporting his impressions to her on his return to Fairmount.

A week after the seniors' organized trip to Washington it was time for graduation. He was asked to read the benediction at the commencement ceremony in the Bethel Tabernacle in the Wesleyan camp grounds, and he took advice from its minister, Rev. DeWeerd, who readily loaned him some books of prayer. In one there was a supplication by the theologian John Henry Newman, and Jimmy chose it for its simple entreaty for "safe lodging and a holy rest, and peace at last." In front of his fellow graduates and a full house of proud parents, including Marcus and Ortense, he received school prizes for his achievements in dramatics, art, and athletics. Academically he was placed 20th out of a class of 49.

Now the big question arose. What was to be his future? Although he was 18 he was at least spared the prospect of having to begin military service – the fate of many of his classmates, who were being drafted without realizing that within a year the US Army would be heavily involved in the Korean War. There was one decision that he was determined to act upon: to leave Fairmount and the Midwest behind him. It came as a disappointment to Adeline, who was hoping that he would go on to a local college, and to Marcus, who wanted his nephew to enroll at his alma mater, Earlham College, a distinguished liberal arts Quaker institution located in Richmond, Indiana.

Toward the end of his senior year, Jimmy realized that without any financial backing his options were limited, but he was seriously interested in an offer received in a letter from his father, to support him at a college in California. Winton wanted to draw closer to his son and to

◄ **WITH LITTLE MARKIE:** Jimmy is pulled around the Winslow farm by Marcus Jr., his kid "brother."

► **GRADUATION DAY:** Jimmy, capped and gowned, poses in the Wesleyan campgrounds after the ceremony that included an address by the Reverend DeWeerd.

▲ **FAMILY SEND-OFF:** Jimmy at the heart of his family. Counterclockwise From right: Mildred Dean (Winton's sister-in-law), Charles Nolan Dean, Grandpa Dean, Grandma Dean, Joan, Marcus Sr., Myron Reece Peacock, Reece Peacock (baby), Jimmy, David Dean, Betsy Dean, Joe Dean, Markie.

achieve the best for him, having seen him infrequently in the near-decade since Mildred's death. Jimmy's initial thought was to study drama at UCLA, but his grades were not adequate to secure admission to the University of California from outside the state. His father was hoping that he would study law, first taking a pre-law course at Santa Monica City College. His aptitude at public speaking had helped him as a qualification when he filled out the application form, and he was accepted to begin there in mid-July, which was when classes started for students from other states. It was not exactly what he had in mind, but he thought that it would be worth a try, if only because it would remove him from what he had increasingly come to feel was the confining atmosphere of Fairmount, where there was no possibility of advancing an acting career. It would also place him in a populous city, where opportunities abounded for him to pursue his own interests.

Joan organized a private family gathering to send him on his way and then, given Jimmy's popularity, and the conviction of many of his classmates and faculty that his combination of talent and ambition would take him to the top as an actor, he was given the honor of a special farewell party, attended by the Winslows and many of his friends. Inevitably the assembly had fun singing "California Here I Come" around the piano, but perhaps they should not have bothered

"Being a good actor isn't easy. Being a man is even harder. I want to be both before I'm done." JAMES DEAN

with the follow-up, "Back Home Again in Indiana." The evening ended with a cascade of good wishes, and a spirited rendering of a popular dirge of the moment, "Now is the Hour." The event was duly noted in *The Fairmount News* social coverage under the heading "James Dean was honored at farewell party Monday night." Earlier that year he had featured in the lead story, which celebrated his triumphant first place in the National Forensic League state competition. The front page also bore his photograph, looking uncharacteristically tidy with his hair slicked back and wearing a jacket and neatly knotted tie, at complete variance with his appearance in the competition itself. Locally he had sufficient star status to warrant news coverage at a modest level.

The day after the farewell party he was driven by friends to Chicago where, at the Greyhound bus station, he boarded the shiny blue-and-white long-distance coach that would take him all the way to Los Angeles.

It was June 1949. The Indiana years were over.

▲ **ON HIS WAY:** Earlier in high school, Jimmy had drawn a removal van en route for Hollywood – a prescient daydream.

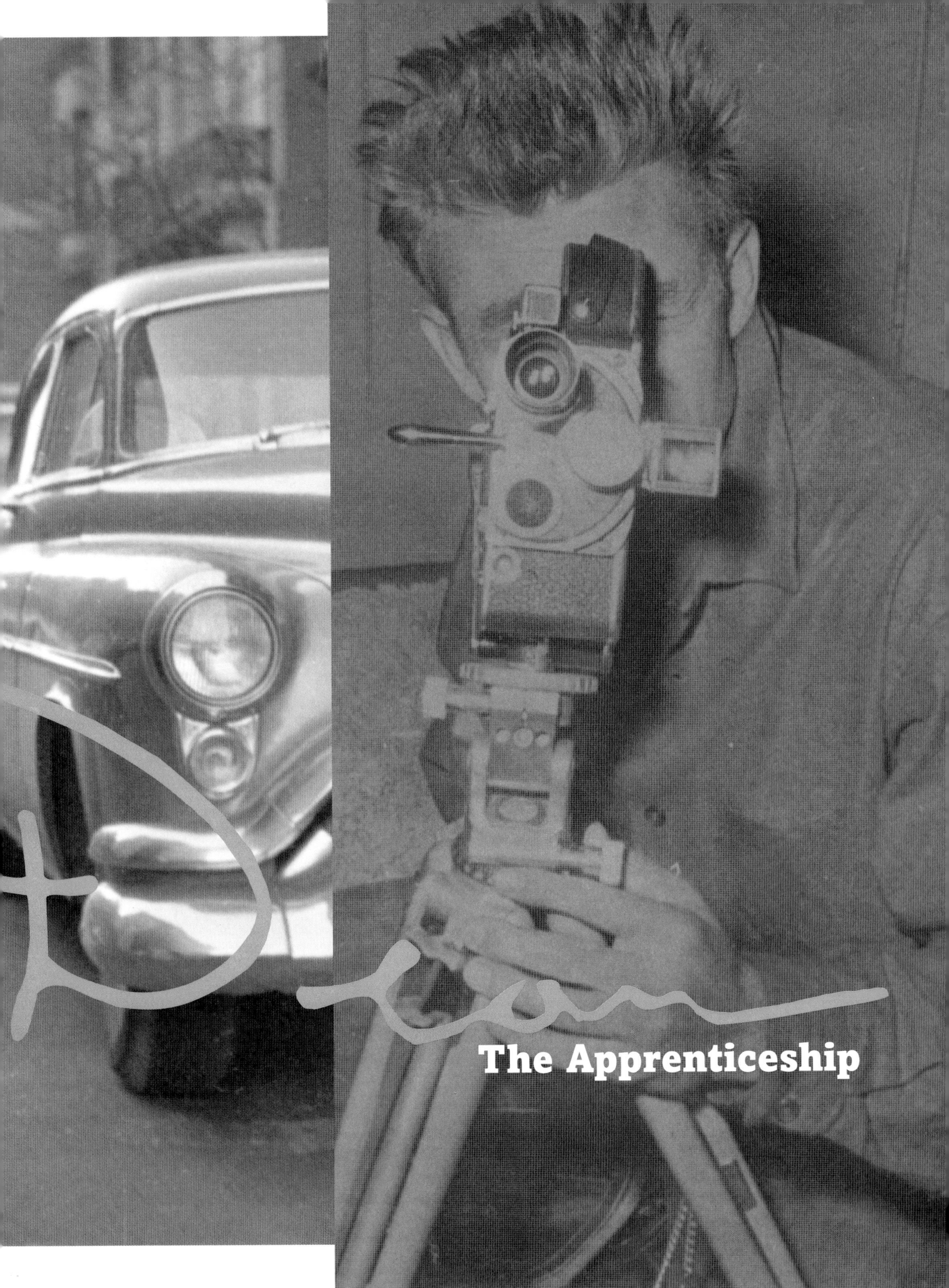

The Apprenticeship

To –
two, very special
people; my precious
grandmother and my
wonderful grandfather.
With all my love forever,
Jimmie

James Dean, 18 years old and newly graduated from high school, arrived in California after the long bus journey to be met by Winton and taken back to his small house at 814-B 6th Street, Santa Monica, where Jimmy was to live. Winton's second wife, Ethel, was wary of his desire to make a career from acting, aware that so many young people turned up in southern California hoping for a glamorous movie career only to meet with bitter disappointment, and her views added to Winton's own skepticism. Ethel was in many respects the dominant figure in their marriage, and Winton often acquiesced for the sake of harmony.

As the safe next step in his son's education Winton had selected Santa Monica City College. In Jimmy's freshman year it had an enrollment of 1,600. It offered two-year courses in a number of areas in which reasonable business careers might be developed, and for Winton it was the obvious choice, although given Jimmy's skills in sports, he had considered courses in physical education such as basketball coaching, which were also available at the college. He appreciated that Jimmy's success in a few school plays counted for little in the real world, and thought he could find a stable vocation without the uncertainties of an acting career. He believed that his son's ambition was just a late adolescent enthusiasm that would fade with maturity.

◄ **CALIFORNIA GREETING:** Jimmy, newly arrived in Santa Monica, sent his grandparents, Charles and Emma Dean, this inscribed photograph, taken at a commercial studio.

Winton made a great effort to improve their relationship by taking Jimmy bowling and trying to teach him golf, but the young man retreated into himself, becoming silent and uncommunicative. His father had given him an automobile. It was a generous gesture, and Jimmy became very fond of the ten-year-old Chevrolet sedan, affectionately naming it "Lena" and using it to drive to and from the college at Pico and 7th Street, adjoining the Santa Monica High School, its location until a new campus was ready. Some of its facilities were shared with the high school. By coincidence, these were the same buildings that would later be chosen as locations for the school in *Rebel Without a Cause*.

There was a 1949 summer session to enable qualification for enrollment in the fall, and Jimmy decided that, should the opportunity arise, he would secure the necessary residential qualification for a transfer to the University of California Los Angeles and its drama department. He soon discovered the Miller Playhouse Theatre Guild, an amateur summer stock company located near the college, and he volunteered his help, hanging around rehearsals and even painting scenery until he was given a job as a stage manager. He billed himself as "Byron James," the only time he adopted a stage name (at one point he had considered calling himself "Marcus Dean," but the Winslows had dissuaded him, believing that adopting a stage name was pretentious).

His activities were reported back home in *The Fairmount News*. A story, headlined "James Dean Joins Theatre Group at Santa Monica, Cal," was based on a letter Jimmy had written to his grandparents, which they had passed on to the news-hungry journal. In a production called *Romance of Scarlet Gulch*, a Californian gold-rush melodrama, he played a drunk under his new stage name and, according to the program notes, he had also been responsible for the outdoor scenery. There had been some help in the set painting from another new arrival in Los Angeles in the summer of 1949,

▼ **ON THE ROAD:** Jimmy with his father Winton in Colorado on a short mountain vacation. Winton's car is a 1950 Ford sedan.

Elizabeth "Bette" McPherson, the Fairmount High PE teacher and art student to whom he had been so attracted. Her contract there had not been renewed – as the Fairmount school board had suspected her of inappropriate behavior with the board's president, with whom she spent weekends painting churches. Called to account, she had responded with indignation rather than contrition, and had been summarily fired. She decided to spend the summer in California, traveling with two women friends who were also teachers at other schools and wanted to enjoy a long break. She contacted Jimmy, who was happy to show them around and drive Bette's car for her. He was particularly interested in Forest Lawn Cemetery at Glendale, with its celebrity interments, the full-scale replica of Michelangelo's statue of David, and the nostalgic evocation of Bonnie Scotland, the Wee Kirk o' the Heather. They partied on the beach and sometimes drove up to Lake Arrowhead, 90 miles east of Los Angeles in the San Bernardino National Forest, where Bette's cousin Marjorie Armstrong had a cabin that they used as a base for water skiing. Jimmy drove fast and was once reprimanded by a patrolman for not heeding a STOP sign. His absences from Winton's house for a night or even two were not criticized.

Although Bette McPherson was years older than Jimmy, he had strong feelings for her and she claimed he had even asked her to marry him. She declined, which she later recalled seemed to hurt him, and she wondered what might have happened had she accepted, believing that he would probably have died young, but might not have become famous. She was not even prepared to live with him – another of his suggestions. The notion of a male teenager cohabiting with a woman nearly in her thirties would have been considered totally unacceptable more than 50 years ago. At the end of the summer, after a friendly parting, she returned to Indiana, and they corresponded. She did not keep his letters and never saw him again, although she once telephoned him, when he was making *Giant*.

He did not lose his virginity to her, although he had confessed to friends that it was his avowed intention to do so before the end of the fall. Other opportunities arose. He made a pitch for the homecoming queen, Dianne Hixon – a tall, spectacular blonde who kept a garter snake as a pet, sometimes carrying it with her on campus in a shoebox – and he went on a number of dates with her, an indication that, in spite of no money and slight stature, he was compellingly attractive.

▲ **DRESSED TO THE NINES:** Jimmy poses in a handsome new double-breasted suit outside his father's home in Santa Monica.

He was taking various courses necessary for the pre-law program to appease Winton, but had added two drama courses, theater, and acting history, taught by Gene Nielson Owen, who was also involved with the college drama club. She told a movie magazine after Jimmy's death that she found him neither rebellious nor moody, and that he was always polite and thoughtful, with a boundless enthusiasm for everything to do with theater. She found initially that he had a speech problem.

"Drinks out of cold mountain streams and sleep under the stars ... you can't beat it." JAMES DEAN

▲ **JIMMY IN THE ROCKIES:** Cooling off by a mountain stream in Colorado, Jimmy is photographed by his father.

Many years later, in 1981, she recalled in the *Los Angeles Times*: "... his articulation was poor, he mashed his words and was somewhat difficult to understand. In an interpretation class, someone pointed this out and blamed it on his Hoosier accent." She discovered the real reason in private, when in her office he took out his dental plate and explained that it made some words hard to enunciate. The prescription she offered was Shakespeare, and exercises on mastering the soliloquies. "One day in class," she observed, "Jimmy read some scenes from Edgar Allan Poe's *Telltale Heart*. He was magnificent – but then he always had a spectacular emotion for any scene he played. Later, during that same class, I asked Jimmy to read some scenes from *Hamlet*. That night, when I returned home, I informed my husband that I had finally found the right student to play Hamlet as I felt it should be played."

She coached him carefully and was astonished by his industriousness as he read the Elizabethan text, and wrestled with its meaning until the essence of the Danish prince's tortured soul entered his own psyche, giving him the understanding to deliver his performance. Alas never recorded, its effectiveness can be guessed at by viewing the few early television plays that show Jimmy as a developing actor, with the beginning of a style that amounted to intense naturalism. The star of a high-school stage in a rural backwater would have been unremarkable in the context of a college in a metropolis that was a nationwide magnet for acting talent. To many of his fellow students James Dean did not cut it, being seen as a small, shy, pallid, and bespectacled kid from nowhere. There were people in his class who had the physique, the stature, and the firm-jawed look of potential movie stars, as there were those who boasted rich, resonant voices that would sound impressive on radio. Gene Nielson Owen was astute enough to appreciate that these attributes were secondary if the power to project was absent. "I never realized what arresting eyes he had until I saw him on a TV show in 1951," she said. "He was never aware of his good looks. It was one of his more charming qualities."

Jimmy also worked hard for a place on the college basketball team, which had a good reputation, having won the Metropolitan Conference championship the year before, and although he made it through to the last 15, he sat out much of the first season. He impressed with his speed and balance, and was awarded a place as substitute guard, which meant that he played in about half of the college games in the second half of the year. He was, however, becoming self-conscious about wearing his glasses, and occasionally tried to play without them. He scored infrequently and did not feature in the statistics. His coach, Sanger Crumpacker, remembered how one day Jimmy came to practice and was so off his game that an explanation was called for. It turned out that he had failed an acting audition, which was far, far worse than any setback he could suffer in sports. "He wanted more than anything else to get into acting," said the coach.

Christmas 1949 came, and Jimmy remembered Adeline Brookshire in Fairmount, sending her some earrings. In January, he looked in on a sermon delivered in Pasadena by the visiting Reverend James DeWeerd, renewing his friendship with the charismatic pastor.

"I ... became close to nature, and am now able to appreciate the beauty with which this world is endowed." JAMES DEAN

When the new semester began in February, Owen found that Jimmy's articulation had improved so much that she recommended him for the college radio station, and he quickly began hosting student programs, on certain days making all the station announcements. He spent his spare time listening to jazz, both live and recorded, and hanging out with friends at numerous coffee shops, notably one called The Cave. He was a founding member of the college jazz club, with a special interest in the traditional Dixieland sound, and would make expeditions to Ray Avery's Record Roundup on La Cienega Boulevard. In March, at his second attempt, he was also elected to the Opheleos, the honor society that consisted of the 21 outstanding male students on campus, which operated under the motto "service without hope of conspicuous reward." They wore royal-blue jackets to mark themselves from the hoi polloi. Just how active he was in the society is not recorded, but merely belonging to it was an indication of prestige. When the banquet was held at the end of the semester, he asked Dianne Hixon, the willowy homecoming queen, to be his guest.

The drama department's contribution to the May Day festivities was a creaky melodrama called *She Was Only a Farmer's Daughter*, staged at the Santa Monica Theater Guild, in which he played a father. Also appearing was his classmate Dick Mangan, who went on to a career as a supporting actor in film and television.

Jimmy had long realized that he would have to leave Winton and Ethel's home if he was to further his ambition, and he had been keeping his eye on the possibility of a transfer to UCLA and its performing arts courses. Owen was not convinced that a move to UCLA was in his best interests. She was a graduate from the department, and knew that it was a tough school, with high academic standards, and she felt that Santa Monica, in spite of its inferior facilities, was the better environment for him. He was unwilling to consider her point of view, and probably felt the transfer would bring him into contact with career opportunities that would never otherwise come his way. When he learned of his son's decision, Winton was furious at first, but knowing that he would be unable to convince him to follow the prescribed path, accepted that he would be leaving home. In any case, Ethel wanted to move to Reseda, near Van Nuys in the Valley.

"I had a job at a military academy.... Couldn't ask for better weather; we were surrounded by mountains and orange grove, really God's country."

JAMES DEAN

Jimmy decided to quit Santa Monica after one year and make the leap. With the help of Coach Crumpacker he engineered a summer job as an athletic instructor at a military academy "boys' camp" east of Los Angeles at Glendora, near the city of San Dimas, where he worked six days a week from June to mid-August. Having put aside the money earned to help his modest tuition fees, he enrolled at UCLA for admission at the beginning of September.

As soon as his camp job ended, instead of returning to Winton in Santa Monica, Jimmy took off on a two-week trip back to Indiana. It was a subdued visit. Many of his high-school friends had been drafted or had moved away. He did, however, go to see Adeline Brookshire, who was studying for a master's degree in theater at Indiana University in Bloomington, 70 miles south of Indianapolis. Fired by her enthusiasm, for a moment he considered a place in IU's drama department and actually discussed it with the faculty head.

▸ **MAKING THE LEAP:** After a year at Santa Monica City College, Jimmy went against the advice of his drama coach and his father's apprehensions, and enrolled in Theater Arts at UCLA.

However, he cast the thought aside when he was told that majors were expected to graduate with teaching certificates, because realistically the chances of finding employment as professional actors were minimal. He also stopped off in Iowa to visit Kletzing College, a Wesleyan foundation now merged with Vennard College, where the Rev. DeWeerd had been installed as president the year before.

During his visit to Marion he saw *The Men*, directed by Fred Zinnemann and scripted by Carl Foreman, one of the victims of the infamous House of Un-American Activities Committee. Its subject was the plight of maimed veterans facing lives as paraplegics. He was deeply affected by the movie, which introduced Marlon Brando to the screen. Born in 1924, Brando had made a dazzling impact on the New York stage in 1947 as the male lead in Tennessee Williams' *A Streetcar Named Desire*, and would repeat the role in Elia Kazan's 1951 film version. For his first movie role in *The Men* Brando had taken the trouble to live among paraplegics, spending all day in a wheelchair to experience what it was like. In Hollywood, just as on Broadway, his unpolished intensity, his improvisational skill, his gift for mimicry, and his ability to submerge his own persona within the character he played, electrified the screen. Brando, schooled in the Stanislavsky technique, was the new face of American acting, and Hollywood was as impressed as the critics had been in New York.

James Dean had found his role model. Brando also came from a Midwest background – Omaha, Nebraska – and his father had discouraged his ambition to act. Like Jimmy, Brando loved motorcycles, leather jackets, and jeans, as well as hanging out in bars and scorning middle-class conventions. Both had a slouched, frowning demeanor, androgynous facial features, and a hypnotic gaze. Brando represented danger, mystery, and power, and already had a coterie of disciples.

▲ **OLD MENTOR:** Jimmy, briefly returning to Indiana, made a point of calling on his former drama teacher Adeline Brookshire.

Marlon Brando

As far as New York theater was concerned, Marlon Brando seemed to fulfill a long-felt need in 1947. Broadway was overshadowed by the authority of the British stage and its acting traditions, upheld by such giants as Laurence Olivier, John Gielgud, and Ralph Richardson. With Elia Kazan's direction of the Tennessee Williams play *A Streetcar Named Desire*, the electrifying presence of Brando seemed like a new dawn for the American stage.

His refreshing style, sensual physicality, striking looks, and sheer unconventionality were like nothing that had been seen before, and gave the Method its legitimacy. The promise turned out to be false. Brando forsook New York for Hollywood, making a distinguished debut in Fred Zinnemann's *The Men* (1950), followed by the replication of his Broadway role in Elia Kazan's film of *Streetcar.* He was to make more films with Kazan, including *On the Waterfront* (1954), for which he won the Academy Award. But Brando's trajectory was ultimately a disappointment, with the lows eventually subsuming the highs as he followed a sad downward path, emerging occasionally from the shadows to startle audiences anew with a performance such as that of Don Corleone in *The Godfather* (1971), for which he won another Oscar, or as the bizarre Colonel Kurtz in *Apocalypse Now* (1979). Even with his shortcomings he remains, after his death in 2004, one of the primary actors of the latter 20th century, and an indelible influence on modern acting style.

► **SCREEN REPRISE:** Brando played Stanley Kowalski both on Broadway and in Elia Kazan's subsequent film of Tennessee Williams' *A Streetcar Named Desire.*

Back in Santa Monica, Jimmy attended a trio of summer lectures by Margaret Mead, the anthropologist Jesse Stuart, the Kentucky novelist and poet, and Will Durant, the historian and philosopher. It was the last speaker who caught his imagination most with the discussion "Is Progress Real?" Jimmy was still quoting Durant in the year that he died.

UCLA occupies a 419-acre campus north of Westwood Village, its home since 1929, and from modest beginnings it has become one of the world's foremost institutes of learning. In the booming postwar years it grew to an enrollment of over 25,000 (today 37,000) and was already enjoying a formidable academic reputation. In September 1950 the new pre-law major James Byron Dean, using his athletic and basketball prowess as credentials, pledged the Epsilon Pi chapter of Sigma Nu, one of many fraternity houses on Gayley Avenue, close to the heart of Westwood Village. Rushing a fraternity was a cheaper option than a campus dorm or off-campus lodgings, but Jimmy disliked fraternity conventions and became something of a social misfit, sneered at for his blue jeans, Indiana accent, and reclusive attitude. The dorm section of the house had six to eight pledges sharing a room furnished with steel lockers and bunk beds, and newcomers were expected to adhere to a strict regime, including household tasks, before they could attain active status. Why, given his maverick, nonconforming nature, Jimmy should have wanted to become a Greek letter member has hitherto been a mystery, but a letter retained by the Winslows reveals that he was put up for it by his friend Bill Harding, a UCLA graduate and the son of Major Harding, who ran the military academy in Glendora where Jimmy had worked in the summer: "Bill got me into U.C.L.A. (avoided red tape; he knows a guy!) Was responsible for me having a good job, night on campus at a dollar an hour (about 75 a month) It's the Visual Aid Dept. (film library) I'm a laboratory assistant which consists of being a projectionist all over campus; and in the library I rewind, splice, file film and so on. Bill also recommended me highly to his old house, at which I was pledged immediately."

▼ **SCOTCH MIST:** Jimmy declaims stage right in a key scene in *Macbeth*, performed in the 1,600-seat auditorium of Royce Hall.

After he was established at UCLA his interest in track sports waned in the face of the superior competition, but he made the happy discovery of fencing, and very quickly grew adept at its precise, agile moves. He became friendly with James Bellah, son of the novelist James Warner Bellah and later a novelist himself. He was already an effective first saber, having started fencing before he was ten years old. Bellah gave Dean instruction, and was surprised and chagrined that his pupil was scoring points off him almost straight away. Dean also joined the ROTC in order to learn marksmanship, and claimed in a letter to the Winslows that he had quickly achieved proficiency, but like fencing it was to be a passing enthusiasm.

"I came up with a wonderful lead in Macbeth, the character Malcolm (huge part)." JAMES DEAN

His choice of pre-law as his major, giving him access to art history and anthropology, was not serious, but a sop to Winton who had initially given him some money. Once that had gone no more was forthcoming so Jimmy was obliged to find part-time jobs, including that of film projectionist for the Theater Arts department. His academic application was almost cursory, as his desire to act now transcended all else. He had enrolled as a Theater Arts minor because it enabled him to audition for the four plays that were staged through the semester. The technical facilities were excellent, and the department benefited from the proximity of the Hollywood studios, which would happily lend costumes when required.

▲ **PLACID HERO:** Jimmy played Malcolm in the UCLA production of *Macbeth*. He thought more highly of his performance than his critics.

The first production in the fall of 1950 was *Macbeth* and, after a week of highly competitive auditioning, in which more than 350 hopefuls had read for parts, Jimmy succeeded in landing that of Malcolm, Duncan's elder son, "The biggest thrill of my life," Jimmy wrote Marcus and Ortense. Malcolm is a key role, and even delivers the play's last lines. Owen had instilled in him the confidence to play Shakespeare, but from contemporary accounts of the five performances in the elegant, 1,600-seat auditorium of Royce Hall, it would seem that he had taken on more than he could handle. One of his problems was his short-sightedness, which required him to wear his glasses in early rehearsals. He irritated his fellow actors by having to put them on each time to check his lines. *Spotlight*, the department's own newspaper, reviewed the production. Jimmy's performance "failed to show any growth, and would have made a hollow king." His inexperience showed, both in his failure to work properly with his fellow actors as part of an ensemble (Joel Climenhaga, who played "Old Siward, the English General," commented that "stage acting was a cooperative art and Jimmy was not a cooperative actor") and in his delivery, which was deemed poor, and marred by the still discernible Hoosier accent. If he resented the criticism he concealed his feelings when he wrote to his aunt and uncle in Fairmount: "I was very much rewarded and proved myself a capable actor in the eyes of several hundred culture-minded individuals. Man, if I can keep this up, and nothing interferes with my progress, one of these days I might be able to contribute something to the world."

During the course of the production he met William (Bill) Bast from the University of Wisconsin, who was also studying acting and was to become a close friend. At a dress rehearsal Bill Bast had watched the strange, kilted figure on stage distort Shakespeare's lines in a peculiar hayseed twang, and when somebody whispered "That's James Dean," he inwardly thought, "James Dean. A name to forget."

Later, over coffee in the Green Room, Bill was introduced to the slouching actor and discovered a rapport. Jimmy was going out with Jeanetta Lewis, a Texan sorority girl, having impressed her by taking her to a Sigma Nu dance, while Bast was attracted to Joanne Mock, cast as Lady Macduff. The couples went on double dates – "one of America's most unfortunate social customs," according to Bill, "... a subtle manifestation of our society's psychological maladjustment." Late one night, on a whim, they drove Joanne's parents' car 90 miles up the coast to Santa Barbara for breakfast and became stranded on the return journey when the oil pan ran dry, leaving them to hitch back. Another time they went 135 miles down the coast to Tijuana, across the Mexican border, and on a further 70 miles to Ensenada, where thick fog prevented their immediate return. They checked in to a motel and although proprieties were observed they felt extremely guilty when the girls' parents found out.

At this time Isabel Draesemer, a minor-level actors' agent who had family connections with James Bellah, entered Jimmy's world. Fortunately she had not seen him in *Macbeth*, and was able to visualize his potential in a non-Shakespearean context. At Bellah's instigation, Jimmy made his way to her office and signed up to become one of her clients. He had already attempted to see a casting director at the Jerry Fairbanks studio in the hope of securing a role in a television film, but without success. Then a Fairbanks executive contacted Draesemer about a Pepsi-Cola commercial that required several teenagers, preferably older than they looked in order to comply with state labor laws, which restricted under-18s to four hours work a day. Draesemer immediately saw a possibility for her new client to win a coveted union card, and, in spite of intensive competition from others, he was among the dozen or so who were selected to appear, for a fee of $10 plus a box lunch. Nick Adams and Beverly Long, also then 19, were among the chosen. Four years later they would both be in *Rebel Without a Cause* alongside Jimmy.

> "Dean was a natural. He grabbed one of the girls and started jitterbugging." JAMES BELLAH

The two-minute spot was shot at the carousel in Griffith Park in January 1951, and all afternoon a group of young people swigged Pepsi and cavorted on the fairground horses. The next setup was a honky-tonk piano around which a group gathered. James Dean supplies the coin to start it and slaps his hand down to get it going, somehow stealing the show by his presence alone. As it bursts into life everyone starts singing "Pepsi-Cola hits the spot.

▶ **LETTER HOME:** Jimmy sends an informative letter back to Indiana to Ortense, Marcus, and little Markie. There is no date, but it would seem to be the summer of 1949, when he was working in summer stock in Santa Monica.

ROBERT OAKLEY *Television Productions*

406 N. LA CIENEGA BLVD. HOLLYWOOD 36, CALIF. CRestview 6-3483

Dear Folks; (Mom, Mark & Marky)

While the boss is away and I'm not very busy, I'll drop you a line or two.

The plays has been under way for three nights now and is seemingly very successful. There will be twelve more nights unless the show is sold and we go on the road. It will then probably be doubled. I got one of the best write ups in the Theatrical Review for my characterization of Charley Smooch. I'll get a publication and send it to you. I am enclosing the program so that you might get an idea of the type thing it is. It is a good show but I personally think it stinks, possibly because I detest that kind of acting.

I seem to be getting a very cheap theater education. The work I doing here is easy and advancement is unlimited as to talent. We get very little pay if any but there isn't much money in television at this stage of the game. I choose to sacrifice the money for the education I am getting in television and movie production also the very valuable contacts that I Make here. When I have learned the ropes and think I am ready I will make my first stab at the film business. (acting always in mind.)

As to my scene painting I am learning very much along with accually doing it. Have done a little work along side Sid Nolton who works for Paramount. He was doing some work for the Theater Guild at the time. When I get the nerve I might ask him let me apprentice under him.

School is starting in Sept. Will have to put aside alot of things while giving all my attention to school work. All that I have learned will sure help when I get into Theater Arts major. I certainly am impatient but getting a foot in the door of the movie world is a tough, long job. Here at the studio, Joan Leslie, David Bruce, Barbara Brown, Hal Price have been rehersing for a show that Oakley is producting. I learn alot from them. I just got to be patient I guess. The never made it until there 20's and 30's even 40's.

Dad is on another three week vacation, Ethel will be on one before long. They will take a trip to Yosimite or somewhere. I don't know whether I will be able to go yet or not.

I could never get along without my little cycle. I guess I'll never sell it. It's like a friend, and brother, friends are hard to find in the theater. The most cattie, criticizing, narcissic bunch of people you ever saw, always at each others throat. But let an outsider try to interfer and they flock to gether like a bunch of long lost buddys. (whatta life.)

ROBERT OAKLEY *Television Productions*

406 N. LA CIENEGA BLVD. HOLLYWOOD 36, CALIF. CRestview 6-3483

How is ole Marky and Tuck hitting it off by now, or has the pig taken Tucks place? When is Markys birthday , infact write and tell me when all your birthdays are. I feel ashamed to have to ask you.

I might get this thing written if that telephone would stop ringing. Agents, actor, singers, etc.
"Everybody wants to get in to the act"

Tell Mrs. Brookshire when you see her that I have never forgotten the Thespian creed.
"Act well your part for there all honor lies."

LOVE

Byron James

P.S.
Disregard the address on the stationary. send any letters to my address.

A big, big bottle and it's got bounce, bounce, bounce, bounce, go get Pepsi for the Pepsi bounce," as drinks are handed round. Because at that time there was a disagreement between the Screen Actors Guild (SAG) and the American Federation of Television and Radio Actors (AFTRA) as to which union should be involved, it was possible for Jimmy to work without a card, and at the same time qualify to join.

Sigma Nu finally lost patience with Jimmy that winter. His solitary behavior and failure to take part in fraternity activities annoyed some of the brothers. He had not performed the domestic chores to the satisfaction of the chapter commander, and he had been late settling his bills. The final straw came when he was involved in a fist fight, which he started. He was asked to hand back his pin and leave. He later claimed that if he had not been thrown out he would have left anyway, as he was totally at odds with fraternity life and its practitioners.

Bill Bast had been planning to rush Sigma Nu himself but, after an uncomfortable interview, had also found that he was not compatible. He was delighted that his friend was no longer part of it, and was very easily persuaded to pool his thin resources with Jimmy's so that they could share a cheap apartment. The search was difficult and initially confined to Santa Monica, a territory Jimmy knew well. Discouraged and almost in despair, they eventually found a three-room top-floor apartment in a house around 4th Street, reached by an outside staircase and a catwalk. Bill has repeatedly tried to find the exact location, but the area is now mostly covered by tall condominiums and looks nothing like it did in the 1950s.

The apartment's rent of $70 a month was more than they could afford, but they decided that the advantages were sufficient to take it. The landlady was an art historian and collector, and the beamed living room had Aztec designs painted on the ceiling, and original Mexican art on the walls. They optimistically called it "The Penthouse," convinced that their luck would change and they would soon be able to support the rent.

Bill had been angling to get into the radio workshop at CBS, and had landed a part-time job as an usher, a break he attributed to the good luck bestowed by the new home. Jimmy, meanwhile, did the rounds and began to learn how hard it was for novice actors to crack the system. He faced intense competition and time-wasting executives who only held negative power, which is to say they could reject freely but did not have the clout to hire. He and Bill would converse intensely about theater and literature. Bill was far better educated, had read more and been to more exotic places. Jimmy was energetically responsive to new ideas, and was constantly drawing, modeling clay, painting, and declaiming. They held parties, often talking girls into providing supper in exchange for an evening's

◂ **STRANGE SIGN-OFF:** Jimmy indicates that he has borrowed both the letterhead and a typewriter, and signs with his temporary stage name, "Byron James," which was soon abandoned.

▲ **APOSTLE ACT:** Jimmy as Christ's disciple John in Father Peyton's Easter television production *Hill Number One.*

original entertainment in the form of sketches, discussions of contemporary literature, and even dramatic readings from Henry Miller's notorious suppressed novel *Tropic of Cancer*.

Jimmy had been disappointed when the only part he secured in the 1951 spring semester productions at UCLA was a one-act student work about Martin Luther called *The Axe of God* by Richard Eshleman. He was cast as a monk who seeks out Luther in exile at Wartburg and is disillusioned by what he finds – an old man more concerned with his creaky gut than communion with God. Eshleman, then the red-hot campus playwright, later recalled that he found Jimmy's interpretation so exciting that he kept attending rehearsals. Given a ride one evening by Eshleman, Jimmy confided his dissatisfaction with fraternity life, his feelings regarding his father, and his general unhappiness at UCLA. Eshleman urged him on the basis of his talent to switch to a Theater Arts major, which would have meant dropping out and re-enrolling.

Then came an important breakthrough. Jerry Fairbanks was producing a special Easter program for *Family Theater Presents*, a religious drama series hosted by Father Patrick Peyton, and it was reported in the trade papers as "the most ambitious and imposing television film undertaking yet planned." With a 30-strong cast, including such established actors as Leif Erickson, Gene Lockhart, Ruth Hussey, Joan Leslie, Roddy McDowall, Jeanne Cagney, and Regis Toomey, *Hill Number One* was an ambitious hour-long work. Jimmy would play the apostle John and deliver a few lines in two scenes. The script was lamentable, delivered in a biblical idiom by strutting Romans and shuffling Jews, but in a way it was a forerunner of Hollywood's obsession in the 1950s with biblical stories, such as *The Robe* that launched CinemaScope two years later.

Jimmy had a severe cold when he was shooting his scenes and received minimal direction. Clean-shaven and wearing a shapeless smock, he looked extremely young (he was 20) in contrast to the other disciples, who are bearded and seem twice his size. Whatever the shortcomings of the production, it netted him a timely $150, which was more than adequate to pay the rent, and gave him his first onscreen credit. After it had aired on March 25, 1951, he even received fan mail of sorts, a request from the seniors at the Immaculate Heart High, a Catholic girls' school, to attend the inaugural meeting of their James Dean Appreciation Society. He took Bill along and enjoyed drinking tea and eating the cake they had baked for him, as well as signing many autographs like a real movie star. Although the reviews had been respectful, none had singled him out for special mention, and the money earned quickly disappeared without fresh offers to replenish it. It was not just his small stature that was held against him; his cultivated air of petulance and rebellion would have almost certainly alienated casting directors not quite ready for a new generation of "cool" actors.

Meanwhile, Bill Bast had met the highly praised actor James Whitmore, who had been in the successful Broadway production *Command Decision*, for which he had won a Tony. Whitmore had made his Hollywood debut in *Undercover Man*, and even won an Academy Award for Best Supporting Actor in *Battleground*. He had studied drama at Yale University, and in New York at the Actors Studio under Elia Kazan and Lee Strasberg. After seeing some productions at UCLA he had formed an informal drama workshop, which followed the precepts of the Actors Studio. A small group of ten dedicated young people gathered in a meeting room over the Brentwood Country Mart at 26th Street and San Vicente Boulevard, and Bill made sure that Jimmy became part of it. Jimmy was captivated by Whitmore's approach, which was totally different to the academic orthodoxy of the Theater Arts department. Whitmore conveyed his love of acting, its power of affirmation, and its extension of the senses, explaining how it could fulfill the performer with the very breath of life, even if the pinnacle was attained though physical pain, emotional torment, and self-sacrifice. Such is the suffering of art. Whitmore, who at 30 had the look of a young Spencer Tracy, was an inspired and inspiring teacher. He convinced Jimmy not only that he had to leave UCLA, but also that he would have to consider going to New York to study at the Actors Studio. Later, Jimmy told the columnist Hedda Hopper: "There's always someone in your life who opens up your eyes. For me, that's Whitmore. He made me see myself. He opened me up, gave me the key."

> "Some high-school girls thought he was sexy and started a fan club. Even then, Dean could go through a lens." JAMES BELLAH

Jimmy quit UCLA, although Bill, who was nearing the end of his four-year course, continued for the time being. They were having an uneasy experience sharing The Penthouse, and Bill found Jimmy's moodiness, bouts of depression, fits of anger, reluctance to perform household chores and to come up with the rent hard to accommodate. As audition after audition produced no results, the touchiness increased, and Bill regarded his housemate as completely antisocial. A further rift occurred over a girl Bill had been dating, with whom Jimmy became emotionally involved.

Beverly Wills was the daughter of the popular comedienne Joan Davis. Beverly also had acting ambitions and was playing a part in a radio show called *Junior Miss*. Bill met her at CBS, became friendly, and was soon enjoying the occasional meal at her mother's expensive home in Bel Air – a relief from the starvation diet he was enduring at The Penthouse (one of Jimmy's ingenious moneysaving dishes was a mixture of oatmeal and mayo or jam). With Beverly's friend Jeanetta Lewis in mind he organized a double date. Jimmy was surly and uncommunicative, until Beverly started to talk about acting, when his interest was suddenly sparked and he became animated. Within two weeks, Beverley told Bill that she and Jimmy were in love. Their love of acting had forged a bond that had grown deep very quickly. Bill was forgiving, and inwardly blamed himself. He felt that he had been interested in her opportunistically and had paid the price.

The new relationship did not last very long. Joan Davis found her daughter's new friend untidy, disrespectful, and sullen, and made little secret of it. He slouched and put his boots up on her table, raided her refrigerator, and used profane language. The dislike was mutual; he despised her wealth and her patronizing manner. His moodiness stifled the development of their affair and Beverly drifted away. He was simultaneously trying to string Jeanetta along, using her as an emotional prop, and she too departed. Beverly Wills was to have a short film career, and died in a house fire in 1963, along with her grandmother and two sons.

Bill and Jimmy were still living on a shoestring, with Bill carrying the financial burden on his own. He finally prevailed upon Jimmy to take a part-time usher's job at CBS. The pay was not high but was at least regular. Unfortunately it was not a role that Jimmy was prepared to perform. He hated the uniform, which he claimed made him look like a monkey. Insubordinate and uncooperative, he was fired within the first week, severely embarrassing Bill, who had fought to get him hired. Generously, he gave his friend a last chance. Bill's mother paid a visit, stocked the refrigerator, and also cooked a few welcome meals. However, she misunderstood Jimmy's taciturn manner, and was very surprised on leaving to be presented with chocolates, flowers, and an envelope, which she opened after her train had pulled out of the Union Station. In it was his photograph, inscribed "To my second mother. With love from Jimmie."

Finally Bill decided that he could no longer live with Jimmy's incessant moodiness, and moved out. Jimmy also decided to find another place and got in touch with Ted Avery, whom he had met at CBS.

▲ **HOUSE CALL:** Jimmy with the mother of his UCLA roommate Bill Bast. Mrs. Bast paid a visit, cooked a few meals, and was surprised by Jimmy's farewell gift.

▶ **HIGH DRAMA:** Jimmy looks stunned, stage blood dripping from his mouth, in an early performance.

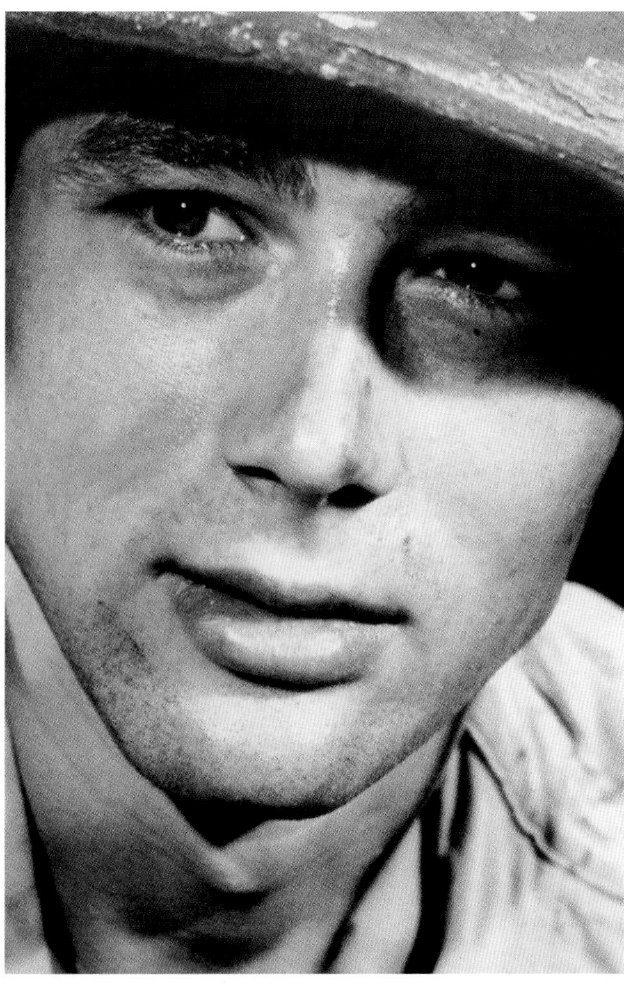

▲ **MOVIE DEBUT:** Jimmy secured a bit part in Samuel Fuller's *Fixed Bayonets!* as a GI in the Korean War, then being waged.

As Avery's wife was away visiting her family, he offered him the sofa in their apartment on North Edgemont in Hollywood, and he also got him a job in the parking lot next to CBS. It suited Jimmy well: no uniform to wear, a tolerant boss, easy hours, and plenty of tips to boost the wages. There was even the possibility of parking the automobile of an influential executive, and catching his attention – the ambition of many a Hollywood carhop.

The tactic worked. He met Rogers Brackett, the radio director of Foote, Cone, and Belding, a leading advertising agency responsible for producing many programs in the golden age of sponsored broadcasting. Agencies handled the entire production from scripting and casting to transmission, with the networks merely providing the air time. The 35-year-old Brackett was distinguished, influential, well connected, comfortably salaried, and homosexual. He was immensely impressed by the youthful, good-looking, ambitious actor, and declared that he could help him. By the time Avery's wife returned from her trip, Jimmy had moved out and into Brackett's apartment on Sunset Plaza Drive. It was a short walk from the renowned, billboard-encrusted Sunset Strip, the then-unadopted part of Sunset Boulevard between Crescent Heights Boulevard and the city limits of Beverly Hills, where nightclubs, restaurants bars, and live entertainment flourished. Brackett maintained his primary home in New York as well as his main office, but his job required his frequent presence on the West Coast.

Brackett represented the springboard into the business that Jimmy so badly needed. Jimmy was ambitious, calculating, and focused on achieving a career break, and Brackett was a convenient means to an end. Brackett immediately found him jobs on radio programs such as *Alias Jane Doe*, *Stars over Hollywood*, and *Hallmark Playhouse*, and he also made money from radio commercials. Late in the summer of 1951 he even managed a bit part in Samuel Fuller's Korean War film *Fixed Bayonets!* although he was uncredited. He was paid just over $44 for his day's work. At the time of filming Jimmy was concerned over the draft, for which he was still eligible, and the onset of the Korean War in 1950 had made the situation more pressing, as his university deferment had expired once he had left UCLA. The director of Selective Service in Indiana at the time, Robert Custer, stated that Jimmy had advanced a conscientious objection argument, which was in accordance with his Quaker upbringing, but that it had been referred to the national board.

At the end of September he played another uncredited role, as a boxing second in the locker room in *Sailor Beware*, a Dean Martin and Jerry Lewis comedy, and two weeks later was given a line to deliver in a 1920s romantic comedy musical *Has Anybody Seen My Gal* directed by Douglas Sirk and starring Rock Hudson (later to play the male lead with Jimmy in *Giant*). Jimmy, again uncredited, played a young man wearing a collegiate outfit of white trousers, sweater, bow tie, and boater, breathlessly addressing Charles Coburn who is serving at a soda fountain: "Hey, Gramps! I'll have a choc malt, heavy on the choc, plenty of milk, four spoons of malt, two scoops of vanilla ice cream, one mixed with the rest and one floating."

> "He sapped the minds of his friends as a blood-sucker saps the strength of an unsuspecting man."
>
> BILL BAST

▲ **CREAM CONFECTION:** Jimmy (right) had an almost impossible line to deliver in *Has Anybody Seen My Gal.*

Rogers Brackett introduced Jimmy to more than just his business contacts. They went down to Tijuana, across the Mexican border from San Diego, and on another occasion to Mexicali, to watch bull fights, a passion Jimmy had acquired from DeWeerd. In Mexicali he met the director Budd Boetticher, a bullfighting fanatic, who made him a present of a bloodstained cape. It had belonged to the Brooklyn-born matador Sidney Franklin, who had been celebrated in prose by Ernest Hemingway. Brackett gave him a copy of *The Little Prince*, Antoine de Saint-Exupéry's enchanting allegorical story

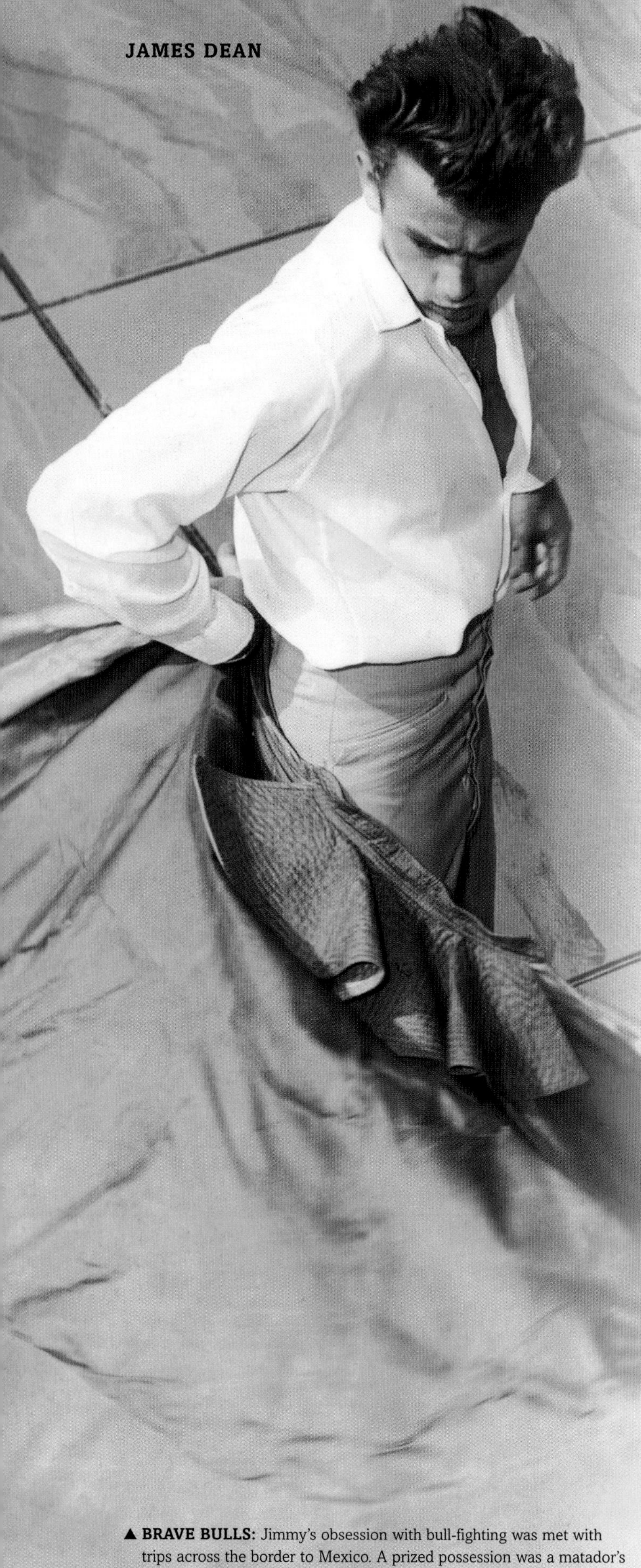

▲ **BRAVE BULLS:** Jimmy's obsession with bull-fighting was met with trips across the border to Mexico. A prized possession was a matador's cape and horns.

written in 1943. It became Jimmy's favorite bedside book, and he frequently read it aloud, or quoted its philosophy to friends. He memorized such thoughts as "Love does not consist in gazing at each other but in looking outward together in the same direction."

Although he was gaining parts, Jimmy realized that they were not the sort that would advance his career. He remembered the advice of James Whitmore – that to make it in acting he should go to New York and learn his craft at the Actors Studio. On *Sailor Beware* he had met another actor, Dick Clayton, who told him that he was giving up acting to become an agent because he did not have Jimmy's talent. When Jimmy told him that he was thinking of going to New York, Clayton recommended one or two agents' names to him, including that of Jane Deacy. He would no longer have need of Isabel Draesemer.

Coincidentally, Brackett was required by his employers, FCB, to go to Chicago and then on to New York. In October they traveled east together and wound up in separate rooms at the luxurious Ambassador Hotel in Chicago, the cost borne by Brackett. While he attended a series of business meetings over several days, Jimmy filled in the time by going to Fairmount, a visit that took the town by surprise, as only a few days earlier they had been reading a somewhat garbled account of his Hollywood sojourn. Adeline Brookshire persuaded the high-school principal to allow him to address the students. He delivered a *tour de force*, relating his experience that ranged from making a Pepsi commercial to acting a scene with Jerry Lewis. He also showed them the art of the matador, twirling his cape and sidestepping an aggressive bull, simulated by a senior who had been brought into the demonstration. Later he was asked to direct a rehearsal for the junior play, *Men are Like Streetcars*, and called upon the techniques learned at his Whitmore classes, taking so much time that anxious parents were calling the school wondering what had happened to their children.

He went on to Indianapolis and caught up with Rev. DeWeerd, who was now in charge of a tabernacle there. Jimmy ranked high in his regard and he gave him $200 toward his expenses. Back in Chicago he was frustrated by Brackett's protracted corporate business. Sensing his impatience, Brackett also provided funds and bought him a ticket on the *Twentieth Century Limited* – the all-Pullman flagship express of the New York Central, which passengers boarded along a red carpet at La Salle Street Station each day at 5pm, and disembarked at Grand Central some 16 hours later. Brackett then called a friend, Alec Wilder, the eclectic composer who had a permanent suite at the Hotel Algonquin on West 44th Street, to help Jimmy on arrival. Brackett intended to follow when he could.

Jimmy arrived at Grand Central Terminal on the morning of the following day. He was feeling happy and energized as he stepped out of the station into the fall sunshine and the bustle of Manhattan. He called Wilder from a payphone at the station and was immediately invited to breakfast at the Algonquin, three blocks away. He made his way across Madison and Fifth Avenue, which in 1951 was still two-way, every intersection ornamented by handsome gilded traffic signals, each surmounted by a tiny statue of Mercury.

Wilder later introduced him to the smaller and more modest Hotel Iroquois a couple of doors along 44th Street, where Jimmy rented a room. But he grew to love the atmosphere of the Algonquin lobby with its dark paneling, coved ceilings, ornate lampshades, comfortable armchairs, and little tables equipped with fixed bells for summoning service. It gave the impression of being unchanged since Frank Case ran the hotel in the days of the Round Table literary wits of the 1920s: Benchley, Parker, Woolcott, Kaufman, Ferber, Sherwood, and Franklin P. Adams, and the literary cast of the New Yorker, led by its singular editor Harold Ross. Jimmy made friends with the bellmen, some of whom had worked there then. On any given day the celebrity count in the lobby was likely to be high. It was the gathering place and listening post for the Broadway aristocracy, where Orson Welles might be pontificating in a corner, Irving Berlin greeting friends, or Rodgers and Hammerstein plotting a new musical.

In those first weeks in New York Jimmy went to the movies, sometimes seeing three in a day. Two of them made a profound impression: *A Streetcar Named Desire* from Warner Bros., directed by Elia Kazan, in which Marlon Brando repeated his electrifying performance as Stanley Kowalski in the film version of Tennessee Williams' play, with Vivien Leigh as Blanche DuBois; and Paramount's *A Place in the Sun*, directed by George Stevens and based on *An American Tragedy* by the Indianan novelist Theodore Dreiser, which starred Montgomery Clift as a poor boy with designs on the lifestyle of a rich heiress, played by Elizabeth Taylor. Brando and Clift represented the emergent new face of American acting, and both were exponents of the Method. Clift, who made his first Broadway appearance in 1935 at the age of 13, had spent more than a decade in New York theater before becoming a movie star with Howard Hawks's classic western *Red River*, and had been

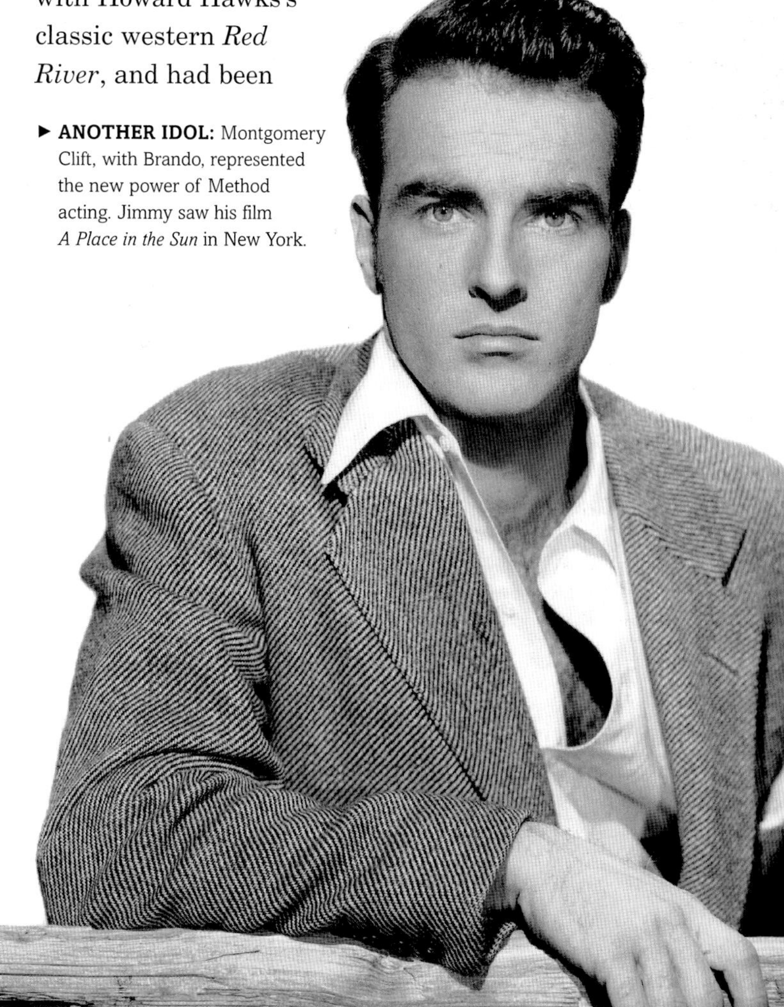

▶ **ANOTHER IDOL:** Montgomery Clift, with Brando, represented the new power of Method acting. Jimmy saw his film *A Place in the Sun* in New York.

Oscar-nominated for his performance in *A Place in the Sun*. He and Brando shared the distinction of being role models for Jimmy, and in later years the trio would be regarded as an entity, the leaders of the Method pack.

Eventually Jimmy moved away from the few midtown blocks around Times Square, and started roaming the city. He became a serious insomniac, consuming vast quantities of caffeine, cigarettes, and alcohol, developing a city pallor and heavy bags under his eyes. The star athlete of high-school and college years was no more. The only job of any consequence to come his way in that period was secured in November 1951, when he was taken on by *Beat the Clock*, a television show in which contestants had to perform silly manual dexterity tasks within a time limit, as an outsized second hand ticked round a dial. Jimmy was required to test the stunts first to see if they were practical, and was paid $5 per hour. He performed so well that none of the contestants came close to matching his speed, and so he was fired.

As his money ebbed away he moved out of the Iroquois in January 1952 and found a berth in the YMCA on West 63rd Street, close to Central Park where he often wandered, the Indianan in him relieved to find a green oasis in the heart of the overwhelming city. He washed dishes in a bar to earn his modest rent.

When Jimmy ate in New York he had a choice of low-priced establishments, particularly the celebrated, now-vanished institution of Horn and Hardart's chain of Automats, where a coin in a slot would open a small, windowed hatch allowing access to the laden dish behind. At Romeo's on Broadway spaghetti was cooked in the window in spectacular fashion, the chef churning and tossing the pasta with panache, as a mouthwatering lure. Hector's at Times Square was a popular cafeteria offering an abundance of cheap fare. Jimmy soon discovered Jerry's Bar on Sixth Avenue at 54th Street, and made good friends with the proprietor, Jerry Lucci, who would often let him eat for nothing more than good conversation. It became his favorite

New York hangout, and when the restaurant was full he would eat his meal in the kitchen. Another well-regarded spot was Cromwell's Pharmacy in the NBC lobby at Rockefeller Plaza. The coffee counter had the reputation of being the poor man's Sardi's, but was more comparable with Schwab's on Sunset Boulevard, as it was a place where resting actors could sit for hours, occasionally putting calls through to their agents from one of a bank of payphones.

These were difficult times for Jimmy, but then Rogers Brackett, still in Chicago, came to his aid. He made the long-distance call that put Jimmy in touch with Ralph Levy, a television director, who in turn passed him on to James Sheldon, an executive at the Young and Rubicam advertising agency. Sheldon asked Jimmy to read for him, and immediately realized that he possessed a sensitive, intelligent talent. At that time Dick Van Patten was about to be drafted, and a replacement was sought for his part in a television sitcom called *Mama*, based on the Broadway play *I Remember Mama* which had starred Brando. Jimmy was given an audition and offered the job on the spot. It was an extraordinary career break, because the show was a national favorite. But bad luck struck again. Van Patten was rejected in category 4-F as unfit for service and went back into the show. Had that not happened, Jimmy's career could well have gone in a different direction.

▲ **NEWS FROM NEW YORK:** Jimmy used the stationery at the Hotel Iroquois, where he stayed for a while in New York, to write to his young cousin back in Indiana.

◄ **FAST FOOD:** One of Jimmy's New York hangouts was Riker's, where he could make a cup of coffee and company last an evening - here with actor Martin Landau.

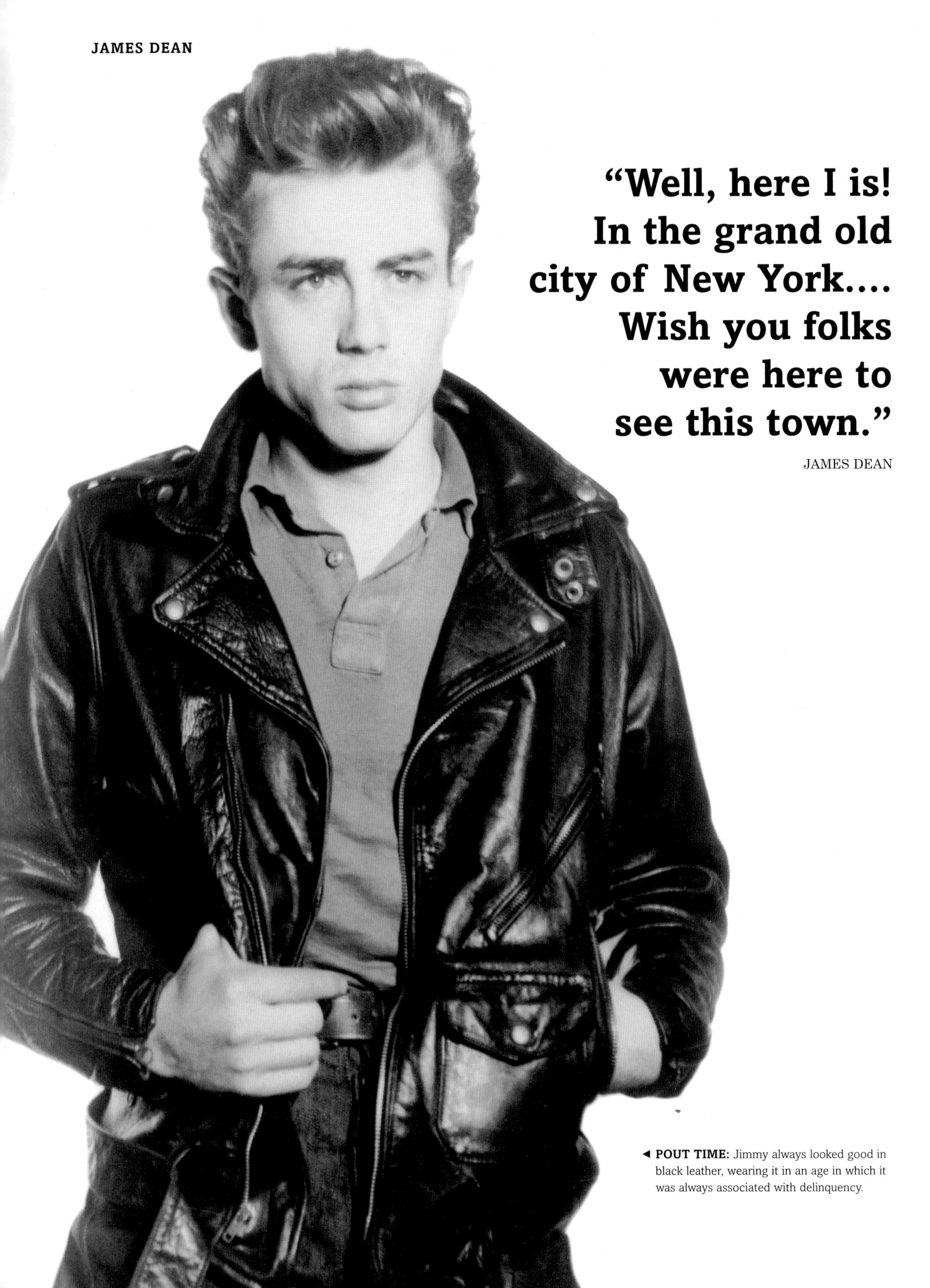

"Well, here I is! In the grand old city of New York.... Wish you folks were here to see this town."

JAMES DEAN

◄ **POUT TIME:** Jimmy always looked good in black leather, wearing it in an age in which it was always associated with delinquency.

Winton would often send him money. He frequently wrote to his father and Ethel (addressed as "Mom") telling them of his progress, urging them to catch a radio and later television performance, and assuring them that he was well. His letters were affectionate and natural, refuting the common perception that he and Winton did not get along. One such, commenting on the reality that at last his ancient Chevrolet ("Lena") had to go, read:

"Dear Mom & Dad
Forgive me for not writing. Sorry to hear about poor "Lena" but we all have to go some time. You did what was wisest and best. She was very good to me. I hope we meet each other again some day. She belonged to the theatre, being as temperamental as she was. My being away was to [sic] much for her. I knew she didn't feel well; but I had hopes she wouldn't get any sicker. She will be very happy once she gets acquainted with a new owner. She needs a slower life and someone who can take good care of her.

Now Ethel, you take good care of Dad! Take him away somewhere and have a lot of fun, relax and play. You and Dad have worked hard all your lives. Now please go and play!

I would like to come home but it isn't quite time yet. I almost went on the road with "Stalag 17" which would have gotten me there, but it wasn't quite the time. Things have been very tough for a while but seem to be picking up. Many nice things are happening to me. You might want to listen to "The Theater Guild on the Air" Sunday May 11th. I'm playing a young Kentuckian. It's about Abe Lincoln "The Paths of Glory" I think. On the radio. Also Crime Syndicate T.V. originates from here Tuesday May 13th, 9-9:30. C.B.S.
All my love
Jim"

Jimmy discovered the Rehearsal Club, located in two adjoining brownstone houses on West 53rd between Sixth and Seventh Avenues. It was a residence for young women in the performing arts, and he had been invited for a meal. It offered secure and reasonable comfort for actresses, singers, and dancers at a modest price, with a 20-bed dorm for short stays, and single, double, and triple rooms for long-term guests. Its vast lobby was the forum for gossip, exchanging contacts, playing checkers, and meeting men friends, who were allowed to stay until midnight but not permitted to put so much as a foot on the staircase. He liked the atmosphere so much that he began to go there unasked, chatting to whoever happened to be around, sometimes accepting a Coke or a sandwich. One of its residents was a tall, dark-haired, young dancer called Elizabeth Sheridan, better known as Dizzy. Although she came from a monied background – her mother was a singer and her divorced father was Frank Sheridan, a distinguished concert pianist – she was making her own way as best she could in a dancing partnership with two men, eking a living by performing in clubs and taking whatever engagements they could find. In the lobby late one wet afternoon she saw Jimmy in raincoat and glasses, huddled on a couch and reading a magazine, his dampness visibly turning into vapor around him. Daringly, he had his feet on the coffee table, which was not the done thing in this genteel establishment. She sat down opposite and watched him light a cigarette, noting his self-assurance and grace in simple gestures. They were the only two present, and she heard him muttering what sounded like jibberish, but was probably Jimmy reading aloud. She responded, prompting laughter and then an introduction. She loaned him her umbrella.

▼ **MOMA ROOF:** Jimmy and friends, including actor Martin Landau and musician Leonard Rosenman, enjoy the sun on the upper deck of the Museum of Modern Art, West 53rd Street.

It was the beginning of an intimate relationship. He went to Harlem and saw her dance in a club and was entranced. She in turn became enamored by his conversation, his wild ambition, and his brilliant napkin doodles. Jerry's became their favorite hangout.

Although she was two years older than him – he turned 21 on February 8, 1952 – they had a similar sense of humor. She consoled him after he lost his job on *Beat the Clock*, and shared his delight when he secured a part in a segment of *The Web*, a drama series on CBS in which he played a bellhop who helps find his brother's murderer. He was hard to rehearse and had trouble finding his marks as well as agonizing over the character. Yet after the show was aired on February 20, he was hired by the producers of *Martin Kane, Private Eye*, but was soon fired because he was considered too difficult, and he only received his money because of his union card. He managed to keep a small role in an episode of *Studio One* called "Ten Thousand Horses Singing," another undemanding role playing

another bellhop, on screen for less than a minute. Better was "The Foggy, Foggy Dew," a half-hour segment for *Lux Video Theatre*, in which he had his first long speaking part, alongside James Barton as the star.

Dizzy and Jimmy grew closer. They talked about bullfighting and *The Little Prince*, music and poetry. They stayed in bars and cafés half the night and wandered around Central Park by day. When they were invited to Sunday dinner by her mother, who lived at Larchmont, outside the city between New Rochelle and Mamaroneck, overlooking Long Island Sound, he suggested taking the train the day before and checking in for the Saturday night at an inn near the Yacht Club, blowing his earnings. It was 1952 and decency demanded a subterfuge, and so they signed the register as Mr. and Mrs. James Dean. The bellboy charitably treated them as newlyweds. The following day Jimmy charmed Mrs. Sheridan, Dizzy's mother, for once putting his rough manners to one side.

He and Dizzy took a room, a so-called studio, in an apartment hotel on West 71st Street. She flitted from job to job, working as a part-time photo retoucher when she was not dancing.

In the spring their romance suffered a serious setback. He told her about Rogers Brackett, who had at last arrived in New York and was living in his apartment on West 38th Street. Jimmy explained how Brackett had helped nurture his career, and how his connections could still open doors for him. Then he delivered his bombshell. He claimed that on the train from Los Angeles to Chicago they had shared a private compartment and Brackett had made a play for him. According to Dizzy, Jimmy had this to say: "He didn't threaten me or anything, but he gave me the impression that our relationship depended on that moment. I decided to go along with it. I succumbed to him. I felt bad afterward. Really strange, like a whore. I felt really uncomfortable selling myself like that, so I left him in Chicago, where he had business to take care of, and came to New York on my own."

Dizzy was anguished and confused. To add to the misery, the following day they were thrown out for rent arrears, and she went alone to find a room near Hell's Kitchen, the seedy midtown West Side district between the Hudson River piers and Ninth Avenue. A day or two later she found Jimmy in a miserable state in a phone booth at Jerry's. By now her bitterness had subsided and she forgave him, after which they went back to her place together. Although it was an unhappy situation, she had decided to come to terms with it, and even agreed to go to Brackett's apartment and meet him, so that Jimmy could demonstrate that he and Dizzy were a couple.

"It's rough going here.... I hope I get work before I run out of money." JAMES DEAN

However disappointed Brackett might have been, he continued to support Jimmy in his quest for work. New York was the center of the rapidly expanding television business, with the proximity of Broadway theater providing a source of drama. There had even been instances of plays written for television subsequently succeeding as motion pictures: Paddy Chayefsky's *Marty*, screened on TV in 1953 and starring Rod Steiger, was later made into an Oscar-winning movie with Ernest Borgnine in the title role; Reginald Rose's *Twelve Angry Men* was translated into film by Sidney Lumet; and Robert Alan Arthur's play *A Man is Ten Feet Tall* was filmed as *Edge of the City*. There was demand from sponsors for drama, which was considered to be an excellent way to enhance corporate prestige. Jimmy's TV appearances gradually increased. In May he had the first of three roles in *Kraft Television Theatre*, then a part in a *Studio One* episode on Abraham Lincoln. Brackett helped him to obtain a role in a *Hallmark Hall of Fame* episode, and also found him a production assistant job at NBC during the summer months.

MUrray Hill 2-7464 BETWEEN FIFTH AND SIXTH AVENUES

HOTEL IROQUOIS
49 WEST 44th STREET
NEW YORK 36, N. Y.

Dear Marcus Jr,

First I want to thank you for the fine pictures.

I feel the urgent need to warn you about something. Anyone at all can draw ~~soldiers~~, guns, and barred gates with Locks on them. Why? because there are alot of those things to see. That shouldn't mean that they are good things to draw. We live in a world where these things become very important. And that is bad. You should be aware of that because you don't have to see too many of those things because you live on land that is greatly blessed by Lord God.

It would be much better if you would spread your talents toward the greater arts. Everyone can't draw trees, clouds, sheep, dogs, all kinds of animals, the earth, hills, mountains, seas oceans. I Beg of you please Do not draw buildings of confindment, Jails, castles or zoos rather draw places of shelter.

~~Do not draw people in uniforms, rather~~ draw people who are free

Do not draw things of Destruction, they are not so important to the good + true artist that he must draw them – rather draw tool, things that build. there are many things to draw at home. All you have to do is look and you will see. They Are harder to draw because they were harder to grow. Have your Daddy help you read this Love

Jim

Sheldon pushed Jimmy toward his agent Jane Deacy, who was employed at the Louis Shurr Agency, having started there as the switchboard operator. Jimmy was familiar with her name, as it had been mentioned to him by Clayton back in Los Angeles. They had an instant affinity, and it looked as though the young actor had found yet another surrogate mother. He even called her "Mom," although she had other clients who addressed her in similar fashion. She recognized the smoldering talent within, and was happy to gently give him the encouragement he craved. Soon afterward she left Shurr to set up on her own in an office on 42nd Street, and Jimmy was willing to stay as her client, along with several other talented new actors, including George C. Scott and Martin Landau. The latter became one of Jimmy's best friends in New York.

Calling on Jane Deacy one day, Jimmy met Christine White using the secretary's typewriter during the lunch break, and discovered that she was an aspiring actress and playwright. They each yearned to join the Actors Studio. The Stanislavsky-based workshop had its roots in the Group Theater of the 1930s and was founded by Cheryl Crawford, Elia Kazan, and Robert Lewis in 1947, and conducted by Lee Strasberg. Membership, by rigorous auditions, was free and for life. Jimmy suggested to Christine that she write a scene for them to use as an audition piece. They spent the next couple of months working on it, rehearsing at every opportunity, trying it on audiences of barflies, automat customers, and old friends at the Iroquois. They formed a close, spiritual relationship. She was five years older than him, and although she later met Dizzy, Christine was unaware that she was his live-in partner. Dizzy was in Ocean City, New Jersey for a summer job and, when she returned, Christine had gone to Hollywood for three months, so Jimmy was spared the problem of having to explain his relationship with either one to the other.

The scene performed by Christine and Jimmy was without scenery or props, and was set on an island beach as a hurricane approaches. In essence it was a dialog between an anxious girl escaping her parents and a beach bum. As there was only one audition, it can be assumed that it was seen by Kazan, Crawford, and Strasberg, and, although the performance went over length, the auditioners were spared the intrusion of the buzzer. They were accepted, among the 15 chosen from 150 hopefuls. Few ever made it at the first attempt. Geraldine Page was alleged to have tried nine times, and much later Dustin Hoffman had seven goes. Jimmy at 21 was probably the youngest recruit.

He wrote to the Winslows:

"You wanted to know what I was doing, also if you could help me in any way. Yes, you could help me very much but first I must tell you what has happened. I have made great strides in my craft. After months of auditioning I am very proud to announce that I am a member of the Actors Studio. The greatest school of the theatre. It houses great people like Marlon Brando, Julie Harris, Arthur Kennedy, Elia Kazan, Mildred Dunock, Keven Mackarthy [sic], Monty Clift, June Havoc, and on & on and on. Very few get into it and it is absolutely free. It is the best thing that can happen to an actor. I am one of the youngest to belong."

It is paradoxical that, having tried so hard to get in, he turned out be a passive member, only attending a few times and contributing little. When he did deliver a mimed piece of his own, extracted from *Matador*, a novel by Barnaby Conrad in which a bullfighter prepares to enter the ring for the last time, it was critically analyzed by Strasberg in fierce terms. So much so that Jimmy listened with increasing misery then walked out, his cape slung over his shoulder, and was hardly seen at the Actors Studio again. Strasberg remarked that he only dissected so fiercely when the performer had a genuine, unique talent.

The nature of the Method – a discipline that involves the total absorption of the actor's inner-most feelings into the creation of character so that all the emotional senses are so closely focused from within that he or she becomes at one with the part –

can play psychological havoc with the practitioner. The most famous Method actors – Brando, Clift, and Jimmy – were never as avid participants in Studio classes as is commonly thought. Jimmy did, however, subject himself to the daily exercises, "ripping away layers to find roots," as he put it. The Method, in a way, was an American response to the academic approach of classical dramatic training, the antithesis of the British style, in which interpretation of meaning transcended feeling. Olivier or Gielgud could play Hamlet and, after the performance walk away, back to normal life. A Method actor, however, would carry the torment home with him on the subway.

Bill Bast arrived in New York in the spring of 1952 seeking work, and for a time roomed with Dizzy and Jimmy in the impossibly small apartment on West 71st. She had a job as an usher in an arthouse movie theater, and Bill eventually found a writing job at CBS. In the late summer Jimmy, on impulse, persuaded the them to hitchhike with him to Fairmount. After an anxious hour or two waiting on the Pennsylvania Turnpike they were picked up in a Nash Rambler by Clyde McCullough, the star catcher for the Pittsburgh Pirates, who was on his way to a game in Des Moines. He enjoyed their company so much that he bought them an ample meal en route at a Howard Johnson's diner.

▲ **CHEZ SCHATT:** Friends gather at New Year's Eve in Roy Schatt's apartment. From left is Barbara Glenn, Tony Ray (son of Nicholas Ray), Bob Heller, Billy Gunn with bongo, Jimmy, Martin Landau. Billy was the subject of Jimmy's oil painting, this time with a saxophone.

In Fairmount Marcus and Ortense were fascinated by Jimmy's friends, to whom he introduced the fondly remembered rural places of childhood. When Jimmy announced that he was coming Marcus had telephoned Winton in California, who agreed to make one of his infrequent visits to Indiana and would take a look at his son's dental bridge, the legacy of his childhood mishap. Dizzy remarked: "Father and son hugged awkwardly, and I was struck by how reserved and self-conscious Winton seemed. His gestures were small and controlled. I don't remember seeing him laugh the entire time we were there." Marcus Winslow Jr. questions her recollection. "Winton joined in the jokes with everyone and wasn't at all like that. It's not the Winton I knew, and I was there."

"I think I'll make it all right." JAMES DEAN

Adeline Brookshire invited them to address the high-school drama class. Bill gave a brilliant exposition on the art of writing, Dizzy demonstrated how dance was another form of communication, and Jimmy recited one sentence: "My name is James Dean and I am an actor" in a score of different ways – melancholic, manic, aggressive, reluctant, hysterical, tearful – and ended by describing Brookshire as the best teacher he ever had. Their respite from New York was cut short by a phone call from Jane Deacy. The producer Lemuel Ayers was casting a play and wanted Jimmy for a key role. Within hours of the call, the trio was thumbing rides back east, accomplishing the 800-mile journey in three stages, the last in a big Cadillac piloted by a Texan who was so drunk that Jimmy took the wheel for the latter part of the journey. Jimmy had met Ayers

▶ **GETTING THE LOOK:** In New York Jimmy worked on his appearance, with encouragement from photographers, especially Roy Schatt, and the cool, easy air of non-deference began to evolve.

▲ **STREET SMART:** The boots, the sweater, the casually slung black overcoat, unremarkable in later years, were greatly at odds with the buttoned-down styles of the 1950s.

through Brackett, and visited his country estate at Stony Point up the Hudson. In spite of being a landlubber, Jimmy had even talked his way into crewing on a 10-day yacht cruise from Cape Cod.

The play, *See the Jaguar* by N. Richard Nash, was about Wally Wilkins, a 17-year-old backwoods boy who is confined in an icehouse by his neurotic, possessive mother so that he will not be contaminated by the world outside. When she dies, he faces the world as a helpless naïf. Jimmy's informal reading of the part led Nash to observe: "He was the only person in the play who caught the spirit of it, I'd say. He had it from the beginning." The omens looked good for his Broadway debut. Alec Wilder had composed the score. Michael Gordon was the director.

The Hartford newspapers singled Jimmy out for praise. The company moved to Philadelphia where Tennessee Williams saw Jimmy's performance, and was enthusiastic when they met at a cast party. Next was the big test – Broadway. With Arthur Kennedy and Constance Ford as the other leads, *See the Jaguar* opened on December 3 at the Cort. At Sardi's, Dizzy had watched him assuming a new celebrity status. The early reviews attacked the play but praised him: "James Dean adds an extraordinary performance," said Walter F. Kerr in the *New York Herald Tribune*; "As the boy James Dean is very good," said John Chapman in the

New York Daily News; "James Dean achieves the feat of making the childish young fugitive believable and unembarrassing," said Richard Watts Jr. in the *New York Post*.

Jimmy and Dizzy went afterward to the Royalton Hotel, opposite the Iroquois on West 44th Street and at that time greatly superior, where Ayers had provided him with a room. It was the way of things then that a room-service waiter should report her presence to the desk, and a manager telephoned insisting that she leave when the meal was finished. Jimmy put her in a cab and wandered back to the room. They were lovers no more. Many years later, as Liz Sheridan, she became known throughout the world for playing Jerry Seinfeld's mother in the TV sitcom *Seinfeld*. She wrote a memoir of her relationship with James Dean, claiming that it was the first time either of them had experienced romantic love. Close as they were, she said that she never uncovered his deepest secrets.

> "The producer told Dean he was too short. Dean ... told him to stand up. The producer came up to Dean's shoulders." JANE DEACY

Jimmy resumed residence at the Iroquois as he could now just afford it (although according to Christine White, who was persuaded to take a room there after returning from Hollywood, he had no refrigerator and kept his milk on the fire escape, spending lonely days lying on his bed playing his recorder). Bill Bast moved in on the same floor, staying until he returned to a job in Hollywood in the spring.

The play was a box-office failure and, after five performances, *See the Jaguar* closed on its first Saturday night. However, Jane Deacy was able to find Jimmy enough television roles to keep him busy and solvent. The medium was still in its infancy, and plays were usually performed live with no possibility of correcting mistakes. Studio conditions were cramped and primitive, and sometimes viewers could clearly hear noises as scenery was moved or the camera dollied to a new position. Recordings were not made on magnetic tape but on film, using a device called the Kinescope, which transferred the cathode-ray image directly to a movie camera. The results were even more degraded than the transmitted black-and-white television image, but at least enabled the plays that Jimmy appeared in to be preserved.

▲ **BOY IN A CAGE:** Jimmy in *See the Jaguar* on Broadway, flanked by Constance Ford and Arthur Kennedy. Although critics noted Jimmy's performance, the play closed on its first Saturday night.

Before coast-to-coast networking had become established, Kinescope prints would be sent from New York to Chicago, Los Angeles, and elsewhere, to be aired on different nights.

In 1953 Jimmy appeared in around 15 drama programs, including episodes of *Danger* on CBS, and on *NBC Campbell Soundstage*, *Kraft TV Theater*, *US Steel Hour*, *Armstrong Circle Theater*, and the premiere of the second season of the prestige program *Omnibus*, hosted by Alistair Cooke. On an episode of *Studio One Summer Theater* – "Sentence of Death," in which he played a youth falsely accused of murder – he met a young actress, Betsy Palmer, another Hoosier. They had an affair which she recalled as sexually muted, he preferring to talk and play records. She felt that he was fundamentally unhappy and sensitive, and, as an introvert herself, she enjoyed being with him.

Other relationships in his New York life included one with Barbara Glenn, an actress he met at Cromwell's Pharmacy. They had an on-off affair until he went to Hollywood in 1954. It was his longest relationship, and he even contemplated marriage. Then there was Arlene Lorca (Sachs), an actress he escorted on dates, and who introduced him to the photographer Roy Schatt. Jimmy was immediately bitten by the camera bug and bought a Leica. Schatt gave him guidance and encouragement on how to use it. It was one of many new passions. In quick succession Jimmy was going to Katherine Dunham with Eartha Kitt to learn dance, taking bongo lessons from the percussion king, Cyril Jackson, and receiving his personal Art Photography 101 lessons from Roy Schatt. A young composer, Leonard Rosenman, was also teaching him to play the piano, and would become a close friend.

In the spring of 1953 he found his final New York berth, a fifth-floor walk-up studio apartment at 19 West 68th Street. It was small, with two circular windows awkwardly positioned for looking out; one wall was lined with bookshelves, another adorned with his bull horns and matador cape, but it had room for a bed, a couch, a record player, and his bongo drums. It was for him a comfortable refuge.

Then came his second and last Broadway appearance. Ruth and Augustus Goetz had adapted André Gide's semiautobiographical novel *L'Immoraliste*, first published in 1904, and Billy Rose, who had a reputation as a controversialist, was the producer. The play dealt with the plight of a young homosexual archeologist, played by Louis Jourdan, who marries in the hope of becoming heterosexual. He and his bride (Geraldine Page) honeymoon in Morocco where a lecherous, thieving, blackmailing Arab houseboy (James Dean) lures him back into the gay world. Jimmy's classic moment was a seductive dance he performed

"... He began to read and he was marvelous. He was instinctively, absolutely right." RUTH GOETZ

in front of Jourdan, wearing dusky makeup and a loose burnoose, snipping the air with pair of scissors held in his hand, in time to the rhythm.

There were production difficulties. Herman Shumlin, the original director, was fired after the Philadelphia tryout, and replaced by Daniel Mann. Jimmy had not liked Shumlin very much but was even less enthusiastic about Mann. He also found little common ground with Louis Jourdan. The French actor was trained traditionally and was entirely unused to Method techniques. At rehearsals he was driven wild by Jimmy's unpredictability and what he took as a willful refusal to repeat an interpretation, claiming that his performance suffered. Mann felt that he had a delinquent adolescent on his hands who was upsetting the entire cast and who very nearly failed to show up for the first New York performance, having ridden off before curtain on his new Triumph motorcycle.

The Immoralist opened on February 8, 1954 at the Royale on West 45th Street to favorable reviews. For Jimmy it was a personal coup, with critics such as Walter Kerr and Richard Watts Jr. again singling him out for special mention. Barbara Glenn remembered how Jimmy went to Sardi's afterwards in torn jeans and a tee-shirt, and was barred entry, necessitating a hasty motorcycle ride up to 68th Street to change into a suit and tie – the only occasion she saw him so attired.

Even more extraordinary was the fact that just as he finally achieved his ambition and received the acclaim of Broadway, he gave Billy Rose 14 days' notice. There was a very good reason for quitting at his moment of glory, and the key to his departure lay in the hands of Elia Kazan.

◀ **SENSUAL ATTRACTION:** Jimmy, as a homosexual Arab houseboy, turns on the wiles in the Broadway adaptation of André Gide's *L'Immoraliste*. He grabbed great notices on opening night. Almost immediately he quit to go to Hollywood.

▼ **MOVING ON:** Jimmy relaxes in the circular window of his New York apartment. He retained it as his Manhattan *pied-a-terre* when he signed his contract with Warner Brothers.

Dean and Roy Schatt

The photographer Roy Schatt taught Jimmy how to use a camera, how to frame his shot, the subtleties of f stops, lens apertures, and film and shutter speeds. Jimmy loved composing and taking pictures, but was less keen on developing and printing them. After one tedious session in the darkroom, he exclaimed that it was a pain in the ass – he just wanted to shoot.

► **AIM AND SHOOT:** A habitual smoker, Jimmy never worried about ash falling into the big Rollei viewfinder.

◄ **SHUTTER BUG:** Jimmy always enjoyed photographing Martin Landau. For one session he used the area around the stoop of his apartment building on West 68th Street.

▼ **PATIENT POSER:** Landau ignored curious pedestrians as he posed.

Dean
The Star

While *The Immoralist* had been in rehearsal in December 1953, Jimmy was already going after a much bigger prize. Warner Bros. were preparing a movie, *Battle Cry*, to be directed by Raoul Walsh from the Leon Uris novel about young marines in World War II, and had set up a casting call in New York. **Jimmy attended, disheveled and unshaven, and delivered a superb reading.** William Orr, Warners' man in New York, had then sent a glowing commendation to the Burbank studios. **"James Dean ... is gaining quite a reputation as a fine young actor," he wrote, observing, "there is a trace of the Marlon Brando school in his work."** Although Jimmy was not cast in either of the roles he tried for, he was not forgotten.

▲ **NOBEL NOVELIST:** John Steinbeck, born and buried in Salinas, California, thought Dean was definitely Cal.

It was not Jimmy's first screen test. The director Fred Zinnemann had seen him in late 1953 when he was casting *Oklahoma!*, the lavish film version of the Rodgers and Hammerstein musical. Jimmy was considered for the role of Curly, the cowboy hero who introduces the action with "Oh, What a Beautiful Mornin'." Before the audition Jimmy had gone to see Zinnemann at the Hotel Pierre, clad in well-worn cowboy gear, and had been politely ejected as soon as he attempted to cross the lobby. Zinnemann recalled that he eventually arrived 45 minutes late, having sneaked in via a service elevator. For his test Jimmy had sung "Pore Jud is Daid" passably well, but it was his presence more than his singing voice that had impressed Zinnemann. Writing about it later, the director thought it was a classic. The part eventually went to the singing star Gordon MacRae.

Elia Kazan had persuaded Jack Warner, the studio head, to allow him to direct *East of Eden*, based on John Steinbeck's new novel – a retelling of the biblical tale of Cain and Abel set in California in the 19th and early 20th centuries. It had been published in September 1952 and by November it was the number one bestseller. The script was written by Paul Osborn who, like Kazan, lived in New York. For the screenplay much of the book was discarded, and Osborn began the action at Chapter 37 in Part 4, around the time of World War I. After he saw Jimmy's performance on stage in *The Immoralist*, Osborn called Kazan and urged him to consider Jimmy for the role of Cal Trask (Cain). Kazan had been thinking of offering the part to Brando, who he had directed in *A Streetcar Named Desire* in 1947 on Broadway and later on screen in 1951, as well as *Viva Zapata!* (1952) and *On the Waterfront* (1954). At Osborn's request, however, he agreed to see Jimmy, and called him to an interview at Warner's New York office. Kazan, who was often known as Gadg, or Gadge, short for a childhood nickname "Gadget," wrote in his autobiography: "When I walked in he was slouched at the end of a leather sofa in the waiting room, a heap of twisted legs and denim rags, looking resentful for no particular reason. I didn't like the expression on his face, so I kept him waiting."

> "He's an odd kid and I think we should make him as handsome as possible." ELIA KAZAN TO JACK WARNER

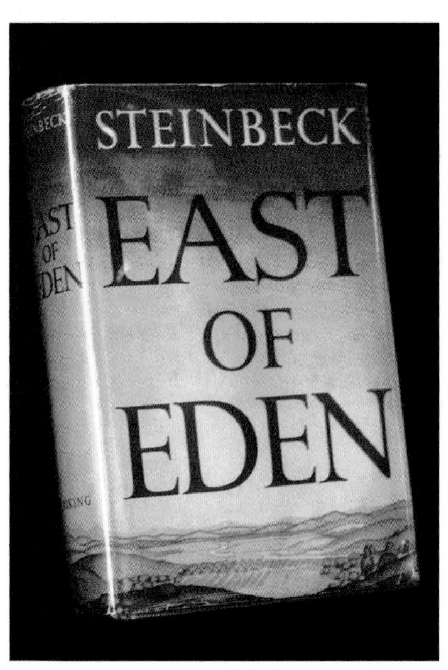

▲ **RAPID BESTSELLER:** Published in late 1952, Steinbeck's *East of Eden* quickly headed the fiction bestseller list. The film covered only the last quarter of the lengthy narrative.

It was a test. Jimmy dropped his belligerent attitude when called in, and after a difficult exchange ("conversation was not his gift," said Kazan), he offered to take the older man on a motorcycle ride. Kazan accepted, game for anything in the name of art, and was shortly afterward roaring down Broadway on the precarious backseat.

Elia Kazan

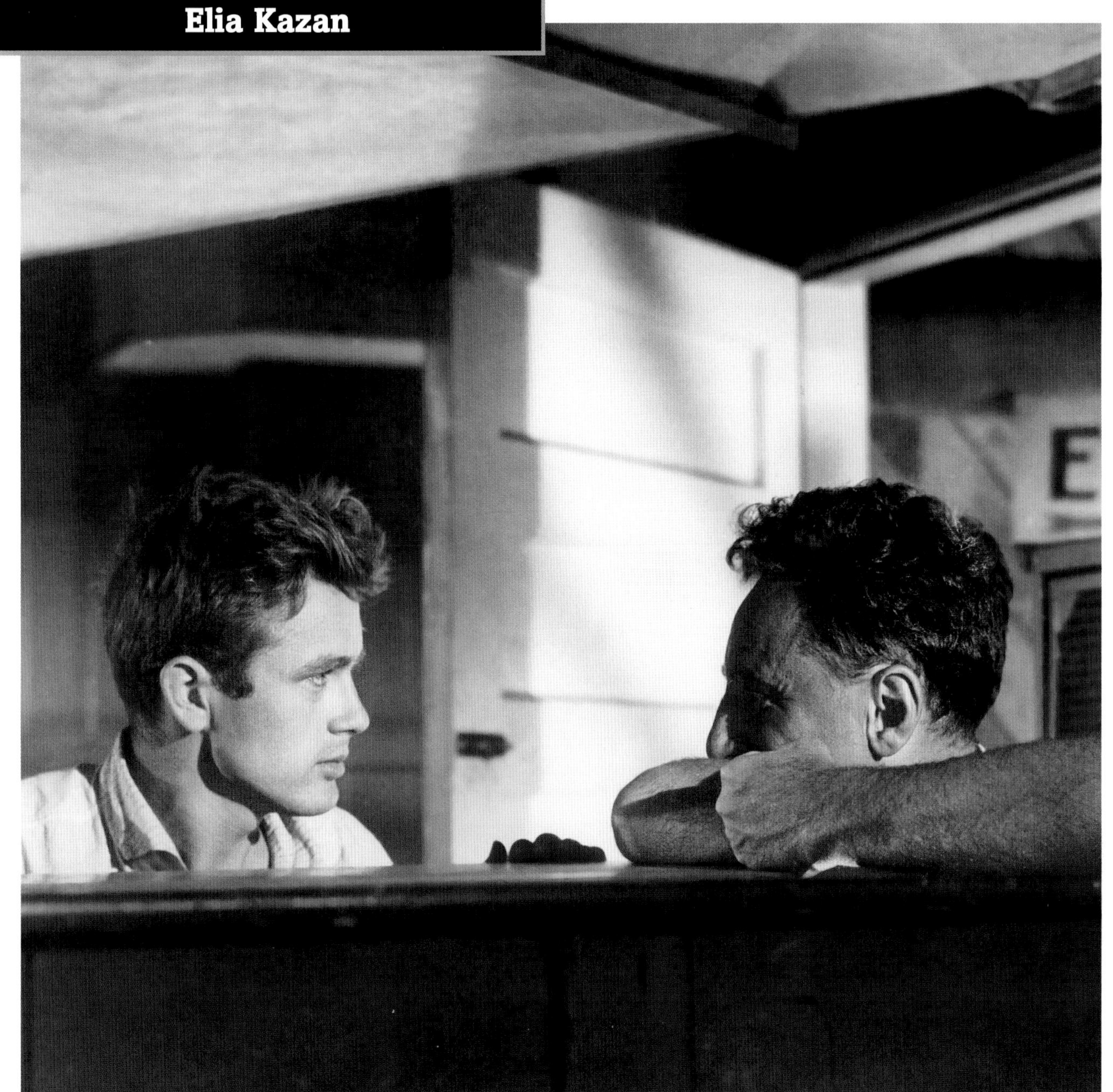

Elia Kazan was a Greek-Turkish immigrant, in America from the age of four, who worked in the Group Theater as an actor from 1932 onwards, becoming a successful stage director in the 1940s.

His first films, such as *Boomerang!* (1947), *Gentleman's Agreement* (1947), *Pinky* (1949), and *Panic in the Streets* (1950), examined social issues using realistic settings, but his cinematic strength was confirmed when he directed the film version of a play he had already staged on Broadway – Tennessee Williams' *A Streetcar Named Desire* (1951) with Marlon Brando. His other Brando films were *Viva Zapata!* (1952) and *On the Waterfront* (1954). Kazan had been a member of the Communist party in his youth and was called to account by the notorious House Un-American Activities Committee. His career was threatened with termination if he pleaded the Fifth Amendment. After agonizing, Kazan named names that were already known to the Committee. Had he not done so he would not have been able to launch James Dean's screen career in *East of Eden*, but the controversy plagued the rest of his life.

▲ **DEAN AND KAZAN:** Whatever reservations Elia Kazan had about James Dean on a personal level, he recognized the suitability of his casting as Cal Trask, and resolved to unleash the formidable talent within the young actor. It was a brilliant directorial coup.

He thought Jimmy was a showoff and, although he did not like him much, felt that he had exactly the quality needed for the part. He sent him to see John Steinbeck, who lived in a brownstone on East 72nd Street. The author agreed that Jimmy was a snotty kid. "But wasn't he Cal?" said Kazan. "He sure as hell was," said Steinbeck. Jimmy, subject to successful screen tests, had won the coveted role.

If anybody could identify the differences between Dean and Brando it was Kazan, and he immediately spotted the vulnerability, pain, and insecurity that underscored Jimmy's self-assurance, suggesting hidden emotional depths. In Steinbeck's novel Cal was just such a troubled youth. His mother had vanished before he even knew her, and he was constantly at odds with his stern, rigidly moralistic father, a lettuce-grower in Salinas, who made no secret of his preference for his other son Aron (Abel), who was a model of dependability and responsibility against Cal's waywardness.

Paul Newman, who had attended the Actors Studio and was appearing at the time in a minor role in William Inge's play *Picnic* on Broadway, was considered to play Aron. Although six years older than Jimmy, Newman still had the fresh face and bright-eyed looks of someone younger, and was given a camera test alongside him. Jimmy in an open-neck shirt, and Newman neatly bow-tied stood in front of the camera and talked off the cuff, occasionally swapping places or turning sideways to display their profiles. As Kazan questioned and prompted them from behind the camera, they seemed friendly and uncompetitive, Jimmy already confident that he had won the part of Cal.

► **TEST SCENE:** Jimmy and Richard Davalos, cast as Aron, played a dialog scene together for Kazan in New York, but it was not used in the final film.

▼ **TWO ON THE THRESHOLD:** Paul Newman auditioned for Aron alongside Jimmy, as this clip from Kazan's interview footage shows.

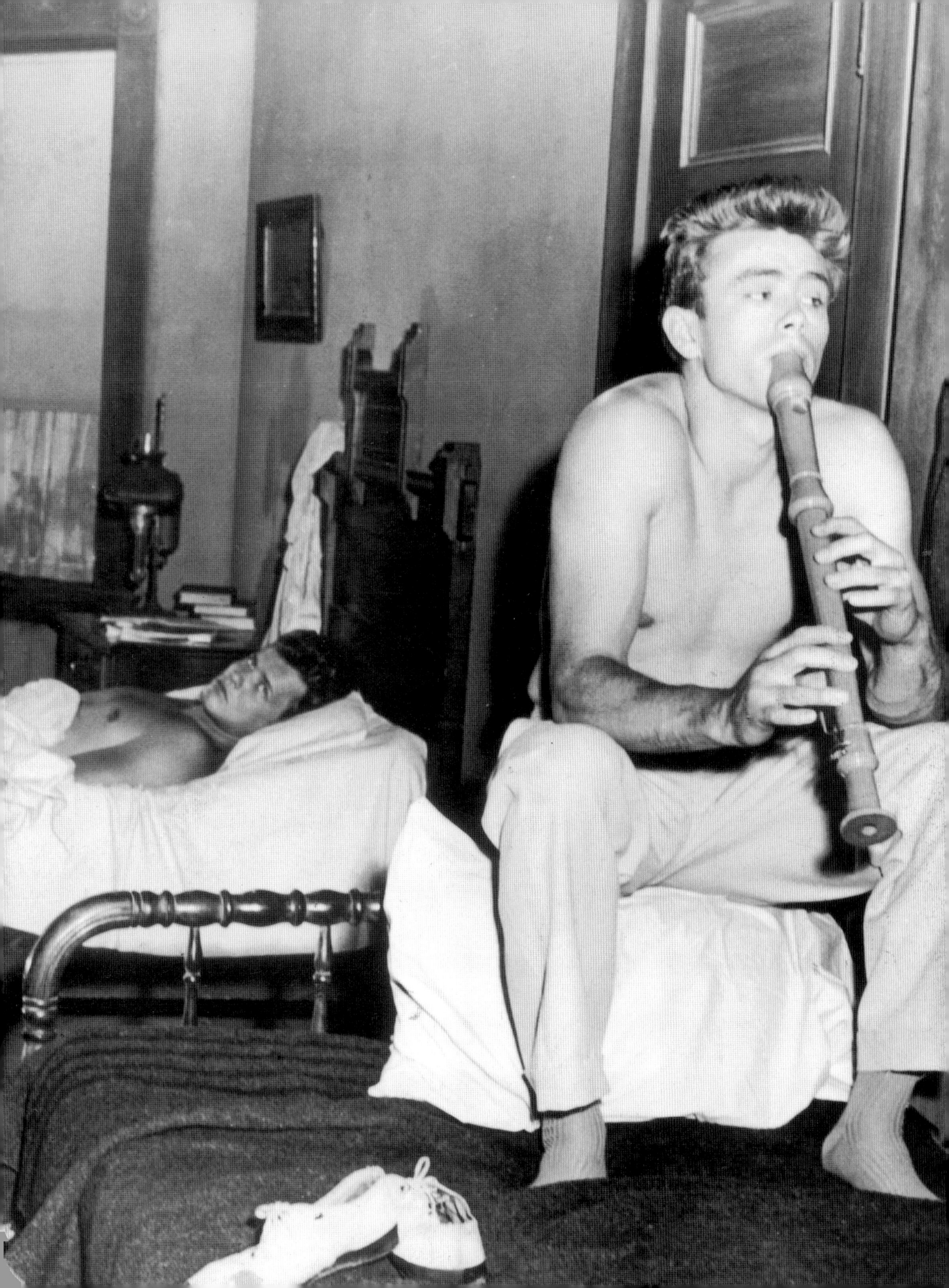

Kazan could have pulled off a spectacular double had he cast Newman, as well as launching not one but two great stars on the screen. Jimmy's success was coincident with Newman's disappointment, and their careers had other parallels. Newman's first film was a lamentable epic, *The Silver Chalice*, a piece of pseudo-biblical kitsch shot in CinemaScope, in which a Greek sculptor fashions the cup used for the Last Supper. The part had been offered to Jimmy, who fortunately was unable to do it because of *East of Eden*. Newman later apologized in the trade papers for his lackluster performance, and has always been testy when interviewers have mentioned it. Ironically, he was to achieve his first real taste of stardom playing the boxer Rocky Graziano in *Somebody Up There Likes Me*, the role planned for Jimmy after *Giant*.

Perhaps Kazan thought that the two actors were too alike to achieve the contrast he wanted between Cal and Aron. The latter had to be unassuming and earnest, and Newman might have caused too much attention to be focused on the character. So Kazan shot an entire scene from the film on a New York sound stage with the part of Aron played by Richard Davalos, who had already been to Hollywood to try out for Cal. The scene was not included in the final version of the film because it was considered unacceptable by the Breen Office (the industry's self-regulating censorship body) due to perceived hints of homoeroticism and incest. In the test footage, in black and white, Cal and Aron are in their bedroom; in the foreground Cal is quietly playing his recorder, Aron is in shadow on the bed. There follows Cal's heartrending lament on how his father loves Aron and rejects him.

"He was a very brilliant actor and a luminous young man ... an angel on earth." JULIE HARRIS

Aron pleads with him to show his father his love, and to gain it in return. It is an intense scene, unusually so for a screen test, and it is unfortunate that the scene was not included when the film was made, as it adds to the motivation of Cal's character.

The other pivotal role in *East of Eden* was that of Abra, Aron's girlfriend who is sympathetically motivated to support Cal. Julie Harris had been identified for the part, and as soon as she finished a play on Broadway Kazan hastened to sign her. To be sure that she and Jimmy could work together he ordered another test, in color but without sound. Jimmy entered into the spirit of the occasion by bringing along a number of balloons, evoking the carnival scene in which Cal and Abra are marooned aloft on a Ferris wheel.

► **CAST LINE-UP:** Richard Davalos, Julie Harris, and James Dean pose woodenly for color and wardrobe testing, a moment that Jimmy lightened by some fooling around.

The part of Cal was not entirely secured, as Jimmy still had to face testing in Hollywood, but he was prepared to take the chance and work out his two weeks' notice in *The Immoralist*. Jane Deacy was anxiously protecting Jimmy's interests, and was negotiating a deal by which, if he signed with Warner, he would still be able to work in television. In the period between leaving the play and embarking for the West Coast, he took a part at the Cherry Lane Theater in a dramatic reading of *Women of Trachis*, Ezra Pound's translation of Sophocles' drama *Trachiniae*. Although it was unpaid, it gave him the opportunity to work with Eli Wallach and Anne Jackson. He also met the composer Leonard Rosenman, then aged 29 and on the brink of a distinguished career. It was the start of an important friendship, and Rosenman, like Jimmy, was to make his film debut with *East of Eden*. In fact, it was Jimmy who urged Kazan to listen to the score of *Women of Trachis*, convincing him that Rosenman was the best possible choice.

An episode in the CBS television series *Danger*, "The Little Woman," in which Jimmy played a delinquent on the run who is sheltered from the law by an eight-year-old girl, kept him in New York until early April 1954. Kazan returned from a month's vacation in the Bahamas, and on April 8 they were scheduled to travel to Los Angeles together.

When Kazan collected Jimmy from his apartment, he emerged not with a suitcase, but with two brown-paper packages tied with string. Their limo then sped to Idlewild Airport (now JFK), where they boarded American Airlines Flight One, the Douglas DC-7 Flagship. It was Jimmy's first flight. He glued himself to the window, watching the ground drop away as the four-engined DC-7 headed westward. When they arrived, a Warner limo driver met them. Jimmy asked if it would be possible to stop on the way to the studio at Winton's workplace so that he could greet his father. Kazan had no objections, and in fact was secretly pleased, as it would enable him to observe the relationship. He was surprised by the tension that he felt existed between the two of them, and from their awkwardness assumed that Winton did not like his son very

"He looked like an immigrant sitting in the back of the luxury limo." ELIA KAZAN

◄ **GREEK PLAY:** Jimmy on stage with Eli Wallach in New York for a reading of *Women of Trachis,* translated by Ezra Pound from Sophocles.

much. The encounter reinforced Kazan's judgment that Jimmy was ideal casting as a son at odds with his father. Marcus Winslow Jr. believes that Kazan had already prejudged the situation, and saw only what he wanted to see.

Although on the brink of earning $1,200 a week Jimmy was initially broke, and was forced to spend the first nights back on the West Coast in a spare room at Winton and Ethel's house. They were then living on South Bundy Drive, two blocks south of Santa Monica Boulevard. Jane Deacy had recommended Dick Clayton at Famous Artists as Jimmy's new West Coast agent. A former actor himself, Clayton had met Jimmy when they had

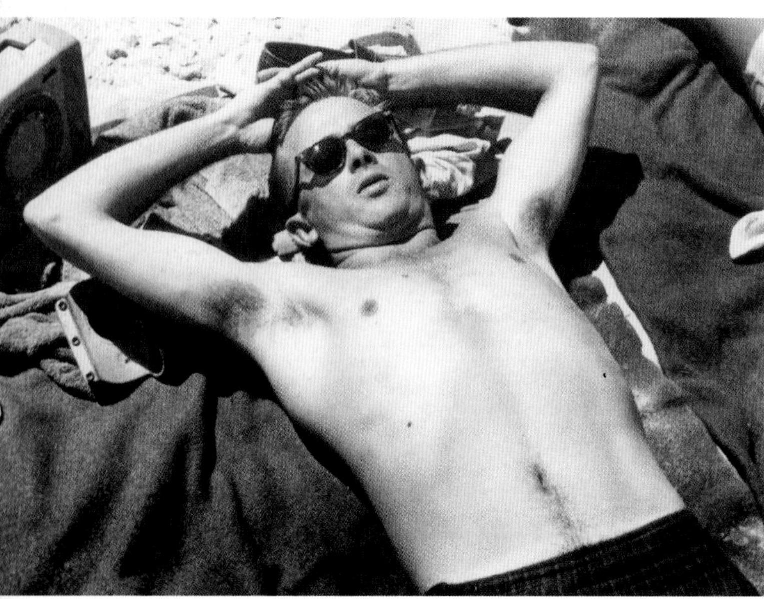

both played bit parts in the Martin and Lewis comedy *Sailor Beware*. Jimmy agitated until Clayton could negotiate some advance spending money from Warners, and he promptly spent it on the first installment on a new MG sports car, and a motorcycle. He also bought a palomino, calling it Cisco after the Cisco Kid, a popular B-movie hero of the time, and he kept it in a stable on the studio lot until Kazan insisted that it be sent to a ranch

▲ **TAN TIME:** Soaking up the sunshine on the beach at Santa Monica, Jimmy attempts to fulfill Kazan's order to lose his city pallor.

► **DRESS CALL:** On location in the midst of the bustle of a movie crew, Jimmy poses for a wardrobe shot that will serve as the costume department's reference for his next scene.

near Santa Barbara. Kazan was quite relaxed about Jimmy's initial living arrangements because he wanted what he understood to be the father-son conflict to rumble on for the sake of influencing his performance in the movie. He was, however, concerned that Jimmy's late-night regime in New York, which he continued in Los Angeles, had left him looking washed out and with flabby muscles, so he dispatched him to Borrego Springs in the desert, some 85 miles south of Palm Springs.

On his return, Jimmy wrote a note to Barbara Glenn in New York. He complained bitterly about Los Angeles, the people, the expense (renting a car for two weeks had set him back $138), and the loneliness. "I HAVN'T BEEN TO BED WITH NOBODY and won't until after the picture and I am home safe in N.Y.C.... Sounds unbelievable but it's the truth I swear." He goes on to say, "Kazan sent me out here to get a tan ... wanted me healthy looking. I look like a prune." He concludes, "Write me please. I'm sad most of the time. Awful lonely too isn't it. I hope you're dying, BECAUSE I AM. Love, Jim (Brando Clift) Dean."

Back in Hollywood, Jimmy resumed his nocturnal wanderings, seeking out bars and clubs, drinking too much, and generally wasting time. He would explore some of the low-grade establishments on the Sunset Strip and Santa Monica Boulevard in West Hollywood. A concerned Kazan decided that it would be better to move him away from Winton and Ethel's home, and with Richard Davalos as his sharer, installed him in a tiny apartment on West Olive, close to the Warner Studios in Burbank. Julie Harris arrived from New York and was moved into a nearby apartment. She remembered that almost as soon as she arrived, Jimmy invited her to take a ride with him in his red MG. She accepted, and he then sped round the tortuous bends of the Hollywood Hills, while she held on, trying hard not to plead with him to slow down – she knew any protest would produce exactly the opposite result.

Googie's, a coffee shop abutting the world-famous Schwab's drugstore on Sunset Boulevard, became one of Jimmy's favorite haunts. It was there that he met Maila Nurmi, a notoriously bizarre

COSTUME DEPT. PROD. 810
NAME JAMES DEAN
PART CAL TRASK
CHG. # 2
SC. 51-66
EXT. RAILROAD YARDS

▲ **LOST PARENT:** Jo Van Fleet played Kate, the madam of a Monterey brothel who turns out to be Cal's mother. Prevailing censorship led to the removal of any hint that her place was anything more than a bar well-staffed with agreeable young hostesses.

▼ **LINE OF SIGHT:** In a memorable moment in *East of Eden,* Jimmy lies down in a beanfield to check his crop growth.

actress, professionally known as Vampira. She was the presenter of late-night TV horror shows, invariably clad in black, wasp-waisted costumes. Their friendship was platonic and not long-lasting, but fanzines put it out that they made love on shiny black bed sheets, and she invoked black magic to put a curse on him when the ardor cooled. In fact she was happily married at the time, and another friend, Jack Simmons, was usually present when they whiled away night hours in outrageous conversation at Googie's.

Shooting began on *East of Eden* in May. The cast assembled in Mendocino on the northern California coast, 150 miles north of San Francisco. It was meant to represent Monterey in 1917 and, with its old wooden houses and New England-style church spires, had kept the look of a fishing port of that time, the appearance and atmosphere that Monterey itself had lost in the course of time. Jimmy stayed with other cast members three miles outside Mendocino at the Little River Inn.

The opening exterior scenes of the film, in which Cal follows a middle-aged woman through the streets to the brothel she owns, were filmed there. The woman is Kate, played by Jo Van Fleet, and proves to be the mother that Adam, Cal and Aron's father, has claimed to be dead. She had moved out of Adam's life many years earlier after shooting and wounding him. Following scenes on location at Mendocino the unit moved south to Salinas, 15 miles inland from the real Monterey, to shoot the scenes in the bean and lettuce fields. One of Jimmy's memorable on-set improvisations has him lying flat in a furrow as though willing his beans to grow. By mid-June location shooting was finished, and for the following two months filming continued on sound stages at Burbank. The most intricate of the back-lot sets was an amusement park complete with carnival rides and a Ferris wheel.

Raymond Massey was cast in the role of Adam and carried an aura of distinction and integrity as

▼ **BUNNY HOP:** Jimmy amuses Julie Harris with some rabbit-like prancing in the boring interval between takes during the carnival scene.

"I doubt that Jimmy would ever have got through ... except for an angel on our set. Her name was Julie Harris."

ELIA KAZAN

a god-fearing conservative. His approach to his craft was traditional and perfectionist, and he soon made clear his discomfort with Jimmy's alternative style. Kazan was unbothered by Massey deprecating Dean, since it helped to emphasize the difficult relationship of their characters on screen – it was exactly what the part called for – but Massey's criticisms were prompted more by distaste for his young costar's lack of professionalism than by animosity on a personal level. He complained to Kazan that on set he never knew what Jimmy was likely to do: "Make him read the lines the way they're written." Their conflict was just what Kazan wanted. "This was an antagonism I didn't try to conceal," wrote Kazan. "I aggravated it, I'm ashamed to say – well, not ashamed; everything goes in directing movies."

In one of the first scenes, Cal infuriates his father by reading from the Bible in a rapid gabble, and insisting on prefacing each verse with its number. Massey, in character, was supposed to be on the edge of a violent rage, and Kazan, in order to raise the tension, secretly prompted Jimmy to insert obscenities into the sacred text. Massey was so apoplectic that he was prepared to walk off the film, and was only placated when Kazan revealed that he had ordered it. It achieved the desired effect. Massey's performance of a man doing his best to control his anger is compelling.

Richard Davalos, as Bill Bast had before him, found sharing an apartment with Jimmy difficult. His moods, unpredictability, sloppiness, and antisocial attitudes finally caused Davalos to approach Kazan, who was also concerned by his star's behavior. When Kazan made a film, his cast was his family and he exercised patriarchal as well as directorial control. More to assert command than to resolve Davalos's discomfort, Kazan re-housed Jimmy in a dressing-room apartment on the studio lot, close to his own. The director ordered an end to the nocturnal motorcycle jaunts and the late-night carousing. With Cisco the palomino exiled, Jimmy next equipped himself with an expensive camera and started taking pictures around the set, which irritated Kazan further, and eventually he put a stop to it.

Containing Jimmy was a problem that had to be balanced against maximizing publicity for Warners' new young star. Stories had to be planted in fan magazines, newspaper gossip columns, and entertainment roundups on radio. Jimmy had strong news value, and the Warner Bros. press office churned out expensive material to feed the publicity machine. Some of it, such as the résumé of his New York stage and television credits, was true, while other details were embellished. Jimmy's farm-boy origins in Indiana were played up and romanticized, and a couple of inches were added to his height so that, as far as Warners were concerned, he was 5ft 10in. The studio was also keen to establish that Jimmy was a normal, red-blooded,

▲ **BIBLE CLASS:** Jimmy's style of reading the scriptures infuriated Raymond Massey as his father in a key scene.

◄ **MONTEREY COOL:** Jimmy's sweater and pants outfit in the Monterey sequence at the opening of the film, although meant to represent 1917, set fashion trends on mid-1950s Ivy League campuses.

America in the 1950s

The mid-1950s were a watershed for young people, now labeled "teenagers," who had been too young to fight in World War II, but were raised during their parents' peacetime adjustment.

The Eisenhower years were marked by unprecedented consumer growth and the spread of middle-class aspirations across sectors of the population that would never previously have considered automobiles, refrigerators, air-conditioners, and big-screen televisions to be within their reach. Politically, it was the era of the Cold War, nuclear paranoia, and the battle for civil rights. The young were uneasy, unsettled, and as the age of deference to parental influences faded, increasingly questioning of adult values. The powerful beat of rock 'n' roll was taking over the airwaves, and MGM filmed *Blackboard Jungle*, a tough, high-school story with a new anthem, the pounding and insistent beat of "Rock Around the Clock" on the soundtrack. But the seminal movie moment came in Marlon Brando's film *The Wild One* (1953), directed by Lazlo Benedek and based on the real-life terrorization of Hollister, California, by hundreds of bikers in 1947. Brando, as leader of a motorcycle gang that descends on a small town and imposes a dominant, threatening presence, is asked what they are rebelling against. He answers, "What've you got?"

▲ **JUNGLE FEVER:** Released in March 1955, *Blackboard Jungle* defined the blues of the big-city teenager.

► **GANG WAR:** Marlon Brando in his iconic role as the leader of a gang of invading bikers that brings violence and fear to a small town in *The Wild One*, premiered in New York on December 30, 1953.

young male, and to emphasize this, nubile starlets were regularly invited to accompany him to premieres and other social events. While *East of Eden* was in production, on an adjoining stage, *The Silver Chalice* was shooting, with Paul Newman in the part that Jimmy had fortuitously not taken. Also in the cast was Pier Angeli, her real name Anna Maria Pierangeli, a promising 22-year-old Italian actress.

As an Italian Catholic, Pier was greatly influenced by her mother, and had already been left dispirited by a broken engagement to Kirk Douglas. Jimmy had received a letter from his most important confidante, Barbara Glenn, announcing that she was getting married, so when Pier and Jimmy met both were feeling bruised from past romances. There was immediate and powerful attraction between them, and the studio bosses were initially delighted that their two new leading male and female stars were getting on so well. The relationship intensified and fed the gossip columns, with the lovebirds spending every spare moment in each other's company – driving in Jimmy's MG, riding on horseback in Griffith Park, relaxing on the beach. Kazan did not approve and noted that when she visited

▼ **TRACK JUMPING:** Jimmy leaps from one train to another, risking a serious fall and doubtless causing acute anxieties for the production accountant. In the film he rides from Salinas to Monterey on a freight train.

James Dean and Pier Angeli

While Jimmy was making *East of Eden*, the young Italian actress Pier Angeli was filming *The Silver Chalice* on a nearby stage. They met, became lovers, and for a time were Hollywood's hottest new couple. Then it turned sour.

◄ **LENS LOVE:** Pier's classic Mediterranean beauty captivated Jimmy, and he spent hours photographing her, using a Rolleiflex and skills learned from his friend Roy Schatt.

▼ **SHAWL THING:** In Jimmy's onset picture of Pier, she is wearing the same paisley shawl from the inset opposite. Her mother proved to be a formidable opponent for Jimmy.

"Was terribly hurt for a while about Pier – but I'm ok now."

JAMES DEAN

▲ **STARRY NIGHT:** Studios liked their young stars to attend premieres. Jimmy was obliged to escort Terry Moore to the opening of *Sabrina*. She basked in the flashbulbs. He scowled and looked unhappy.

► **BEEFCAKE:** The fanzines eagerly sought torso shots, and Jimmy had to oblige. His slight frame hardly placed him in the champions' league, but it still caused plenty of hearts to flutter.

Jimmy's dressing room it would resound with the echoes of either lovemaking or quarreling, and he could not be sure which. "I could hear them boffing but more often arguing through the walls." Pier's mother was an even more formidable opponent. She had already opposed Pier's engagement to Kirk Douglas, and liked Jimmy even less. She had made it plain her daughter should marry a nice Italian Catholic boy, not a wild Quaker rebel. She disparaged his prospects and was certainly bothered by his uncouth manner.

Perhaps Mama Pierangeli had put him off the idea but, more likely, he had decided that his career should come first. Their relationship, anyway, started to cool, and when the Billy Wilder film *Sabrina*, with Humphrey Bogart, William Holden, and Audrey Hepburn, opened with a glitzy premiere, Clayton made sure that Jimmy was seen with a glamorous alternative young star on his arm – in this instance Terry Moore, famous as the girl in *Mighty Joe Young*, the *King Kong*-style adventure. Jimmy had known her long before Pier came on the scene, but press photographs on the night show her looking radiant and possessed, while he looks as though he would much rather be somewhere else.

The relationship with Pier finally ended when, after shooting on *East of Eden* had finished, and Jimmy was in New York for a television play, Pier announced she was going to wed the singer Vic Damone, who safely met her mother's criterion of a suitably Italian heritage. Jimmy sullenly waited across the street from St. Timothy's Church at Pico and Beverly Glen Boulevards, and loudly revved his motorcycle when the newlyweds emerged, before riding off in a cloud of anger. Descriptions of his behavior were later considered apocryphal because they hardly squared with his press comments at the time: "Pier's still okay with me. She broke the news to me the night before she announced her engagement but she wouldn't tell me

"How can you measure acting in inches?"

JAMES DEAN, CRITICIZED FOR BEING ONLY 5FT 8IN

who the guy was. I was floored when I learned it was Vic Damone. Oh well, maybe she likes his singing."

Pier's romantic life was complicated and by no means exclusive. She was dating Eddie Fisher during her early days with Jimmy, although he would later marry her close friend, Debbie Reynolds. Pier's marriage to Damone proved to be disastrous, ending in divorce in 1958. After a further marriage and divorce she died of a barbiturate overdose in 1971, aged only 39.

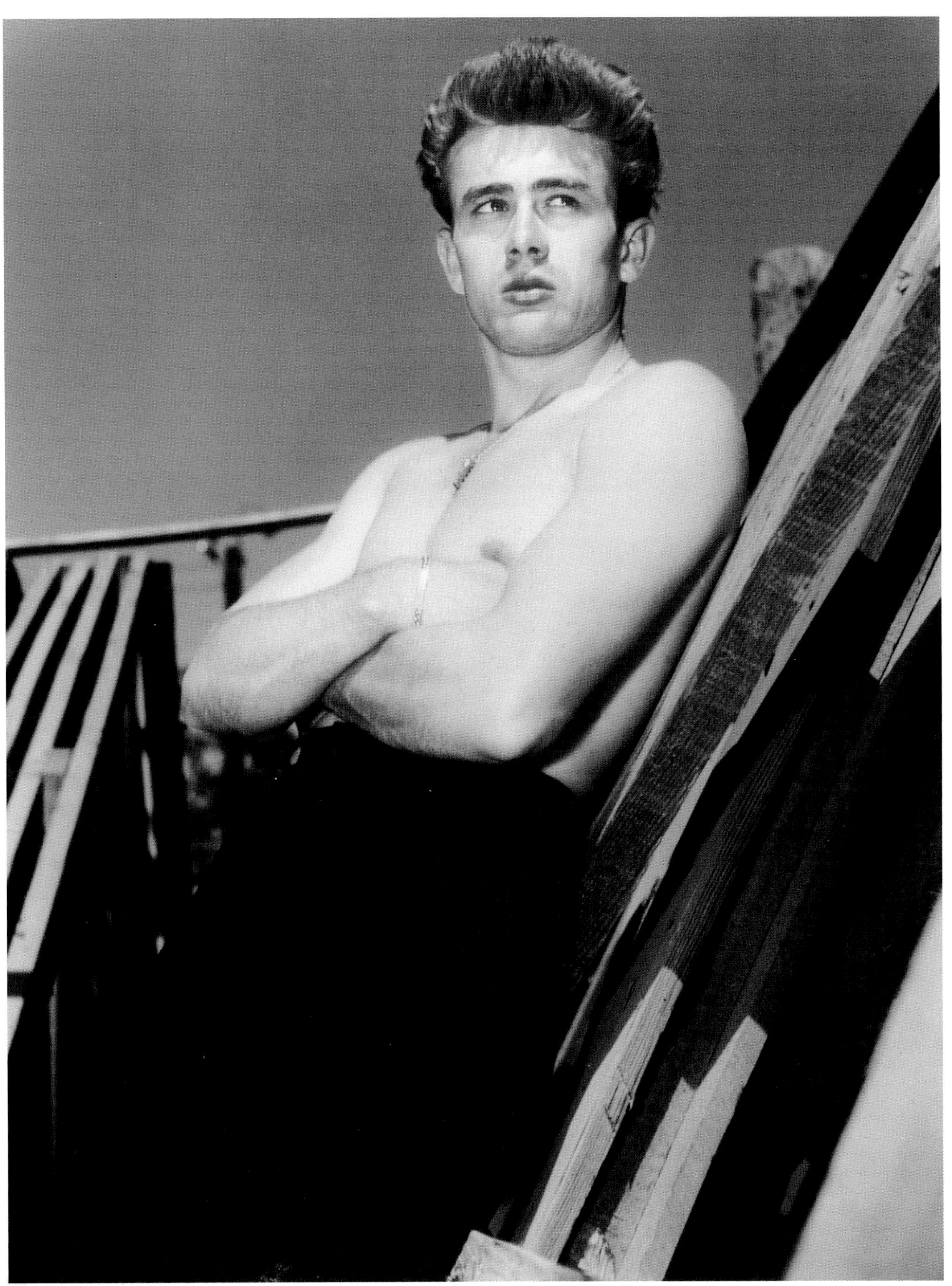

"Marlon ... was very gracious to Jimmy, who was so adoring that he seemed shrunken and twisted in misery." ELIA KAZAN

The memory of Jimmy stayed with her, and three years before she died she said: "He is the only man I ever loved deeply as a woman should love a man. I never loved either of my husbands the way I loved Jimmy."

Jimmy's relationship with Kazan, never warm but initially fueled with a certain amount of mutual respect, worsened as *East of Eden* progressed. As a special treat, Kazan invited Marlon Brando, then filming *Desirée* at another studio, to pay a visit to his set. Brando was a role model and almost a demigod in Jimmy's eyes. Kazan noted how Jimmy's voice would drop to a cathedral hush when talking about him. Brando had been told that Jimmy was obsessed with him, but responded graciously without being patronizing. Observed Kazan: "[Jimmy was] so adoring he seemed shrunken and twisted in misery." A photograph of the event shows a relaxed Brando, flanked by Kazan, his arm resting lightly on Brando's shoulder, and Julie Harris, gazing at the visitor as though he is the most important man on earth, while at the edge Jimmy looks the other way, seeming uncomfortable and dejected. In his autobiography Kazan was scathing and ungenerous. He said that Brando, well trained by Stella Adler, had excellent technique. "Dean had no technique to speak of." He went on:

▲ **FACE AT THE WINDOW:** In order to get Jimmy to play the scene in which he climbs up to Abra's window to talk to her, Kazan took him out to an Italian restaurant and plied him with Chianti. The scene worked superbly.

◄ **STAR TURN:** Jimmy's idol and Kazan's Oscar-winning star of *On the Waterfront* came on set. He delighted Kazan and charmed Harris, but sent Jimmy into confusion.

"On my film, Jimmy would either get the scene right immediately, without any detailed direction – that was ninety-five percent of the time – or he couldn't get it at all. Then I had to use some extraordinary means – the Chianti, for instance." That was a reference to the scene where Cal climbs up on to the porch overhang to talk to Abra through her bedroom window. After a disappointing start, Kazan took Jimmy to an Italian restaurant and plied him with wine, then returned to the set to shoot one of the most memorable scenes in the film.

Kazan seemed to regard Jimmy's acting achievement as accidental, and was surprised by his success, in spite of having gone to almost improper lengths to heighten his vulnerability so that it would communicate in his acting. "I doubt that Jimmy would ever have got through *East of Eden* except for an angel on our set. Her name was Julie Harris, and she was goodness itself with Jimmy, kind, patient and everlastingly sympathetic."

When the final day came in August 1954, and the shooting was over, she found Jimmy sobbing in his dressing-room. She recalled that he was crying, "It's over." She tried to reassure him that it was just the start of a great career, but he was inconsolable, and she realized that for him, the end of shooting was like the breakup of a family.

Leonard Rosenman, whose powerful, atmospheric score would contribute much to the success of the film, had also seen Jimmy's vulnerability and insecurity at close hand. Rosenman believed that the root of his acting technique was his intuitive assumption of Cal's troubles as his own, and the personal anguish was a projection of the alienation experienced by the character he was portraying. Massey was overwhelmed by the passion in Jimmy's acting in the climactic birthday scene: Cal has been secretly working to replace the money his father lost in his brave, pioneering attempt to transport frozen lettuce by rail, by growing and selling beans to the British Purchasing Agency as food for the soldiers in the trenches of France. When he hands his father the money, wrapped as a birthday present, his father spurns it, declaring that he can have no part in profiteering from the war. Jimmy suddenly and without rehearsing flings his arms round Massey and sobs as dollar bills fall around them. The startled Massey calls on him to stop, and Jimmy turns and leaves the room, a terrible, hurt cry bursting from him. Massey, although startled, had remained in character and Kazan had no need for another take.

"You never know what he's going to say or do." RAYMOND MASSEY TO ELIA KAZAN

▲ **MONEY SHOT:** The veteran actor Raymond Massey found Jimmy's unpredictable improvisations unnerving, particularly in the great scene when Adam rejects Cal's offer of money. Massey remained in character in spite of his surprise, and the result was a climactic moment in American film acting.

◄ **EROTIC POWER:** Julie Harris proved to be a calming influence on Jimmy, and their scenes together, although never going beyond a chaste peck on the cheek, generated an erotic power.

As soon as he finished filming Jimmy went to New York for television appearances arranged by Jane Deacy. A loan-out to MGM to appear in a Vincente Minnelli film, *The Cobweb*, was declined in spite of Jimmy's desire to play the psychopathic patient in a psychiatric clinic. Warner Bros. wisely sensed that it would not be a suitable follow-up for their new star, but they were not yet ready with the project that would be. He went to New York to appear in "Run Like a Thief," a segment of *Philco TV Playhouse*, and auditioned unsuccessfully for the Broadway production of *The Teahouse of the August Moon*. Burgess Meredith won the role and in the film it was taken by Brando. In any case, Jimmy could not have taken the part, since his Warner contract allowed a stage appearance only after the third film, and there were two to go.

Other television appearances included an episode of *Danger* called "Padlock" in New York, and an adaptation of a Sherwood Anderson story entitled "I'm a Fool" produced in Los Angeles for *General Electric Theater*, in which he plays a young man who devises a bogus persona to impress a girl and, having won her love, realizes that it can go nowhere because he is not who he says he is. The girl was played by Natalie Wood, a 16-year-old veteran of 20 films. They had not met before, but it was the beginning of a friendship that would develop when they made *Rebel Without a Cause*. She was impressed by the way he had turned up late for the first day of rehearsals, wearing tattered jeans held by a safety pin, and making his entrance through an open window rather than the door.

During this period he also began dating another foreign actress, Lili Kardell, then 19. It was a sporadic romance, not helped by his elusiveness, sudden disappearances, and moody preoccupations. Hers was a very minor career in comparison with another of his "exotic" European girlfriends, Ursula Andress from Switzerland.

◄ **SCENE-STEALING:** After *East of Eden*, Jimmy played the spoiled young scion of a wealthy family accused of stealing money. "The Thief" was an episode of *The U.S. Steel Hour* on ABC.

► **COSTAR:** Jimmy talks to Mary Astor, who starred with Paul Lukas, Diana Lynne, and Patric Knowles. Jimmy sought to upstage all of them.

She impressed Jimmy enough to make him want to learn German, and, although only 19, she had been to Paris and sat at Jean-Paul Sartre's feet, and could enlighten Jimmy on the philosophy of existentialism. Before marrying John Derek in 1957 she had dated a forgetful Brando, who, when writing his memoirs in the 1990s, had to telephone her to ask if they ever slept together. She did not become an international star until 1962, when she established an iconic image by emerging from the sea in *Dr No*, the first James Bond film.

Then came the first previews of *East of Eden*. Kazan recalled the scene at Huntington Park on December 6: "The instant he appeared on the screen, hundreds of girls began to scream. They'd been waiting for him, it seemed – how come or why, I don't know." Clayton said: "I couldn't believe the guy on the screen was the same guy I knew."

On March 9 *East of Eden* had its world premiere in New York at the Astor on Times Square, a glittering benefit for the Actors Studio attended by Kazan, Steinbeck, and Jack Warner, together with Raymond Massey, Jo Van Fleet, and Richard Davalos from the cast. Although he had walked past the theater only a day or two before to note his name and image prominently displayed on the marquee, Jimmy was conspicuously absent from the premiere. Partly it was due to his distaste for dressing up for formal occasions, but another factor was that he had contacted Barbara Glenn. Her first engagement had come to nothing, but she had now found the man she really was to marry, and her seriousness had affected Jimmy. He asked to meet her fiancé over dinner, and she agreed, although she was concerned that Jimmy might behave badly. To her relief, he appeared to be in good spirits, but insisted on seeing her alone later. She went to his West 68th Street apartment to find him greatly distressed. He pleaded with her not to marry. It was to no avail and Glenn made an acrimonious departure. She never saw him again. Jimmy returned to Hollywood to begin preparation for his next film.

▲ **EXOTIC DATING:** For a while, Jimmy was interested in the Swiss actress Ursula Andress, who was on the verge of her career, and for a moment he thought of learning German to impress her.

◄ **PLAYING WITH CONVICTION:** Another television appearance was in "Life Sentence" for *Campbell Soundstage* on NBC. Jimmy played a former prisoner. The acress is Georgann Johnson.

"This son of a bitch is absolutely crazy."

PAUL LUKAS, COSTAR IN *THE THIEF*

Reviews of *East of Eden* were excellent and Jimmy's contribution was hailed as seismic. Frank Quinn in the *New York Daily Mirror* said that he was "destined for a blazing career." In *Time* he was described as "a young man from Indiana who is unquestionably the biggest news Hollywood has made in 1955." In *The Hollywood Reporter* Jack Moffitt said: "He is that rare thing, a young actor who is a great actor, and the troubled eloquence with which he puts over the problems of misunderstood youth may lead to his being accepted by young audiences as a sort of symbol of their generation."

Of what a girl did–what a boy did–
of ecstasy and revenge...
WARNER BROS. PRESENT
ELIA KAZAN'S
EXPLOSIVE PRODUCTION OF
JOHN STEINBECK'S
"EAST OF EDEN"
CINEMASCOPE
AND WARNERCOLOR
THE NEW HIT– THE BIGGEST HIT– FROM THE ACADEMY AWARD DIRECTOR OF ON THE WATERFRONT, ELIA KAZAN!
JULIE HARRIS · JAMES DEAN · RAYMOND MASSEY
ELIA KAZAN
JAMES
DEAN
RAYMOND MASSEY
JULIE HARRIS
BURL IVES
Et mesterværk...
Man tryllebindes...
Blandt de største...
skrev pressen
ELIA KAZAN'S
ØST FOR
paradis
efter JOHN STEINBECK'S roman
"EAST OF EDEN"
ASTOR
LOEW'S
DRAMA OF THE TEEN-AGE TERROR!
Blackboard Jungle
Glenn FORD
IT'S DYNAMITE!
SHERATON ASTOR HOTEL
ROOF OPENING MAY 25

In the *Los Angeles Examiner* Dorothy Manners exclaimed: "Everything you have heard about young Dean is true. He is a great young actor whose portrayal of the troubled, inverted 'bad brother' is a rare achievement – and would be for an actor of twice his age and experience." Bosley Crowther in the *New York Times* sounded an off-key note: "He scuffs his feet, he whirls, he pouts, he sputters, he leans against walls, he rolls his eyes, he swallows his words, he ambles slack-kneed – all like Brando used to do. Never have we seen a performer so clearly follow another's style. Mr. Kazan should be spanked for permitting him to do such a sophomoric thing." Natalie Wood later identified the similarities of Jimmy with Brando as a consequence of them both having Elia Kazan as their director.

> "I was totally unprepared for his success."
>
> ELIA KAZAN

◀ **THE CONTENDERS:** Times Square, New York in the spring of 1955. At Loew's *Blackboard Jungle* is playing, and opposite *East of Eden* has just opened at the Astor. Jimmy's next film surpassed *Blackboard Jungle* as a message to the young people of America.

Astor
20 000 LEAGUES
UNDER THE SEA
CINEMASCOPE
APPLIANCES

In late 1954 Dennis Stock was a 27-year-old photographer who had moved to Los Angeles from New York, having **won first prize in *Life*'s Young Photographer contest**, after a long apprenticeship to the innovative *Life* photographer Gjon Mili.

He had already achieved considerable success in Hollywood, shooting photo-essays on stars such as Humphrey Bogart, and through Mili had joined Magnum, the world-renowned photographers' cooperative. It was a singular honor to belong to such an elite agency and he was its youngest member. To Californian publicists his credentials and contacts with New York publications were impressive, and he was in the privileged position of being able to gain access to stars and filmmakers almost at will.

Nicholas Ray held regular Sunday afternoon soirees at his bungalow at the Chateau Marmont, on the Sunset Strip, with the intention of allowing people of talent who had an accord with his own maverick disposition to meet, make alliances, and trade ideas. Over jugs of wine, fierce and often controversial discussions took place that would not have been possible in the context of the work environment during the week, and Ray saw himself as a creative catalyst.

"The story, as I explained it, was to reveal the environment that affected and shaped the unique character of James Byron Dean." DENNIS STOCK

Although by now extremely skilled as an observer, Stock was not particularly comfortable at these events, and found it difficult to interact. On one occasion, he said, "Nick noticed my reserved appearance and led me up the small flight of stairs to a corner where a young man reclined, in a mood that seemed similar to mine." The introduction to James Dean over, Ray departed, leaving them to talk. "There was nothing terribly imposing about this bespectacled young man. At first, his responses to my brief inquiries and observations were monosyllabic. But as the wine flowed more abundantly, so did our conversation. Relaxed, Jimmy asked about different aspects of photographic techniques, and I happily answered as best I could."

Jimmy mentioned his involvement in the unreleased *East of Eden*, although Stock had neither read the book nor was aware that a film had been made from it. Jimmy then persuaded Stock to make a point of seeing it at a midweek sneak preview that was to take place in Santa Monica.

◄ **ALONE:** James Dean stalks Times Square, the heart of Broadway, on a wet, wintry New York morning in early 1955. The photograph is among the 20th century's most famous celebrity images.

Stock accepted the invitation, and a few nights later was bowled over by the freshness and vitality of Jimmy's performance: "The entire audience applauded as the house lights signaled the end." He realized he was witnessing the initiation of a new star, and he sought Jimmy out after the screening, very much aware of the contrast between the passion he had seen on the screen, and the reticent shyness of the man he had met at the Chateau Marmont. He found him on his Triumph motorcycle in the alley beside the theater. An idea had already formed in Stock's mind that a photo story on James Dean would be viable, but there was no chance of putting the proposition to him while he was being congratulated by the many well-wishers who had seen the film, so they agreed to meet for breakfast the following morning at Googie's, Jimmy's favorite coffee shop on Sunset Strip near Crescent Heights.

The following morning, almost as soon as Jimmy arrived at the popular hangout for young actors and industry hopefuls, he was assailed on all sides by admirers who had been present or had heard of the previous night's ovation, and again Stock had no opportunity to press his idea. Finally his patience gave out and he made to leave. Jimmy at once paid the check, then steered Stock through the door to his motorcycle in the parking lot. He told Stock that his agent had a beautiful place up in the hills where they could talk without being bothered, and urged him to climb on the back. It was the first time Stock had ever been on a motorcycle, and he clung on to Jimmy in terror as they raced at white-knuckle speeds up Laurel Canyon and the high winding roads that took them to Dick Clayton's house, with its panoramic view across western Los Angeles to the shimmering Pacific. He and Jimmy sat down on the hillside, and for several hours talked about themselves, their backgrounds and their beliefs. Jimmy revealed much of his past, and as their conversation developed, Stock realized that in order to give the story depth they should go together to Fairmount as well as New York, and so

► **CLOSE SHAVE:** On impulse, Jimmy stopped at a Times Square barbershop and insisted that Dennis Stock photograph him as he received a hair trim and a shave to remove a three-day beard growth.

acquire a full visual perspective on his path to stardom. The logical placement for such a story in Stock's view had to be *Life*, then the leading weekly picture magazine. As soon as he could he contacted the editors, but they took a week to approve the idea and agree an advance against expenses. Stock also cut a deal with Jimmy that he should have the first exclusive rights for a photo-essay on him, precluding the possibility of a rival magazine beating him to it.

In fact he was not the first with the idea. It had already occurred to Jimmy's photographer friend Roy Schatt, who had first sparked his interest in photography. Some weeks earlier Schatt had presented the proposal of a new-star story to *Life*, but because Jimmy had been pictured in such a disheveled and dissolute-looking state the editors of the Henry Luce publication, subscribing to their proprietor's beliefs in the propagation of wholesome images, had rejected the story. As far as *Life* was concerned, young actors were expected to have short hair, buttoned-down collars, narrow ties and lapels, and neat jackets in the "Ivy-League" look then in vogue. Jimmy, whose favorite attire was a tee-shirt and faded denims, was a decade or so ahead of his time in fashion terms.

He and Stock took off for New York in January 1955. By then word was beginning to spread to the East Coast that Jimmy was on his way to becoming a huge star. He had rapidly become fast friends with Stock, and a mutual trust had evolved. Stock felt that Jimmy was much more at ease in New York than he had been in Los Angeles, and followed him around his old haunts. He saw that when they roamed the streets of midtown Manhattan Jimmy would watch people and often discover unusual vignettes of life that would have escaped other pedestrians. When Stock visited the tiny apartment five floors up on West 68th Street, which Jimmy had retained as a convenient *pied à terre*, he felt that with its two circular windows it reminded him of a ship's cabin. He photographed the cape and bull horns hanging on the wall, the overflowing bookcase with its well-thumbed

"He lived like a stray animal ... come to think of it he was a stray animal." DENNIS STOCK

volumes of plays, Shakespeare, Kafka, and Walt Kelly's *Pogo*, the radical comic strip of the day. Jimmy, as a concession to his guest, cleared away its usual detritus of empty beer cans, overflowing ashtrays, and unwashed dishes.

Stock was with him when, on impulse, he suddenly decided to have a haircut in a barbershop off Times Square, choosing the full works with hot towels, and the removal of his three-day growth with a freshly stropped razor. Bizarrely, he insisted on posing in the window of a furniture store, but blasé New Yorkers ignored him and scurried past without interest. He was photographed sitting in on a class at the Actors Studio, taking a dance lesson from Katherine Dunham in a class that included Eartha Kitt, receiving tuition from Cyril Jackson on the bongo drums, chatting to Geraldine Page in her dressing room at the Cort Theatre while she readied herself for her evening performance in *The Rainmaker*, and hanging out at places like Jerry's Bar and Cromwell's Drugstore.

"Jimmy was an insomniac – the worst I've ever met – so at odd times and on odd places he would simply pass out, for a few minutes, or a few hours,

◀ **TOP FLIGHT:** Jimmy's cramped, one-room, fifth-floor walk-up apartment on West 68th Street reminded Stock of a ship's cabin with its porthole-shaped windows and bunk bed.

▲ **INSTANT SLUMBER:** Jimmy had the alarming capacity to fall asleep in places like Jerry's Bar on West 54th Street in an instant. Stock attributed it to the insomnia that kept him awake all night.

then wake up and set out again. He lived like a stray animal. Come to think of it, he was a stray animal," said Stock when his Dean pictures were published as a book.

The most famous photograph was taken on a cold and wet February day in the center of Times Square. Jimmy walks through the downpour, his shoulders hunched, his hands buried in the pockets of his overcoat, collar raised, with a sodden cigarette between his lips. There is nobody else in sight, and even the neon signs have lost their luster in the gray dreariness of the weather. More than any other image it has been held to represent the loneliness and introversion of James Dean, and has been continually reproduced.

The February climate in Indiana can also be unwelcoming. Jimmy and Stock set out for a chilly Fairmount, and stayed with the Winslows at the Jonesboro farmhouse. "The Winslows were the kindest, warmest, most generous people, and it was very moving how much they loved Jimmy," said Stock. Jimmy walked around the familiar town but he felt almost like a stranger, sensing that he had moved on and no longer belonged there in spite of the warmth of his family welcome. He attended the Sweetheart Ball, commemorating St Valentine's Day, at the Fairmount High School, and its distinguished alumnus dutifully signed autographs and exchanged pleasantries with those teachers who remembered him. He even managed a few energetic bursts on the bongo drums, eliciting enthusiastic cheers from the students. He was not yet a household name, as *East of Eden* sill awaited its national release, but the knowledge that he had made his first Hollywood film, and the fact that he had been seen on television in so many plays, rendered him the object of idolization. For the ball he was spruced up in a jacket, dark shirt, and pale tie, but for most of the time in Fairmount he preferred to stroll around town in a cord

windbreaker, zipped up to keep the cold out, and a flat felt cap. Another famous iconic photograph has Jimmy in the same garb, with the inevitable cigarette in his mouth, strolling along Washington close to the intersection of Main, the heart of Fairmount, with the delicate onion dome of the Citizens Bank on the corner behind him. The building is still there, but the traffic light, one of a pair, has been replaced and now rests by the Fairmount Historical Museum. (Its mate was destroyed in an auto accident – Fairmount is the kind of small town that still remembers the day years ago when a car knocked down a traffic light.)

One of Stock's photographs captures an extraordinary moment during a visit they made to the long-defunct Hunt's Furniture Store, which, because the same family owned the local funeral home, kept a selection of caskets on show. Jimmy jumped into one and urged Stock to take a picture. "A prank, yes," said Stock, "but there was a sense of

◄ **STEPPING OUT:** The singer Eartha Kitt, one of the "New Faces of 1952," and Jimmy take part in an energetic Katherine Dunham dance class in a Broadway studio.

▼ **CLASS ACT:** Sessions at the Actors Studio are rarely photographed. Jimmy, in the front row, pays close attention, but the reality is that he lost interest soon after membership.

PRESCRIPTIONS
DRUGS
NO PARKING ANY TIME
BANK
STATE
BANK

something else." That photograph would be constantly reproduced to support the common perception that Jimmy had an unhealthy preoccupation with death. Similarly, another photograph that was taken in the Park Cemetery close to the tombstone of Cal Dean, his great-grandfather was regarded as another signal. The reality was that both Jimmy and Stock were struck by the juxtaposition of his surname and the first name of the character he played in *East of Eden*.

Stock was deeply impressed by the Winslows. "It is probable that Jimmy never got over his mother's death, but it is nonetheless hard to imagine a better home for a boy, in such a situation," he wrote. He quoted the words of Grandma Dean speaking of Marcus and Ortense Winslow. "Both are wise and gentle. Theirs is like a Quaker home should be. You never hear a harsh word there."

It was the relationship with Marcus Winslow Jr., "Little Markie," then seven years old, that Stock found really delightful. "Very simple and uncomplicated," he said. Jimmy was just like an older brother, helping him to build a model Jaguar from a kit, fixing his bicycle and pushing him around the snow-covered yard in his soapbox derby racer. He imagined that in Markie Jimmy saw himself at that age. As a farm boy Markie was already acquainted with tractors, and was fascinated by mechanical movement, an interest that remains with him. Marcus Winslow Jr. is a car enthusiast and the owner of an impressive collection of historic Fords.

Stock also observed the ease with which Jimmy handled the barnyard animals. He would sit amid the patient cattle and thump away obliviously on his bongo drum, and he posed proudly with an enormous and slightly belligerent sow in front of the barn door. The animals accepted him because he was a farm boy, and he respected them without any fear or apprehension.

Back in California, Stock photographed Jimmy during the shooting of *Rebel Without a Cause*, including the knife fight at the planetarium in Griffith Park, and the opening night sequence when Jimmy lay drunk in the roadway playing with a toy

"As Jimmy and I roamed the town and farm and fields of Fairmount ... I came to know, or at least to glimpse, the real James Dean."

DENNIS STOCK

▲ **COINCIDENCE:** In Park Cemetery, Fairmount with Markie, Jimmy spotted an old family tombstone linking his last name with the role he played in *East of Eden*.

◄ **HOME IN INDIANA:** Jimmy at Main and Washington, the center of Fairmount, the small rural town in Grant County, Indiana, where he was raised.

DRIVERS
CLUB

monkey. Jimmy even arranged for Stock to have a screen credit as dialog director, a strange position for a photographer.

With the assignment completed, Stock submitted the pictures to the magazine. By then *East of Eden* was receiving its early press and trade previews and the buzz was mounting that his debut performance was proving to be the most exceptional for years. Jimmy's shyness alternated with moments when he assumed the ego of a star. At one point he urged that Stock should stipulate to *Life* they guarantee a cover, and that the text accompanying the story should be written by a friend so that he could control it. Stock quietly ignored him.

The pictures were published in the *Life* issue of March 7, 1955, with the headline "Moody New Star." Sadly for Jimmy it did not make the cover, nor was it heavily flagged at the front of the magazine, but appeared as a routine feature among many in the fat publication.

"They never really liked the story very much," said Stock in 2004, "so they weren't going to give it the best display."

Stock continued a very successful career after Jimmy's death. For the first 20 years he adhered to black-and-white reportage, alternating picture essays on top movie stars and American jazz greats with "road" stories on subjects such as the Hell's Angels bikers.

▲ **READING TO HIS COUSIN:** To Marcus Winslow Jr. ("Markie") Jimmy always seemed like his big brother.

◀ **WHEELS FOR MARKIE:** Jimmy gives young Marcus assistance with his soapbox derby racer.

▼ **FIRST STAGE:** Jimmy went with Stock back to Fairmount High School and the auditorium where he received ovations in school plays.

“His own corpse would be taken there seven months later.” DENNIS STOCK

▲ **PORTENT:** Jimmy startled Stock by climbing into an open casket on display at a Fairmount store. The photograph has often been cited as

He turned to color and movement in the 1970s and lived in Europe, embracing with fervor the new medium of video recording. His career has been prolific, with a book published or a show staged almost every year into his mid-seventie He lives in Connecticut at Old Saybrook. His brief, positive friendship with James Dean has been a constant force throughout his life. He recalls Jimmy’s humbling, pessimistic take on the human condition: “There really isn’t an opportunity for greatness in this world. We are impaled in a crock of conditioning. A fish that is in water has no choice that he is. Genius would have it that we swim in sand.... We are fish and

"He could never really go home again." DENNIS STOCK

▲ **SCHOOL CELEBRATION:** Jimmy with Dennis Stock at the Sweethearts' Ball on St. Valentine's Day at Fairmount High. Jimmy had brought his bongo drums and played along with the band, then signed many autographs.

► **GOODBYE INDIANA:** Robert Middleton had driven Jimmy and Dennis to Indianapolis to take the flight back to Los Angeles. This was the last photograph taken by Middleton of Jimmy in his home state.

The idea of *Rebel Without a Cause* being made as a movie had begun as early as 1946, when Warner Bros. bought the rights to a book by Dr. Robert Lindner. **The story was about a young psychotic in a prison psychiatric unit, and several attempts had been made to turn the account into a screenplay.**

Marlon Brando had even been considered for the lead and had tested for it in 1947. Then Nicholas Ray, a maverick director who had worked as an actor, wrote a 17-page treatment of Lindner's book. Ray's directorial work included the poignant story of a fugitive couple, *They Live by Night* (1949), the bleak *film-noir* set in Hollywood, *In a Lonely Place* (1950), and the metaphor-laden, baroque western *Johnny Guitar* (1954), and had a tense edge almost bordering on the chaotic. He was adept at portraying vulnerable social loners. Leon Uris and Irving Shulman had both failed in their attempts at a screenplay, but, with the help of Stewart Stern, Ray finally managed to create a story that could be filmed, concerning a troubled high-school boy, at odds with his peers and his parents. It owed little to the original book except its inspirational title.

Ray's aim was to demonstrate that even teenagers from middle-class backgrounds could run wild when alienated from parents preoccupied with professional achievement and social status. It was, he felt, an increasingly common yet inadequately understood problem. The Culver City police department was approached and provided much support, including consultations with social workers, psychiatrists, and counselors, and it also opened up interview sessions with delinquents. Ray recognized that unwitting neglect by parents could lead to a sense of purposelessness and despair in the young, sometimes resulting in

"I went and hung around with kids in Los Angeles before making the movie.... These aren't poor kids, you know." JAMES DEAN

an explosion of antisocial behavior that was – to use a phrase that later became a casebook cliché – a cry for help. In confining the action to little more than 24 hours, he wanted to emulate the dramatic tension of *Romeo and Juliet*, believing that Shakespeare's play was the best expression of the theme of juvenile delinquency.

Nicholas Ray was determined that he would secure Jimmy to play the lead role, and spent much time preparing his actor for the part. He traveled to New York to talk Jimmy through it, and observed

◀ **REFRESHING PAUSE:** Natalie Wood and Jimmy take an on-set breather by the water cooler. They had met a few months earlier when they appeared in *I'm A Fool* on NBC.

Nicholas Ray

Nicholas Ray studied architecture under Frank Lloyd Wright, acted on stage with Elia Kazan, assisted John Houseman on the wartime *Voice of America*, worked with Kazan again as assistant director on *A Tree Grows in Brooklyn* (1945), and made his film directing debut with *They Live by Night* (1949).

He was one of the most interesting mainstream American directors in that, however much he was constrained by the system, much of his best work seemed detached from standard Hollywood attitudes, such as *Knock on Any Door* (1949), *In a Lonely Place* (1950) and *Johnny Guitar* (1954). The British critic Geoff Andrew, one of Ray's most dedicated admirers, describes him as the first home-grown film-poet of American disillusionment, and suggests that this is why he has always had such a powerful influence on European cinema, and in later years became a totem figure for American independent filmmakers.

▲ **MASTER'S VOICE:** Jimmy and Nicholas Ray got on well during filming, and the director encouraged his star's wild behaviour, believing it suited the character of Jim Stark.

► **END GAME:** Director and star confer in front of the Planetarium, prior to shooting the finale of *Rebel Without A Cause*,

"Dean always wanted to make a film in which he could personally believe, but it was never easy for him." NICHOLAS RAY

characteristics that could be incorporated into the performance. Simultaneously Warner Bros. had allocated a role for Jimmy in their major epic *Giant* – to be directed by George Stevens – a grandiose interpretation of Edna Ferber's epic novel set in Texas, and scheduled for shooting that summer. Jimmy was anxious to play the role of Jett Rink, even though it meant third billing after Rock Hudson and Elizabeth Taylor. Taylor's pregnancy caused a delay to the *Giant* schedule, which enabled Ray's film to fill the gap.

Back in Hollywood, Jimmy's preparation for *Rebel* included outrageous behavior that went far beyond hanging out in Googie's for much of the night. At every appearance in public he was constantly "on," an actor giving a performance, testing reactions, striving for effect. He had become copy for the hundreds of press stringers who hung around the watering-holes.

Lloyd Shearer wrote in *Parade* magazine: "Jimmy dresses like an unmade bed; lives in a one-room $30 a month garage apartment; roars to work on a high-powered motorcycle. 'You can sit with Dean all afternoon,' one publicity man told me, 'and he won't open his mouth. He's worse than Brando who at least is articulate.'"

Stardom seemed to be going to Jimmy's head, and his manners had not improved. His circle included many hangers-on, who openly exploited his acquaintance, or abused his hospitality by leaving him to pick up the drinking tab. However, among his most tender friendships was one with Toni Lee Scott, a blonde who had lost her leg as a passenger in a motorcycle crash. They met at

► **PALE RIDER:** Jimmy would ride to the locations around Los Angeles on his motorcycle, helmetless, eyes shaded, the inevitable cigarette clamped firmly in his mouth.

Googie's and Jimmy, sensitive to her situation, helped to boost her confidence. In 1970 she wrote in her autobiography: "He turned me in the right direction. There was never any romance between us. There was friendship." He said of her stump: "It's beautiful, and you're beautiful. And don't let anyone convince you otherwise." It was Scott who introduced Jimmy to the artist Kenneth Kendall, who would sculpt his bust.

To add excitement and to oblige his passion for speed, in February 1955 Jimmy bought a white Porsche 356 Super Speedster, which he entered in races. On many occasions his road riding and driving were considered risky. On at least one occasion he came off his motorcycle, fortunately without injury. He was also seen to come to a standstill not by applying the brakes, which had failed, but by riding straight through a gas station into a wall.

At the end of March *Rebel Without a Cause* began shooting, starting with the knife fight outside the Planetarium in Griffith Park. Jack Warner, confident in the favorable reception of *East of Eden* and impressed with Ray's first footage, ordered *Rebel* to be made in CinemaScope and in color (then preferred for all films produced in the anamorphic or "squeezed" wide-screen format that had been introduced in 1953). The black-and-white footage was scrapped, and shooting began anew. It was the right decision, and from it came what is probably the key image in the James Dean iconography – his slouched pose in a blazing red zip-up jacket and blue jeans.

Jimmy played Jim Stark, a name that had been cobbled from his own and from his character in *East of Eden*. The story is acted out within the time frame of two nights and a day. He plays the son of middle-class parents, who have just moved into the neighborhood of an unnamed Californian city that is clearly Los Angeles, and at the start of the story he is already in trouble with the police, who have picked him up late at night, drunk in the street. Early scenes in the juvenile hall, as the parents come to collect their son, establish the strained relationship with his forceful but unimaginative mother, played by Ann Doran, and his pliant, well-meaning, and clumsy father, played by Jim Backus, known generally to moviegoers as the voice of the myopic Mr. Magoo in Stephen Bosustow's popular animated shorts. It is not that they are oppressive parents – if anything his father is overindulgent – but they are clearly from a different world than their son. There is a history of Jim's teenage problems and subsequent, hasty relocations to make fresh starts.

The following day Jim, nursing a hangover, starts at his new high school. He meets Judy, played by Natalie Wood, a neurotic girl he had seen detained by the police the previous night, and attracts the derision of new classmates for siding with an unpopular loner, nicknamed Plato – played by Sal Mineo – a rich boy neglected by his divorced parents, who had also been pulled in for

▲ **IN REVERSE:** Carefully backing up in the narrow driveway at Sunset Plaza Drive, Jimmy takes a ride in his new, cherished Porsche 356 Speedster.

◄ **COOL CAT:** Jimmy, caught by the camera by his trailer, confirms the impression of one commentator that he often looked like an unmade bed.

THIS IS TO CERTIFY THAT

JAMES DEAN

IS A MEMBER OF THE

NATIONAL AUTOMOBILE CLUB

PORSCHE ROADSTER '55

ISSUED BY sdm-1 VOID IF ALTERED

MEMBERSHIP NUMBER 8252-J

EXPIRATION DATE NOV 22-55

GENERAL MANAGER

ABOVE LISTED CARS ENTITLED TO FREE EMERGENCY ROAD SERVICE

WHEN CHANGE IS REQUIRED RETURN CARD TO CLUB FOR CORRECTION

▲ **ROADSIDE ASSISTANCE:** Jimmy's National Automobile Club membership card.

◄ **CAR FOR A STAR:** The Speedster was an expensive import; Jimmy, now a star, could afford it.

disturbed behavior. Later, on an educational visit to the Planetarium at the Griffith Observatory, he is forced into a knife fight with Buzz, played by Corey Allen, leader of his antagonists and Judy's boyfriend. The fight is inconclusive, and for honor's sake he takes part in a "chickie run" that evening, in which the duelists drive at top speed toward a cliff edge, leaping at the last second – the one who goes first being the loser. The belt on Buzz's coat-sleeve gets caught, making it impossible for him to jump, and he dies as his car plunges off the cliff. Jim flees to his parents and is unable to make them understand the seriousness of the situation. In despair he runs off and hides out in a deserted mansion with Plato and Judy. The question is, who will find the sad trio first – Buzz's lethally minded friends seeking revenge, or the police, searching on behalf of anxious parents, knowing that Plato has his father's gun. Tragedy seems inevitable.

There was a strong rapport between Jimmy and Ray. In spite of Kazan's warnings regarding Jimmy's wild habits, and the need to keep a close check on his excessive behavior, Ray was unfazed.

► **DEFINING THE FUTURE:** Jimmy, more than anybody, helped to define the accepted sartorial appearance of the young for generations to come – tee-shirt, jeans, and boots.

Natalie Wood

Natalie Wood was born in San Francisco in 1938 to Russian immigrant parents who spoke little English. She made her film debut in 1943 in *Happy Land*, in a bit part as a child who drops an ice-cream cone.

After *Tomorrow is Forever* (1946) significant parts followed in a succession of films, including *The Ghost and Mrs. Muir* (1947), *Miracle on 34th Street* (1947), and *No Sad Songs for Me* (1950).

By the time she made *Rebel Without a Cause* she was already a movie veteran, although only 16 years old. Later she starred in memorable films such as *The Searchers* (1956), *West Side Story* (1961), and, for Elia Kazan, *Splendor in the Grass* (1961). Other parts included the title roles in *Gypsy* (1962) and *Inside Daisy Clover* (1966), and the social comedy *Bob & Carol & Ted & Alice* (1969). She was a small (5ft 0in), dark-haired, and dynamic beauty, and at one time was the hottest young female star in Hollywood, in constant demand. Twice married to the same man, the actor Robert Wagner, she shared Dean's misfortune by meeting an early, tragic death, in her case from drowning in a bizarre accident, the circumstances of which have never been properly explained.

▲ **ADORING FAN:** Natalie Wood was passionate about Jimmy, but there was no affair, claimed her biographer Gavin Lambert.

He did not even appear to mind that his star was racing his new Porsche at Palm Springs on the weekend before principal photography began, and in fact commiserated when Jimmy only made it to second place on a technicality. The relationship between them meant that Jimmy trusted Ray's directorial methods and he, in turn, was allowed to apply his own touches to many of the scenes, firing his ambition to become a director himself when he suspected acting would begin to pall. Backus contended that Jimmy actually co-directed the film, and others in the cast said that Ray was so extraordinarily receptive to input from his actors that Jimmy's suggestions were always treated with the utmost respect. Of the three film roles Jimmy played, his part in *Rebel Without a Cause* comes closest to his own reality. The photographer Dennis Stock – given a screen credit on the film as "dialog supervisor" – had got to know him well during their photojournalism foray for *Life*, and said that he could see Jimmy as he really was in his portrayal of Jim Stark.

▲ **SCRIPT CHECK:** Natalie, Jimmy, and Nick confer before shooting a key scene. Ray was close to both of them, and they enjoyed each other's friendship, as well as having an accord with their director.

At the core of the film is the interrelationship between the three: Judy, first glibly hostile to Jim in order to stay in with Buzz's gang, is then drawn to him because she recognizes an alienation similar to that she has toward her own parents, particularly a father who refuses her love; and Plato, who, as far as Hollywood censorship of the day allowed, is homosexually attracted to his new protector. In real life the three actors all had childhood traumas.

▲ **AT ODDS WITH THE WORLD:** Jim and Judy, both alienated from their parents, seek mutual solace.

▶ **WAITING FOR COLLECTION:** Jim Stark, found drunk in the streets, waits in Juvenile Hall for his parents.

▼ **"YOU'RE TEARING ME APART":** Jim turns away in increasing anguish as his father (Jim Backus) looks on in disappointment at his son's misbehavior, in the scene at the police house.

Wood was pushed into films at the age of four by her Russian immigrant parents who barely spoke English. Mineo's Sicilian father was a casket maker. Thrown out of parochial school at eight, young Salvatore became a member of a tough Bronx street gang and was persuaded to take up acting as an alternative to serving time in a reform school. The screenwriter Stewart Stern is said to have based Mineo's character, Plato, on Jimmy's friend Jack Simmons, who was actually auditioned for the role but was rejected for being too mannered in performance. Simmons was, however, taken on to play one of the film's teenage gang members.

It is as though the trio of misfits, holed up in the abandoned mansion (the empty swimming pool was the one used in Billy Wilder's *Sunset Boulevard*, outside the long-demolished house at 641 North Irving Boulevard that had been owned by J. Paul Getty) becomes a surrogate family, with Plato role-playing as the child of Jim and Judy. Censorship constraints insisted that any erotic overtones were carefully purged from the finished film.

BOOTS 25¢
SAM BROWNE 20¢
GET "CHIT" AT DESK

▲ **CONFRONTATION:** Jim defends himself against a knife attack by Buzz (Corey Allen) during the school's Planetarium visit.

Documents in the Warner Bros. archives reveal how sensitive the restrictions were. There could be no suggestion that Judy had been arrested for soliciting, instead she was hauled in by the police for breaking curfew. It had to be made clear that the high-school girls sneaking a smoke were using ordinary cigarettes, not marijuana. The knife fight had to be edited so that detail was omitted. In the racing sequence it had to be obvious that no innocent parties were at risk. There could be no suggestion of sexual activity between Jim and Judy in spite of their attraction. And so on. Considering the imposed inhibitions, it is amazing that the film was still able to make such a powerful impact.

One of the first sequences to be shot occurs near the beginning of the film, when Jim is interviewed by Ray (the director seems to have lent his name to a compassionate adult, played by Ed Platt), a detective specializing in juvenile cases. Jim, still drunk and angry, tries to take a swing at him, but Ray tells him that if he wants to blow off his rage he should take it out on the desk. Jimmy erupted with such passion that when he smashed his hand into the furniture he almost broke his bones, but carried on with the scene in spite of the pain, and later had to be taken to hospital for X-rays, which revealed bad bruising and contusions but no fractures. He had accomplished the scene in one take, but that was after keeping cast and crew waiting for hours while he stayed in his trailer preparing.

The real-life liaisons and attractions on the set of *Rebel Without a Cause* colored the shooting, bringing their own tensions. Wood, still only 16, was having an affair with the 44-year-old Ray. Jimmy and Ray, meanwhile, were very friendly collaborators, but if she was jealous of their closeness she did not let it show. She soon became attracted to Jimmy and found a generous side to his acting, as he often helped her with her technique. Mineo, a closet homosexual (a necessity because in

"The only way to make a scene realistic is to do it the way you know it would really happen." JAMES DEAN

▼ **PROTECTION:** Jimmy is helped into an armored vest prior to shooting the knife fight – necessary if it is to look realistic and frightening.

1955 homosexuality was still illegal) was hopelessly in love with Jimmy, but remained unrequited. As for the rest of the cast, the 19-year-old Dennis Hopper, gaining his first screen credit, while not lusting after Jimmy, was fascinated by his charismatic power as an actor. Hopper was actually in love with Wood, but nothing serious came of it because of her involvement with the director. Steffi Sidney, one of the girls in the gang, was infatuated with Hopper. To compound the complications, another actress in the cast, Beverly Long – who had appeared with Jimmy in the Pepsi commercial five years earlier – had previously dated Corey Allen, the chickie-run opponent, and was also very good friends with Jack Grinnage, who played Moose. That such a tangled web of intrigue was being woven as filming progressed greatly amused Ray, who tapped into its energy to raise the tension on the set.

◄ **NEARING THE END:** Jim, having emptied Plato's gun, prepares to open the planetarium door so that they can surrender to the police, unaware that his friend is about to be shot for being in possession of a deadly weapon.

▲ **HERO WORSHIP:** The script called for Plato, who was played by Sal Mineo, to adore Jim homosexually without actually saying so, given censorship constraints of the time. Mineo was a homosexual in reality, and was infatuated with Jimmy, who let him remain unrequited.

There were changes in the finished film. Under the opening credits, Jim is discovered lying in a deserted street at night (the corner of Franklin and Sierra Bonita in Hollywood), hopelessly drunk, and playing with a toy monkey on the roadway. Where the toy came from is not explained – a prologue, in which a businessman hurrying home laden with gifts for his children is assaulted by a teenage gang, was removed in the final cut. Ray also shot an alternative version of the climactic moment, which has Jimmy on the roof of the Planetarium vainly calling down to the police, trying to tell them that he has taken the bullets from Plato's gun, just before they shoot him. The closing shot of this version shows the view from inside the dome as its aperture slowly closes. The ending that was used is superficially more conventional, with Plato mown down in front of Jim as they attempt to leave the building. In the shock of the aftermath, Jim's parents move in, and there seems to be a rapprochement leading perhaps to a better understanding. Jim introduces Judy to them:

"Parents are often at fault, but the kids have some work to do, too." JAMES DEAN

"This is Judy. She's my friend." The tragedy is over, barely 24 hours since it began, and the anger of the rebel seems to have been purged by the death of Plato. It is as if the adolescent Jim has suddenly grown up and accepted his responsibilities. As the cars move away and the end titles go up, a man in a trench coat with a briefcase is seen striding purposefully toward the Planetarium. A detail denied the casual moviegoer is that this is Nicholas Ray, the director applying his signature to a film that was to stand as a seminal comment on a generation.

James Dean appears in almost every scene and delivers a performance so intrinsic to the structure of the film that it is difficult to visualize any other actor in the role. Of the three feature roles he played, Jim Stark is the one that carried the entire film. Middle-class teenage angst had found its spokesman.

At the end of shooting Jimmy had hoped to go to the Indy 500, but the 11-day overrun of the *Rebel* schedule made it impossible for him to leave California, as he was urgently required for wardrobe and makeup tests for *Giant*. Memorial Day was his last chance to race before the film's director George Stevens placed a ban on him, and he competed at Santa Barbara, pushing the Porsche Speedster so hard in the last lap that it blew a piston, ending his chances.

▸ **TOP OF THE WORLD:** Jimmy relaxes on the parapet of the Planetarium roof while the next shot for the unused sequence is set up.

Edna Ferber's great American novel *Giant* is a saga set in Texas, and covers three decades in the life of a rich cattle baron, who accrues even more wealth when he blankets his ranch with oil derricks. **Texans were not overly fond of Ferber's portrait of their state, but the version directed by George Stevens was regarded with much more approval.**

By May 1955 the monumental production of *Giant* had already been a year in preparation, and it was the biggest of Warner projects. By 1956 it had overrun its budget, having reached an astronomical $5.4 million. Filming had been delayed on account of Elizabeth Taylor's pregnancy in her marriage to the English actor Michael Wilding, but by June extensive location shooting had begun around Marfa, Texas. It was a remote place in the western part of the vast state, a three-hour drive from El Paso, and 60 miles from the Mexican border. Marfa then, as now, was a crossroads desert town of around 2,500 inhabitants, and the shooting of *Giant* is still regarded as the biggest event in its history.

Out on the Worth Evans Ranch, 20 miles from Marfa, the Reata mansion was built to Boris Leven's design, a massive Victorian gothic house that could be seen from miles away, looming over the empty, dusty landscape like a giant liner in mid-ocean. It was actually a three-sided structure with a hollow interior, matched by a more finished version on a Burbank sound stage. Remnants of its skeleton still stand, much as it was left after the skin was stripped from it at the end of filming, the remaining timbers having been eroded more by souvenir hunters than the dry desert winds.

Jimmy's role, in spite of his best efforts to have the script modified, was subordinate to that of Rock Hudson, who plays Jordan "Bick" Benedict, inheritor and patriarch of the giant Reata ranch, which at 595,000 acres was roughly the size of New Hampshire. Also taking star billing over Jimmy was Elizabeth Taylor, who played Leslie Lynnton, the beautiful, bright, strong-willed bride Bick finds in Maryland on a visit to buy equine bloodstock. She must make serious adjustments to her lifestyle, exchanging the gently undulating, green landscape of Maryland foxhunting country for the flat, featureless monotony of the Reata's sandy expanse.

Jimmy played Jett Rink (making a trio of monosyllabic character names), a surly ranch hand, who is as much a Texan as his employer Bick. Their antagonism is mutual and bitter, because Jett is dirt-poor, only one step up from the despised Mexicans who supply the manual labor. He regards the gulf between him and the fabulously wealthy Benedict family as too extreme. The real-life inspiration for Jett Rink and his sudden wealth was the "King of the Wildcatters," Glenn

◄ **THE OUTSIDER:** Jimmy slips into a crucifixion posture in a scene in which Elizabeth Taylor as Leslie calls on him on the tiny parcel of Reata land he inherited to the horror of the other Benedicts.

George Stevens

George Stevens, the director who had, before World War II, made such lightweight confections as *Swing Time* (1936), *Quality Street* (1937), and *Gunga Din* (1939), was a craftsman whose output drastically changed after his experience in uniform making films for the US Signal Corps in Europe.

The frivolity vanished in his postwar work, and he became known for a painstaking and careful approach to big subjects. His work included *A Place in the Sun* (1951), the adaptation of Theodore Dreiser's *An American Tragedy*, with Montgomery Clift as a social climber who resorts to murder to attain marriage to a rich girl played by Elizabeth Taylor, and *Shane* (1953), a celebrated western in which a stranger, played by Alan Ladd, rides in and vanquishes the men who are terrorizing decent smallholders who yearn to replace frontier anarchy with law and order. His film of *Giant* reflects many of his postwar characteristics: the big theme, a love of America, a liberal approach to issues such as racial bigotry, male chauvinism, and capitalistic greed. In spite of the casting of Clift in *A Place in the Sun*, Stevens was not much in accord with Method acting, and his first choice for Jett Rink was Ladd, who was eight years older than Rock Hudson.

► **PLANNING THE SCENE:** George Stevens and Jimmy discuss a scene on location at Marfa.

▼ **STUDIO DIRECTION:** On a soundstage at Burbank, Stevens discusses Jimmy's climactic scene as the middle-aged, wealthy Jett Rink.

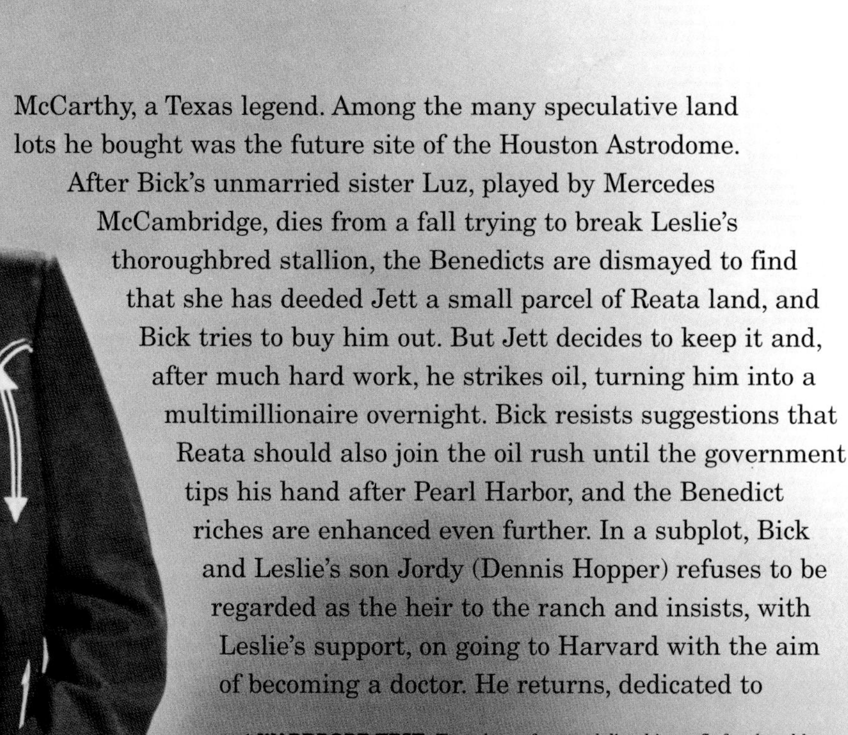

McCarthy, a Texas legend. Among the many speculative land lots he bought was the future site of the Houston Astrodome. After Bick's unmarried sister Luz, played by Mercedes McCambridge, dies from a fall trying to break Leslie's thoroughbred stallion, the Benedicts are dismayed to find that she has deeded Jett a small parcel of Reata land, and Bick tries to buy him out. But Jett decides to keep it and, after much hard work, he strikes oil, turning him into a multimillionaire overnight. Bick resists suggestions that Reata should also join the oil rush until the government tips his hand after Pearl Harbor, and the Benedict riches are enhanced even further. In a subplot, Bick and Leslie's son Jordy (Dennis Hopper) refuses to be regarded as the heir to the ranch and insists, with Leslie's support, on going to Harvard with the aim of becoming a doctor. He returns, dedicated to

◄ **WARDROBE TEST:** Two days after modeling his outfit for the older Jett Rink, Jimmy was on set in Marfa, Texas. Time was short.

improving the squalid conditions in the Mexican village on Reata property, and marries Juana, an educated Hispanic woman (Elsa Cardénas) who is also a doctor. Bick is obliged to come to terms with a mixed-race grandson.

When the absurdly wealthy Jett, in a fit of megalomania, invites the cream of Texas society to the opening of an airport named after him, the Benedicts attend with trepidation. On Jett's orders Juana is humiliated in a beauty salon because of her race. Bick attempts to fight him, but Jett is too drunk to engage and shortly afterward passes out in public, just as he is about to make his speech at the gala banquet, his run of success supposedly concluded. Bick, his heart pumping with a new surge of liberalism, stops at a roadside diner, accompanied by Leslie, Juana, and his light and dark-skinned grandchildren, and intervenes when the racist proprietor tries to eject a Mexican family. He loses the ensuing fight, but his gallant action is rewarded by the reaffirmation of Leslie's love for him.

The role of Jett is secondary to the main dramatic thrust, which is concerned with the relationship between Bick and Leslie, played by actors well-established at the box office, who were being paid considerably more than Jimmy's

▼ **TWO TOGETHER:** Luz Benedict, played by Mercedes McCambridge, was Jett's closest friend, bequeathing him Little Reata.

guaranteed minimum of $15,000. In contrast, Elizabeth Taylor's salary was $175,000 and Hudson's $100,000.

What is noticeable in *Giant* is that Jimmy's style of acting is at odds with that of the other performers, and his character of Jett is a creature of hesitation, diffidence, verbal stumbling, and sudden unexplained bursts of laughter, twitches, shrugs, and slouches. He is forever tilting his hat forward or pushing it back. He reclines rather than sits, extending his legs toward any object that allows him to elevate his feet. In the key scene in which he is informed of the terms of Luz's legacy, he plays with a piece of rope to which a rock is tied, performing tricks such as making loops by means of abrupt jerks, while everyone patiently waits for him to speak. Almost without exception, the rest of the cast acts in a straightforward, understated fashion, and Hudson in particular displays a foursquare, dignified straightness in his performance, which gives him more conviction than he has in any of his other films. But whereas his is an acceptable, accomplished, but conventional representation, Jimmy invests Jett with an uncanny realism. He moves as though he has spent half his lifetime on a horse. His skin has the leathery look of someone accustomed to working in the hot sun, and his cowboy hat is like an extension to his head,

▲ **STRETCHING OUT:** Jimmy takes a break from a heavy schedule. He joined *Giant* well into shooting – *Rebel Without A Cause* did not finish until the end of May.

"I sat there like a bump on a log watching that big, lumpy Rock Hudson making love to Liz Taylor." JAMES DEAN

Elizabeth Taylor and Rock Hudson

Jimmy's role in *Giant* was secondary to those of Elizabeth Taylor and Rock Hudson – both already big stars, guaranteed to attract huge moviegoing audiences, and who commanded salaries to match their status.

Elizabeth Taylor was born to American parents in London in 1932. Her father, an art dealer, was establishing a gallery there. At the age of seven, with the onset of World War II, the family relocated to Los Angeles while the United States was still neutral, and made her film debut in *There's One Born Every Minute* (1942), followed by *Lassie Come Home* (1943). She achieved stardom in the leading role in *National Velvet* (1944). In common with Natalie Wood, she achieved the rare feat of surviving from child actress to top adult star. By the time she made *Giant*, although still only 23, she had become a Hollywood diva with a private life that was persistently public. Her transition to adulthood had occurred with an earlier George Stevens film, *A Place in the Sun* (1951). In spite of her outstanding beauty and stellar presence her health was always fragile, and her absenteeism through illness caused Stevens far more headaches than James Dean's waywardness. Years later, when making *Cleopatra* for a record-breaking $1 million salary, her almost fatal illness temporarily closed down the production, making it the most expensive film ever made.

Rock Hudson was born Roy Scherer Jr. in Winnetka, north of Chicago, in 1925. Although the polar opposite of Brando in acting terms, he was actually far more talented than he was prepared to allow audiences to believe; they only saw a tall, amiable, sympathetic, and handsome leading man, as adept at rugged action adventure as gentler domestic drama. His earlier films had been unremarkable, but he caught the eye of the stylish German director Douglas Sirk, who had arrived in Hollywood in the late 1930s, and in his romantic melodramas such as *Magnificent Obsession* (1954), *All That Heaven Allows* (1956), and *Written on the Wind* (1956) his contributions were capable and satisfying. George Stevens provided him with one of his most rewarding parts in *Giant*. He was by no means limited in range. In a series of light screwball farces with Doris Day, such as *Pillow Talk* (1959), *Lover Come Back* (1961), and *Send Me No Flowers* (1964) his comedic gifts delighted the box office. Ultimately Hudson, having concealed his homosexuality successfully from the public, was destined to become one of the earliest celebrities to succumb to the AIDS virus, in 1985.

◄ **CAUGHT:** Jimmy enjoyed monopolizing Elizabeth Taylor's company, leaving Rock Hudson in the cold. She, in turn, enjoyed the rivalry between the two men.

often only removed when he has been indoors for what seems like several minutes. Jimmy draws the eye, even when he is not the center of the scene. William Mellor's deep-focus cinematography often allows the placement of characters at various points within the depth of field, and Stevens sometimes holds the frame in long-shot rather than inter-cutting with close-ups. Quite deliberately, he chose not to use the then highly fashionable CinemaScope format, because he disliked having to compose within a letterbox shape. Also, the anamorphic lens intrinsic to CinemaScope tended to distort faces, a fault that was corrected with its successor, Panavision.

Rock Hudson was ostensibly a ruggedly handsome heartthrob, but Jimmy was under no illusions that it was a deception, a studio-made façade. Hudson was in fact a closet homosexual who, in 1985, would shock the world by becoming an early victim of AIDS. In the 1950s the studio had gone to considerable efforts to conceal his orientation from legions of female fans, and was relieved when he had married. Jimmy's knowingness added to the tension between the two men. Another factor was Hudson's friendship with his costar Elizabeth Taylor, who at 23 was six years younger than him. Taylor has always seemed to get on well with men of ambiguous sexuality, but her cozy amiability with Hudson riled Jimmy, and he resolved to snatch her from him.

◄ **OLD COWHAND:** Jimmy as young Jett wore the cowboy outfit as though he had been born in the saddle, and horrified Jane Withers by never having his shirt washed.

► **FOOLING WITH LIZ:** Jimmy and Elizabeth Taylor whiled away the tedium between setups with improvised acrobatic stunts, to the chagrin of the production team.

It proved rather easy. She found that he was opening himself up especially for her, and confiding intimate secrets that she was sure he had shared with nobody else. She responded to the story of his maternal loss in childhood with great sympathy, and did not appreciate that he was playing a game with her, the one called "Make Rock Jealous."

Arguably Jimmy was also propping up his character motivation. In the film, Jett is secretly in love with Leslie, who is unattainable, but unconsciously she supplies the motivation for him to achieve his wildcat oil-driller's dreams, much in the way that she fuels Clift's character's social ambitions in *A Place in the Sun*. One of the most remarkable scenes in the film shows Leslie visiting Jett in the little shanty house he has made for himself on his inherited plot, which he has called "Little Reata," much to Bick's disgust. When he goes off to make some tea, Leslie finds a pile of self-improvement books on his shelf. He, meanwhile, is fortifying himself with a surreptitious swig or two of hard liquor, a foretaste of his eventual downfall from alcoholism. Leslie is in fact *Giant*'s strongest character, the air of change that blows in from the outside world with ideas on racial tolerance, an improved life for the peons, and a role for women beyond childbearing and deferring to their husbands. That she likes Jett is not in doubt, but whether her feelings go beyond that is not made clear, even though the scene crackles with electric tension.

The sprawling narrative – the film runs for 3 hours 18 minutes – falls into two distinct halves, and in the second the cast ages. Hudson is allowed to keep his clean, rugged looks with the addition of a little fat around the midriff and gentle graying of the temples. Elizabeth Taylor, padded to add more curves to her figure, maintains the unwrinkled face of a 23-year-old, although her hair becomes a fetching shade of silver. Jimmy does not age gracefully at all, even in the over-cosmeticized Hollywood manner. As Jett's oil pumps start to

◄ **SMALL KINGDOM:** Jett climbs his windmill to look across his inherited land, which he called Little Reata, further angering his former boss, Bick Benedict.

however, play a magnificent tête-à-tête scene, in which he makes a halfhearted marriage proposal to the Benedicts' elder daughter, Luz II, played by Carroll Baker, using his skills in improvisation and spontaneity to the full. Although Baker was making her screen debut and actually acting in her first scene, she handled his tricks with polished unfussiness and assurance. Unlike the rest of the cast, she had trained at the Actors Studio, and Jimmy draws on that experience to stretch her. It is one of the most effective scenes in his screen career.

Later, when Jett endures his humiliating public downfall, Jimmy fumbled it and actually failed to deliver the last speech that had been written for him. The few words that are said had to be looped by another actor, Nick Adams, after Jimmy had died, as his rendering was too indistinct to be usable. The screenplay had

disgorge the black glop that will make him rich, he sports a rakish little mustache, then as the years advance his hair also becomes silver, losing some of its abundance, but his face stays unlined, assuming a permanent lecherous sneer. It is possible that the makeup artist was concerned not to mar the hot new Warner Bros. property, but the effect is unconvincing. A plausible excuse could be that the commitment to *Rebel Without a Cause* left too little time for Jimmy's makeup tests, in which a better aged appearance could have been achieved by experimentation. Jimmy is far surer in the first half of the film when he is playing approximately his own age. His attempt to portray Jett in advanced middle age, quite apart from the unsatisfactory makeup, exposes his inexperience. He does,

▲ **WILDCAT STRIKE:** His gusher erupts and in seconds Jett becomes a rich man.

► **GENTLEMAN CALLER:** Matured into wealth and status, Jett visits the Reata mansion and is greeted by Luz II, Bick and Leslie's daughter, played by Carroll Baker.

▲ **DEAD DRUNK:** The elderly Jett Rink sways as he stands to give his speech at the banquet – a sign of his downfall from alcoholism.

required him to become progressively more inebriated, and Jimmy simply took it too far.

To some extent this was the fault of the director. Jimmy and George Stevens did not always see eye to eye. Stevens, always the perfectionist, required many takes from different angles to cover each shot. He greatly enjoyed the editing process, and liked to shoot excessive footage to give him the widest possible choice. Jimmy called him the "round-the-clock" director because of his need to circle each setup with alternative takes. Stevens was infuriated by Jimmy's inability to deliver the same performance twice, which meant that successive takes became hard to match. For Stevens, the cutting room was the arena of true creativity and, having shot over 600,000ft of *Giant*, he spent a further year editing it until he had the preview cut of 3 hours 35 minutes, and then removed a further 17 minutes in time for the premiere.

Delayed by the over-run of the *Rebel Without a Cause* schedule, Jimmy had joined the film late. Locations around Charlottesville, Virginia for the Maryland scenes in which he was not involved had long concluded. Marfa was not an easy place to accommodate a big Hollywood production, with its cast and crew of 250 people, and the only acceptable hotel to stay in, El Paisano, was immediately filled, leaving everyone else to be lodged in rented homes after careful negotiations according to their status. Even the stars were expected to share their residences. Jimmy lived in the same house as

"I don't recall ever working with anyone who had such a gift." WILLIAM C. MELLOR, CINEMATOGRAPHER

Rock Hudson and Chill Wills, who played a genial Benedict uncle. Domestic air conditioning was then almost nonexistent. The sole movie theater in the town was commandeered for the screening of dailies. There was very little after-hours activity in Marfa, other than a bar or two, and the nearest place with anything resembling nightlife was too far

away for an evening's drive. In the daytime it was unbearably hot. At the time of shooting the thermometer was usually above 100 degrees, and it had not rained for the past five years. Life in Marfa was tough, but the locals were used to it and regarded their visitors as pampered city folk. But Jimmy preferred the company of the Texans to his colleagues, and while the rest of the cast shared the misery, he rarely mingled with his colleagues. Jane Withers, who played Bick's earlier love, Vashti Snythe, actually managed to wash Jimmy's favorite shirt, but only after he had been wearing it nonstop for two weeks. He was popular with the inhabitants because he always took time to speak to them. Lucy Garcia, then a Marfa teenager, recalled how Hudson and Taylor were unapproachable, surrounded by an entourage, and never mingled with the townsfolk, while Jimmy made a point of meeting them, talking, and signing autographs without the slightest hint of impatience.

His interest in the locals was justified in that it enabled him to study the distinctive accent they used, and to replicate the physical mannerisms, in particular the odd, lopsided gait of the cowboy. He learned the difficult art of rope twirling, how to ride Texas-style, and even how to strum a guitar, a talent not required in the film. The preparation added to the contrast in his performance with that of the others.

▶ **CANDID CAMERA:** Jane Withers, who played Vashti Snythe in the movie, lovingly films Jimmy, in a contemplative mood.

> **"I've gotten to like the state and the people so much I'm apt to talk like a proud Texan even after *Giant* is completed."**
>
> JAMES DEAN

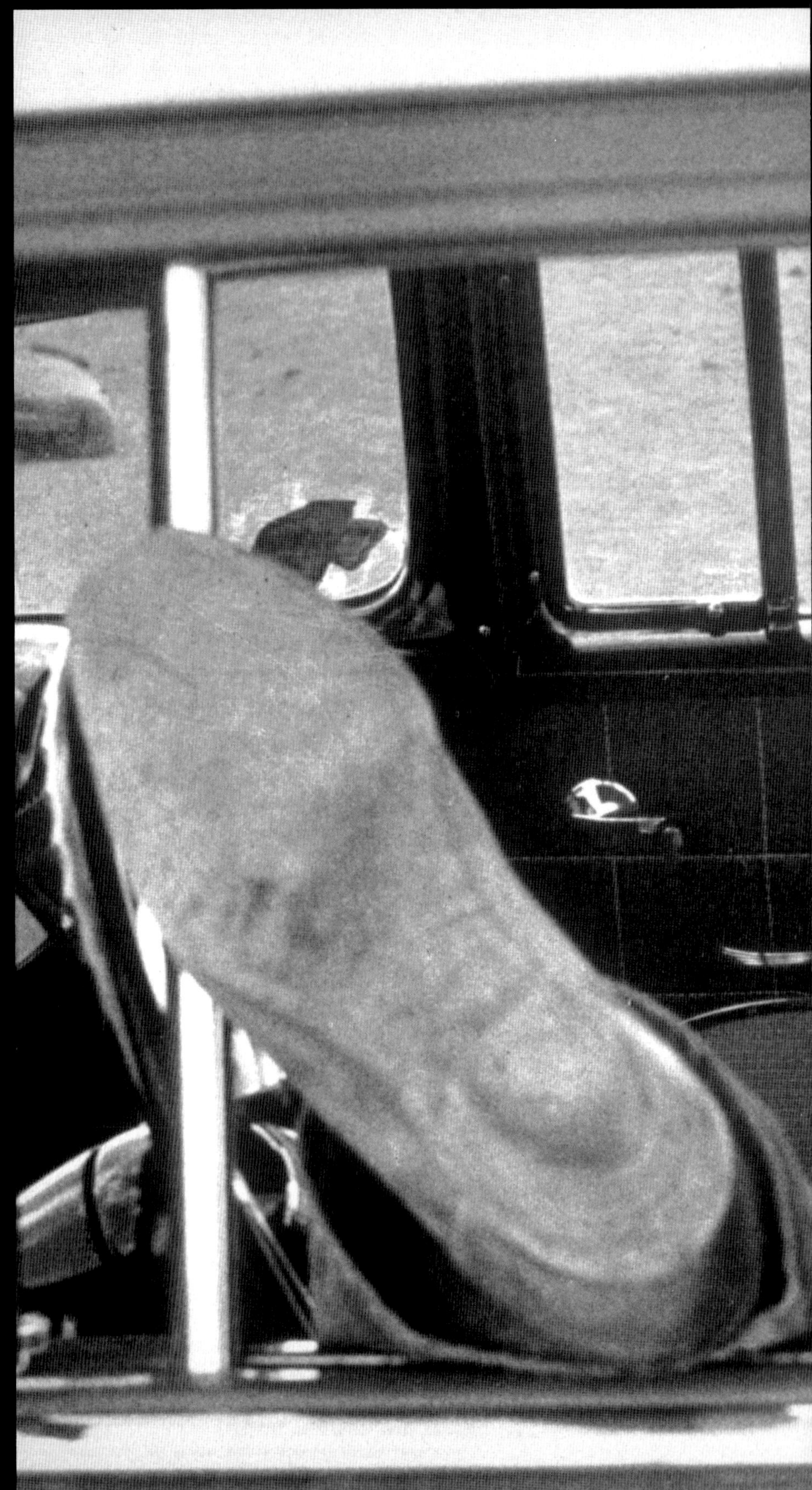

▶ **GOING NATIVE:** Dozing in the noonday heat of Marfa, Jimmy takes it easy as he awaits his next call to be on set. He had the ability to take instant naps.

Although he was the lead, Rock Hudson had very little acting technique, having been groomed merely to be a star. Tall (6ft 4in), dark-haired, good-looking, rugged, yet gentle in manner, he had become a sex symbol on account of his imposing screen presence and charm. Bick was one of his best roles, and the only one for which he was Oscar-nominated. On screen he and Jimmy were an ill-matched pair, which suited the needs of the plot. Of Jimmy's three films, *Giant* is the only one where his short stature is constantly apparent. It is not surprising, and also in accordance with the storyline, that the two actors did not respond well to each other. Hudson hated all the improvised business Jimmy would get up to when he was supposed to be listening to Bick's lines. A well-mannered person himself, he thought Jimmy was uncouth and inconsiderately rude.

Hudson also disapproved of the way Jimmy constantly denigrated George Stevens. The absence of an affinity with the director contributed to the edginess of his performance and the success of the film. Jimmy found Stevens' authoritarian attitude on set distracting, and many of his habits irritating. Stevens liked to have his cast standing by, ready in costume and makeup whether they were wanted or not. It was his safety device should a scene not work and hasty rescheduling become necessary. But in the heat and dust of Marfa it was exhausting to be expected to hang around all day on such an off-chance, and Jimmy annoyed Stevens by absenting himself after three days of inactivity in a row. He received a very public scolding the next day, in which the director attempted to impose his command, but it was not the best way to win Jimmy's respect.

Edna Ferber made a point of visiting the set, breaking the rule she had observed when other novels of hers had been filmed. She had not liked the initial script and wanted to observe progress firsthand. She and Jimmy got on well, and she was delighted by his eagerness to have her define precisely what Jett was about. "I don't think there is another actor in the world who can convey Jett as well as he did," she said, qualifying her praise by adding "... like most geniuses, Dean suffered from success poisoning."

▲ **AUTHOR'S NOTE:** Edna Ferber rarely visited sets of films from her novels, but *Giant* was an exception. She liked Jimmy, and described him as as "Definitely gifted. Frequently maddening."

◄ **LAID-BACK COWBOY:** Jimmy enjoys a moment of relaxation – still wearing his cowboy boots – on the set of *Giant*. George Stevens insisted his actors be ready in full costume, even if their scenes were not scheduled for that time.

▲ **EYE TO EYE:** At the Villa Capri, Jimmy clowns with his friend Sammy Davis Jr. and a 35mm Leica.

The location shooting in Marfa wrapped in the second week of July, and a relieved cast and crew reassembled on the Burbank sound stages on July 11. Jimmy was now dating Ursula Andress, mainly at weekends because the *Giant* schedule was still very demanding. A dinner for two at the Villa Capri had alerted the gossip columnists. It was not a lasting romance.

Having already frustrated Stevens with his tardiness on set, Jimmy again incurred the director's wrath in July by taking an unauthorized day off, fully aware that he was on call. He was moving house from 1541 Sunset Plaza Drive to a rented bungalow, designed like a hunting lodge, at 14611 Sutton Street in Sherman Oaks. He pleaded that he had been too tired to work and shrugged off charges of unprofessionalism. Stevens angrily vowed never to work with him again, although in the months that followed, when he was closeted in the cutting room, he marveled at the extraordinary qualities Jimmy projected on screen.

Jimmy's presence on set was, however, far better than that of Elizabeth Taylor, who had 21 days of absence during shooting owing to her constant ill health and a range of medical complaints. On two occasions her unavailability caused the production to be halted, on the second occasion for over a week when only a day or two was needed to finish its shoot.

As the protracted film neared the end of its production period, Jimmy was planning his future career. The next movie he was scheduled to appear in was a screen biography of the boxer Rocky Graziano called *Somebody Up There Likes Me*, with Pier Angeli appearing as the hero's wife. It was to be made for MGM, with Jimmy as a loan-out as a trade for Elizabeth Taylor's appearance in *Giant*. He had already started training with a boxing professional. Through his agent Dick Clayton and executives at Warner Bros. he was also exploring the possibility of a film based on the life of the western outlaw Billy the Kid. The roles in each of these films were to be taken by Paul Newman after Jimmy's death; the latter, *The Left-Handed Gun*, was Arthur Penn's first feature as director. Jane Deacy came out from New York to negotiate an appearance for him in a big television production of *The Corn is Green* by Emlyn Williams, with Judith Anderson as the tough schoolmarm who drives a poor Welsh boy toward an Oxford scholarship. Because it was taking place in October in New York, he was concerned that it would put a temporary hold on his racing plans. Deacy also worked with Clayton on a new six-year Warner contract worth $1 million for nine films. He would also be allowed to appear in a Broadway play of his choosing in 1956.

▲ **SOCIAL CIRCUIT:** Back in Hollywood Jimmy dines out at the Villa Capri with Ursula Andress, his "exotic" Swiss date.

Jimmy spent what were to be the last weeks of his life mostly working. Although the stunt driver Bill Hickman had been teaching him various motor-racing techniques, he was still under the prohibition enforced by Stevens, and on Labor Day, when he was not required for filming, he went to Santa Barbara to watch a friend, Lew Bracker, compete in his first race. He was itching to get back behind the wheel as a competitor and was contemplating trading his Porsche Speedster up to a more powerful model. Bracker was an insurance man, and in order to underwrite the risk of Jimmy's sporting passion, had been drawing up a life policy for him, which would leave $85,000 to Marcus and Ortense, $10,000 for Marcus Jr.'s education, and a further $5,000 to his grandparents, Charles and Emma Dean. Sadly it became a case of unfinished business. The bequests were dependent on his signing a will, which he never did, and after his death the entire value of the policy by law went to Winton, who had not even been named as a beneficiary. Bracker urged Jimmy to check out Competition Motors in Hollywood as soon as possible because they had taken delivery of a new Spyder, on display in their showroom window. Jimmy decided to buy it, and announced a roster of racing meets that he intended to enter.

"Take a good look at me. You may not get the chance again." JAMES DEAN TO WILLIAM C. MELLOR

That July the National Safety Council had popularized the slogan "The life you save may be your own," which had been featured on billboards, in press advertising, and in celebrity-endorsed television commercials. Jimmy was persuaded to take part in one, having acquired a reputation for his love of fast cars and motor racing, and having become a symbol for his generation. In full makeup and costume as Jett Rink, as though he had just wandered in from a neighboring sound stage, he was interviewed by the actor Gig Young on an office set. Jimmy, slouched in a chair and playing distractedly with his rock on a rope while Young questions him, delivers a few muttered answers. Summing up, Young says: "Jimmy, we probably have a great many young people watching our show tonight, and for their benefit I'd like your opinion about fast driving on the highway." Jimmy answers, dragging on a cigarette: "I used to fly around quite a bit, but you know, I took a lot of unnecessary chances on the highway. Then I started racing, and now when I drive on the highways I'm extra cautious 'cause no one knows what they're doing half the time. You don't know what this guy's gonna do or that one. I find myself being very cautious on the highway. I don't have the urge to speed on the highway. People say racing is dangerous. But I'll take my chances on the track any day than on a highway." He gets up to leave, but Young halts him with one more question: "Do you have any special advice for the young people who drive?" Jimmy turns, halfway through the door, and says with his head slightly lowered: "Take it easy driving. The life you might save might be mine."

The evening of September 17 he went with Ursula Andress to the Village Theater in Westwood, where the final cut of *Rebel Without a Cause* was given a sneak preview before an audience. Following the triumph of *East of Eden*, it had

▼ **LOOKING AHEAD:** After three big films in a row Jimmy looked forward to a period of rest after *Giant* and the chance to indulge his love of motor racing.

▲ **PERSONAL TOUCH:** After taking delivery of his new Porsche Spyder Jimmy had George Barris, who customized cars, apply in his workshop his racing number and the affectionate name "Little Bastard."

▶ **DOCTOR'S APPROVAL:** As further evidence of his fitness to race Jimmy had his physician write a letter certifying his good health.

IRVING S. BERMAN, M. D.
9884 SANTA MONICA BLVD.
BEVERLY HILLS, CALIFORNIA

Sept. 27, 1955

Sport Car Club of America, Inc.
San Francisco, Calif.

Gentlemen:

This is to certify that
Mr. James Dean
14,611 Sutton St.
Sherman Oaks, Calif.
has been given a complete physical examination this date.

He is in excellent health. His neuro-muscular reflexes are all physiological. All organs and systems are normal.

He is therefore physically qualified to engage in competitive automobile racing.

Very truly yours,

Irving S. Berman, M.D.

become one of the most eagerly awaited movies of the fall, and the audience response was favorable.

On September 21 he bought the silver Spyder 550, trading in his Speedster 356 and adding a check for $3,000, representing the full value of the new car at $6,900, an extraordinary price then for an automobile, when a top-of-the-range Cadillac sedan could be bought for less than $4,000. It was a tiny vehicle, with a topless aluminum body as fragile as an eggshell, a rudimentary windshield in the form of a six-inch plastic strip, and an entirely hand-built air-cooled engine. He had his personal touches applied at the workshop of George Barris, who specialized in customizing stars' cars. His racing number "130" was painted in black over the hood, on the doors, and above the midships engine grille. Across the rear of the car the name he gave it was applied in script-style lettering, "Little Bastard," a reference to an obscure private joke between Jimmy and Bill Hickman.

He was inordinately proud of his new automobile and drove it around town to impress his friends, some of whom were apprehensive. Beulah Roth, wife of the photographer Sanford Roth, who had been shooting him for a picture essay on *Giant* and became a friend, was taken on a quick ride to the market, but was so terrified she insisted on walking back, vowing never to drive in it again. Ursula Andress flatly refused to get into it.

September 23 was Jimmy's last day on *Giant*. He drove his terrifying little car to the Warner Bros. lot and, now that the driving ban no longer applied, insisted that Stevens take a spin with him around the studio. The director was delivered rather shakily back to the sound stage, where a crowd had gathered to look at the car. Also joining the throng were two studio guards. Stevens later reported their words to Jimmy: "'You can never drive this car on the lot again; you're gonna kill a carpenter or an actor or somebody.' And that was the last time I saw Jimmy."

The following week Jimmy decided to race at Salinas on the weekend, but it was too late for his name to go on the program. The town, which he had also known as the location of *East of Eden*, was 300 miles north of Los Angeles, a long haul in the era before the I-5 freeway. He wanted others to be there to see him race and compiled a list of those who would be invited to go – a roll that even included his father. In the end only Hickman and Roth agreed to accompany him, along with the Porsche mechanic, Rolf Weutherich. On the eve of his departure, one of his last acts was to deliver his Siamese cat for safekeeping to Jeanette Miller, an actress girlfriend. It had been a gift from Elizabeth Taylor, and he had named him Marcus, or Markie, after his uncle. With the cat was a note from Jimmy, advising her what food he should have and a reminder to take him in for his shots the following Tuesday.

On the morning of September 30 Jimmy left his home in Sherman Oaks and drove in his Ford station wagon to Competition Motors on Vine Street in Hollywood, where he picked up the Spyder. After a sandwich at the Hollywood Ranch Market across

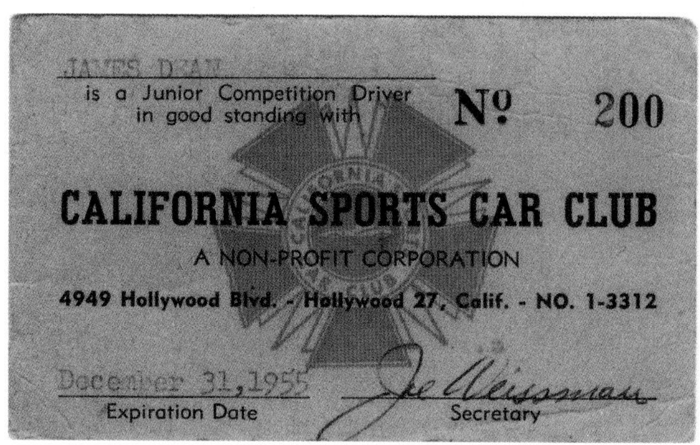
JAMES DEAN
is a Junior Competition Driver in good standing with
Nº 200
CALIFORNIA SPORTS CAR CLUB
A NON-PROFIT CORPORATION
4949 Hollywood Blvd. - Hollywood 27, Calif. - NO. 1-3312
December 31, 1955
Expiration Date
Secretary

▲ **BACK ON TRACK:** Jimmy renewed membership to allow him to race again as soon as he was no longer bound by Stevens' prohibition order.

the street, he and Weutherich went to Roth's house. Because the engine needed more mileage to reach optimum performance, Jimmy had decided that rather than have it towed on a low-loader behind the Ford station wagon he would drive the car, with Weutherich as his passenger. Roth and Hickman followed in the Ford as Jimmy and Weutherich set off in the tiny high-performance Spyder, their heads well above the minuscule windshield, and headed north for Salinas.

Dean and Racing

James Dean was a fast, steel-nerved driver, and many devotees of motor racing felt that he had what it takes to be a champion. After acting, it was his life's passion.

He only had time to compete in three main events, at Palm Springs, where he finished in second place after his rival's disqualification, at Bakersfield, where he finished overall third but first in his class, and Santa Barbara where, lying fourth, a piston blew, forcing him to a standstill. For a beginner it was an impressive record.

▲ **AUTO MANIA:** Jimmy had been car and motorcycle crazy since childhood, when his uncle had taught him to drive a tractor. Hollywood gave him the money to fulfill his mechanized desires, opening up the chance to win.

Dean and Racing

▲ **ON THE MOVE:** Jimmy chats to motorcycle ace Johnny McLaughlin at Minter Field, Bakersfield. He is wearing a Salinas tee-shirt.

◀ **PRIZE HAUL:** For so short a racing career, Jimmy amassed quite a few trophies. Inset is the program for the two-day Palm Springs event in March 1955.

JAMES DEAN
The overnight sensation of 'East of Eden'
Warner Bros. put all the force of the screen into a challenging drama of today's juvenile violence!
James Dean Memorial Issue
THE STARS
THE REAL
JAMES DEAN STORY
MES DEAN
HOW HE LI
BOB ROMEO ON FLUTE
CONGA DRUMS
AD-LIB
Le Petit Prince

REBELS UNITED
INDIANA
DYLAN TODD SING
the ballad of james dean
Dean
The Legacy

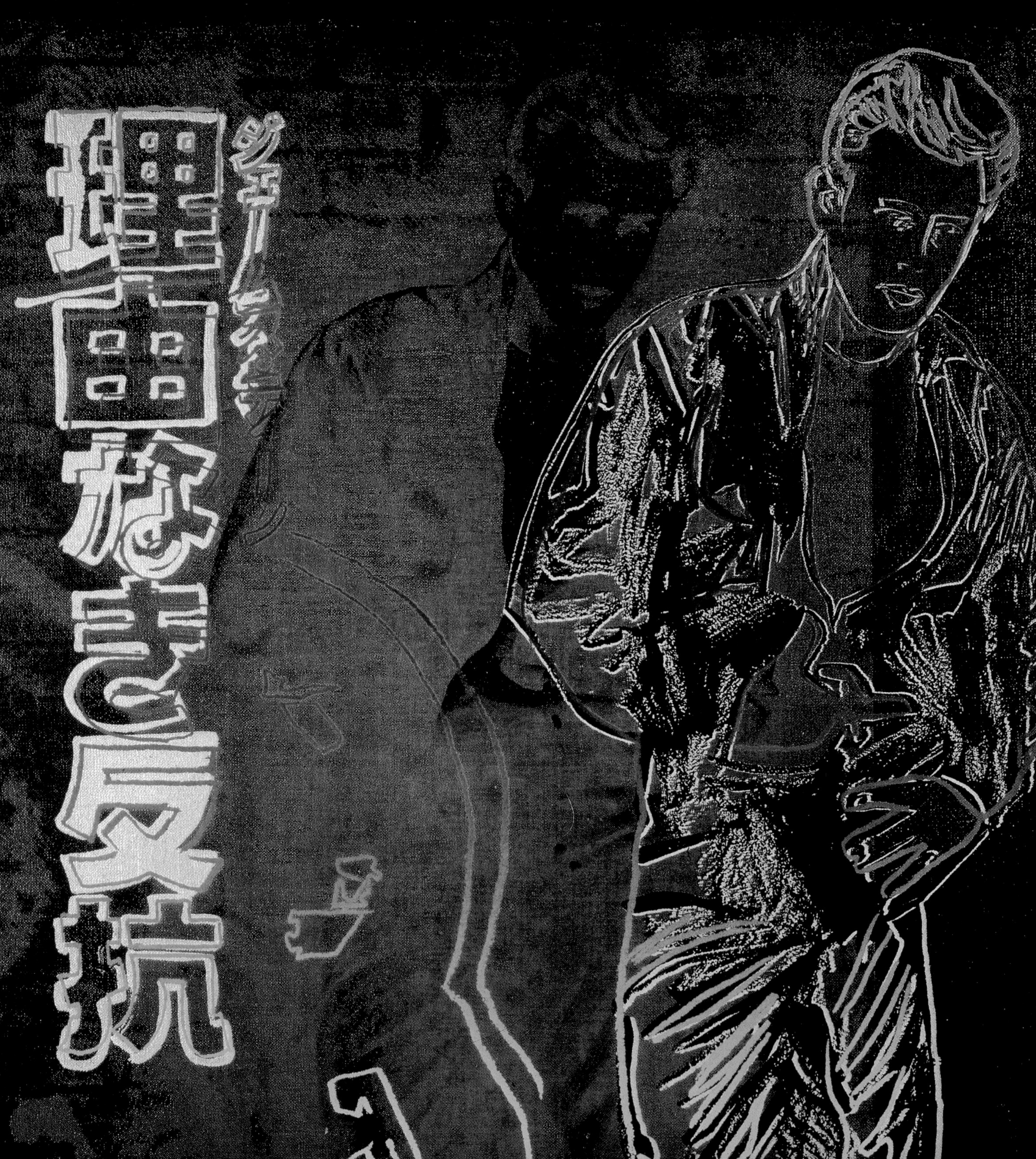
理由なき反抗

"So long. I think I'll let the Spyder out..." JAMES DEAN

For someone so young, Jimmy had an unusual preoccupation with mortality. More than once he had told friends that he did not expect to live beyond 30. He was fearless when he was racing and perfectly prepared to accept the associated risks. **When the subject of a fatal crash on the circuit had arisen, he had said: "What better way to die? It's fast and clean and you go out in a blaze of glory."** He was greatly attracted to bullfighting, and underlined a passage in his copy of Hemingway's *Death in the Afternoon*, which read, "The only place where you could see life and death, i.e. violent death now that the wars were over, was in the bullring."

Given Jimmy's obsession with speed and racing, many of those who knew him fully expected him to meet his end in a road or track accident. He had come off his motorcycle on more than one occasion, once sliding sideways across the busy Barham Boulevard, having missed a "Stop" sign. His passengers, whether on the back of the motorcycle or in the front seat of his car, were invariably left quivering with fear.

◄ **DEAN THE ICON:** Andy Warhol's famous 1984 visualization of Jimmy adds to the mountain of iconography that has accumulated in the years since his death.

▲ **SAD MEETING:** Mourners file into the Fairmount Friends Church for Jimmy's funeral service.

His favorite route to test his driving skills was through the Hollywood Hills, following the spectacular serpentine Mulholland Drive along the ridge of the Santa Monica Mountains. He pushed his motorcycle or automobile as hard as he could and was still unsatisfied, and his taste for speed was constantly reflected in the urgent manner in which he conducted his working and social life.

On that Friday evening of September 30, 1955 George Stevens, key crew-members, and some of the cast of *Giant*, had assembled at Warner Bros. Studios in Burbank in a projection theater for the screening of the six o'clock dailies, the rushes of recent filming. At some point during the session, a telephone call came through to Stevens at the mini-console, which had direct access to the booth. He pressed a buzzer. The screening abruptly stopped and the lights went up. All eyes turned on him. Ashen-faced and in a state of shock, he managed to articulate the terrible news that there had been a car crash, and Jimmy Dean was dead. As Carroll Baker described it, "death was present in that room."

Elizabeth Taylor went to her dressing room and threw up. Too upset to work the following day, she broke down. Her grief was so profoundly felt that she had to be hospitalized. As the long shooting schedule was nearing its conclusion her increasingly frail health, which had been causing concern for Warner's administration, now gave way completely, forcing a closure of production even though only a couple of days remained to finish the film. The report of Jimmy's fatal accident was late in making the Saturday-morning editions of the east-coast newspapers, and only the barest facts were noted, but his death was announced on radio and television, casting a pall on social events in Hollywood that Friday evening. On Sunday the story and obituary tributes were given exceptional coverage throughout America and around the world – an interest that was remarkable considering only one of his three features had been seen by the general public.

Winton Dean was told of his son's death by the agent Dick Clayton, who had received the call from Henry Ginsburg, the producer of *Giant*. Clayton made the decision to drive over to Winton's house rather than break the news by telephone. Winton then called Joan late on the Friday evening, and asked her to notify her parents. Marcus and Ortense had been in Los Angeles for a month and were driving back to Indiana. On the highway they heard a radio newscaster say that a young actor had been killed; Marcus turned the car radio off before hearing the name, yet he felt an uncomfortable premonition. His fear was confirmed when they reached Fairmount on Monday evening. He telephoned Winton, who initially wanted Jimmy to be buried next to his mother in the cemetery at Marion, and persuaded him that Fairmount would be a better resting place.

The flags at the Warner studio flew at half-mast, and Jimmy's body was flown back, accompanied by Winton and Ethel, to Fairmount, Indiana to lie in Hunt's Funeral Parlor from Thursday until Saturday, October 8, the day of his burial in the Park Cemetery. *The Fairmount News* adopted a black-bordered masthead, "IN MEMORY OF JAMES DEAN," and the lead story, headlined "James Dean Killed As Result Of California Car Accident," appeared alongside his portrait and an appreciation. The writer was borne aloft by a dubious muse when he made the observation: "His brief career was as bright as a meteor which flows like a golden tear down the dark cheeks of night."

The funeral service was held at Fairmount Friends Church (not at Back Creek, which was far too small), and was conducted by the Reverends James DeWeerd and Xen Harvey, the local pastor who had also spoken at Jimmy's graduation. The closed coffin lay in front of the congregation, covered with flowers, and the organ softly played "Going Home" from Dvorak's *New World Symphony*. The little church was packed with 600 people, and at least four times as many mourners gathered outside, listening to the proceedings relayed by loudspeakers, together with the newsreel and television cameras, and phalanxes of press photographers and reporters. If the throng had been hoping for a gathering of Hollywood stars, they would have been disappointed. From *Giant* only the producer Henry Ginsburg made the journey. Elizabeth Taylor sent an array of fine orchids to add to more than a hundred floral tributes, mostly from people who had never met Jimmy, but had been overwhelmed by his performance in *East of Eden*. Edna Ferber, the author of the novel on which *Giant* was based, also sent flowers. Among others who had flown in from California were Jimmy's friends Nick Adams, Lew Bracker, Jack Simmons, and Dennis Stock.

Reverend Harvey's eulogy was entitled "The Life of James Dean: A Drama in Three Acts," and he closed with the words: "The career of James Dean has not ended. It has just begun. And remember,

"His brief career was as bright as a meteor which flows like a golden tear down the dark cheeks of night." *THE FAIRMOUNT NEWS*

▲ **MOURNERS DEPART:** The service over, those who attended made their exit. Ruth, Mildred Dean's sister, weeps.

God Himself is directing the production." In his address Reverend DeWeerd made the percipient point: "Although Jimmy's life was a short one, he accomplished more than most persons do if they live to be seventy or eighty."

For Dennis Stock, who had been in Fairmount eight months earlier to shoot his famous photo-essay on Jimmy, the service was a harrowing experience. At its conclusion he found Marcus inconsolable. "It was as though he was in a state of shock," he said, "almost incapable of taking in the fact of Jimmy's death." Stock helped to support him through the next ordeal of the interment at the Park Cemetery. The six pallbearers who carried the coffin to the graveside were all Fairmount contemporaries of Jimmy's, four of whom had been basketball teammates.

The inquest of James Dean took place on Tuesday, October 11 in the Council Chamber of Paso Robles city hall. It was an unsatisfactory business. Donald Turnupseed attested that he never saw Jimmy coming until it was too late to avoid a collision. The job of the San Luis Obispo sheriff-coroner, in whose county jurisdiction the death had occurred, was to determine cause, and to decide whether or not it was a result of a criminal act. He had a jury of 12 citizens, three of them women. The district attorney also took part swearing them in, and all had been to the crash site to inspect the road layout.

"It was impossible for Dean to avoid the crash. Speed was not involved." POLICEMAN AT THE SCENE

The inquest was thick with charts, photographs, and expert witnesses. In spite of the accident having taken place in daylight on a clear day, the question of visibility became an issue. The sun had at that time been low enough behind surrounding hills not to have got in anyone's eyes, and the road surface was dry. Much was made of the Spyder's low profile and silver paintwork, which were alleged to have made the car hard to see. It seems there was no mention of the very distinctive roar of the four overhead cams and two dual-throat carburetors of its handcrafted power unit, which could be heard long before the little car came into view. That, and the low-slung body, gave the impression of speed even when it was chugging along at a modest rate. Consequently, some witnesses hugely exaggerated how fast it was traveling. One even thought it was doing 140 mph, impossible given the car's top speed. There was also the suggestion that Jimmy was not wearing his glasses. Jimmy's eyesight was so poor that he would simply have been unable to drive without them. Indeed, had he not been wearing them, the officer who stopped him near Bakersfield would have given him another citation, since it was a required condition on his driver's license. From road marks it was deduced that he had not attempted to apply the brakes. In fact the positioning of the cars indicated that Jimmy was trying to swerve out and around the Ford. Given the stopping distance, abrupt breaking would have made a collision unavoidable, and it is probable that Jimmy was accelerating to reach safety.

The verdict, after the jury had deliberated for just 20 minutes, was: "We find no indication that James Dean met death through any criminal act of another, and that he died of a fractured neck and other injuries received." The conclusion was that the accident was caused by Jimmy's excessive speed, and that Turnupseed was entirely without blame. It was the inadequate conclusion to a process that had taken, from start to finish, two hours and 15 minutes.

The jury's verdict flew in the face of the accepted logic of highway accidents, which holds that when a left turn is executed in the face of oncoming traffic it is the turning driver who is responsible should a

▼ **PALLBEARERS' BURDEN:** Jimmy's coffin leaves the church. Four times more people turned up than could be admitted.

collision occur. But this was a country courthouse, suddenly thrust into the national spotlight. Their reasoning would have been that James Dean, from the decadent metropolis of Los Angeles to the south, and a movie actor prominent in the Hollywood environment, was an alien figure in San Luis Obispo County. Donald Turnupseed, navy man, Cal Poly student, unblemished reputation, was a local boy. Jimmy had been driving an absurdly expensive, ostentatious, imported European racing car on a public highway, while Turnupseed had been making his way home after a day's toil in a workaday American Ford. Jimmy, widely known for his love of speed, had already been booked that afternoon by a police officer for driving over the limit, and later had endangered a family with his reckless passing. What they saw was an overpaid, spoiled young man who was an associate of suspicious acting types in Hollywood and New York, and himself a fast-living Bohemian. The burden of proof in an inquest is far less than that required in a trial, and the good citizens were persuaded by the evidence set before them, so their verdict was hardly surprising.

It was also demonstrably wrong. Using the excellent police diagrams made at the time, which were certified as accurate, it is possible to analyze the crash much more comprehensively by using computer techniques not available in the mid-1950s. Jimmy's speed was certainly not excessive, as can be established by the distance the Porsche traveled after the impact, around 45ft. The much heavier Ford went 39ft. Had the flimsy Porsche been moving at the high speeds claimed, it would have ended up many times further from the point of collision, and would have sustained even more damage – to the point that it would have been unrecognizable as a car.

This was the actual sequence of events: Jimmy, moving downhill toward the junction, saw Turnupseed ahead of him in the center lane preparing to make an unsignaled turn, but could not read his intentions accurately. He assumed Turnupseed was going to let him pass. Then Turnupseed started to move again, and Jimmy, instead of braking, attempted to steer round him by veering to the right. It was Turnupseed's

▼ DEATH MAP: The police diagram of Cholame, accurately showing where the crash occurred, and where the vehicles ended up.

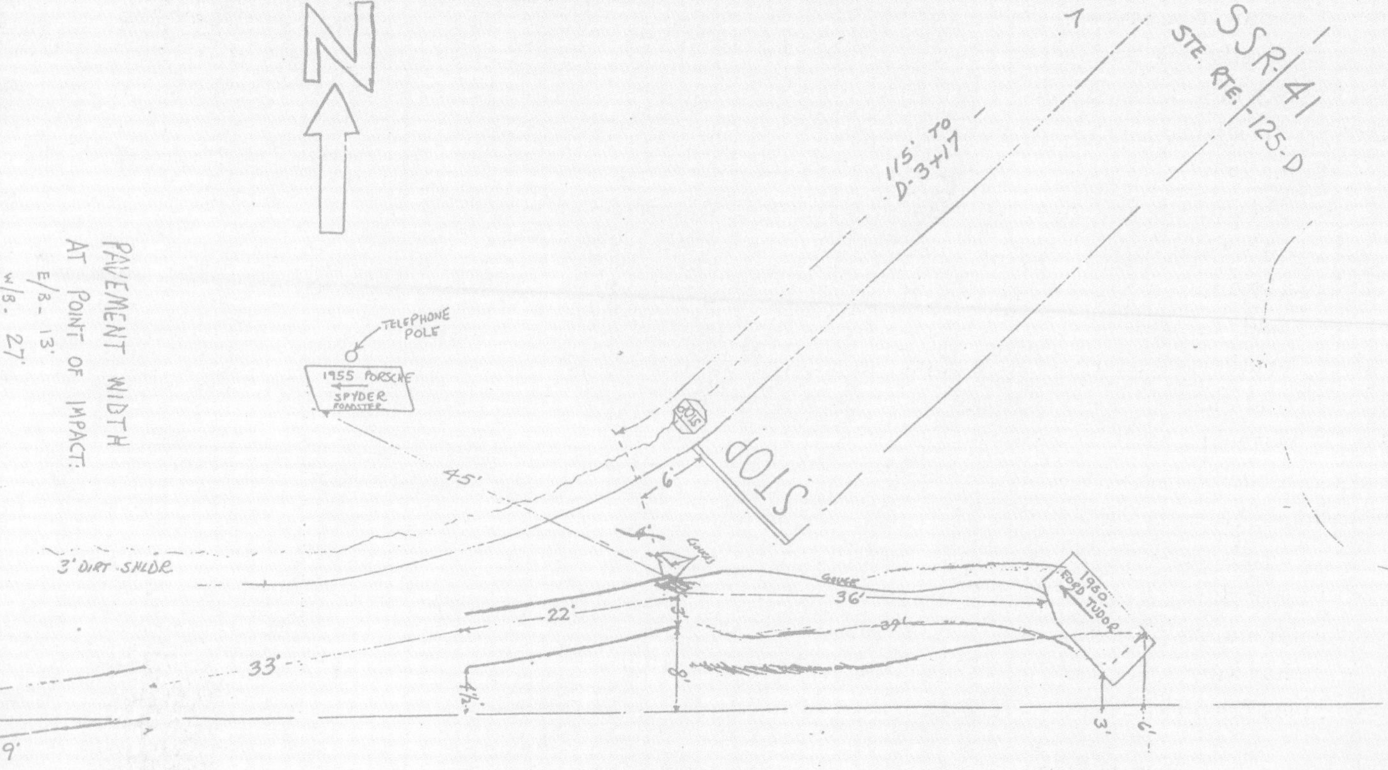

“They couldn’t stop Jimmy – he didn’t fear death the way people normally do.” SAL MINEO

wavering that was the cause of the accident, and had it been another local driver, rather than a wealthy stranger who had been hit, he would almost certainly have faced prosecution. Many road accidents occur because one driver misinterprets the likely actions of another, as was the case here.

This is not to say that Jimmy was not as likely to crash at another time in another place. He had an established reputation for pushing cars and motorcycles to their limits, and was under no illusions that his need for speed could bring about his early demise. He had even told friends that he did not expect to survive beyond 30.

Turnupseed, dazed after the accident, had to hitchhike the rest of the way to his home in Tulare and, in spite of pressures, refused ever to give media interviews, although a few months before he died in 1995 he gave a radio interview to a Californian presenter, Maria Moretti. He said that his statement that he had not seen the Spyder was untrue. He made a misjudgment through lack of concentration, having been listening to Kay Starr and Doris Day on the radio. He also said that he thought Weutherich, in a red shirt, was the one who was driving, and was flung clear. Turnupseed had kept his silence over the years on account of the hate mail and even physical attacks from Dean devotees. Yet in 1958 his insurance company settled with Jimmy’s, waiving further claims. In his deposition to an attorney three years after the crash, he had stuck to his line that he had not noticed the other car closing from the opposite direction and made no mention of the question about who was driving. He spent the rest of his days in obscurity, never discussing the mistake that had blighted his life.

Weutherich spent a year in hospital while his broken body slowly mended. The crash did not diminish his appetite for fast cars. Even before the one that killed Jimmy, he had experienced two serious crashes while racing in Germany. He went back to Porsche, having failed to sue Turnupseed because he did not file his papers within the time limit, and remained in their employment until 1968. After a number of unsuccessful marriages and a spell in a psychiatric hospital, he was killed in a traffic accident in Kupferzell, Germany in 1981. As in 1955, he was not wearing a seat belt.

▲ **POSTHUMOUS ACCLAIM:** After Jimmy’s death *Rebel Without A Cause* was released around the world and acclaimed as the finest statement on the dilemma of the diaffected young.

The anticipatory buzz for *Rebel Without a Cause* had been intense even before the accident, and now Nicholas Ray’s new film became the center of a media frenzy. The premiere was due to take place on October 26 in New York at the Astor, where *East of Eden* had opened the previous March. Warner Bros. initially feared that the death of their star would be damaging for the box-office, but decided nevertheless to build the publicity campaign around James Dean. As the focus of the film, Jimmy had expressed his willingness to participate in the publicity junkets and media interviews preceding its release. His absence proved to be no disadvantage in selling the film, and the manner of his death even seemed to be in keeping with the characterization of Jim Stark. "This kid has a chip on both shoulders!" shouted the advertisements. Some of the announcements noted that the initials J.D. could equally stand for "Juvenile Delinquent" or "Just Dynamite."There was a fine line separating good taste from commercial opportunism.

Had Jimmy not died, *Rebel Without a Cause* would still have found a substantial young audience. The timing was auspicious. MGM's *Blackboard Jungle*, directed by Richard Brooks, had been released only six months earlier, and had touched a nerve in appealing directly to young, postwar Americans, now labeled "teenagers." *Blackboard Jungle* had been made in black and white at a time when color was becoming standard for all movies from major studios. It was set in a troubled urban high school and starred Glenn Ford as a teacher trying to control a hostile classroom in which switchblades ruled, with Sidney Poitier and Vic Morrow among the students. Much of its success was due to the soundtrack, which featured the pounding beat of the relentless, ground-breaking rock 'n' roll number "Rock Around the Clock," performed off-screen by Bill Haley and His Comets. In *Rebel Without a Cause* most of the music was composed by Jimmy's friend Leonard Rosenman; the score was dramatically appropriate but it was not the reason crowds flocked to the box-office. *Blackboard Jungle*, to some extent, warmed up audiences for *Rebel Without a Cause*, although the latter switched the focus from urban slum to white-collar neighborhood. It was clearly the better film of the two, with higher production values and a commanding central performance. *Rebel Without a Cause* attracted a much larger audience, with parents as keen as their children to see this new flag-waver for American teenage angst.

The reviews were generally excellent. "Extraordinarily good acting by the late James Dean, Natalie Wood, and Sal Mineo," said Jack Moffitt in *The Hollywood Reporter*. The authoritative trade newspaper *Daily Variety* observed that James Dean would have matured into an actor of stellar importance, and that the Brando mannerisms noted in *East of Eden* had gone. Bosley Crowther in *The New York Times* dissented: "We do wish the young actors, including Mr. Dean, had not been so intent on imitating Marlon Brando in varying degrees. The tendency, possibly typical of the behavior of certain youths, may therefore be a subtle commentary, but it grows monotonous."

The defining of James Dean the Legend did not take long. Almost immediately fanatics emerged who could not accept he had died. Some believed that he had survived the crash but had been seriously disfigured, and that Warner Bros. had whisked him away to a secret medical location where he was receiving the best plastic surgery money could buy. At some point in the future, they alleged, he would be reintroduced to the world and would resume his career. Such wishful thinking led to fanciful reports of an anonymous patient, bandaged from head to foot, lying in a bed in a guarded wing of a secluded and remote sanatorium. In the weeks and months after his death, Jimmy's fan mail received at Warner Bros. actually increased, surpassing that of the living stars on the lot. Just a month after his death 3,000 letters were arriving each week. Mail was addressed directly to Jimmy as if he was still alive. By the following July the number of letters had increased to 7,000 a week.

George Stevens, who had begun the laborious post-production preparation of *Giant*, was inundated by demands not to trim Jimmy's performance in any way. Few directors in Hollywood were as meticulous in the editing process, and it took Stevens a further year to complete his film for release.

There were reported sightings of Jimmy. A face on a crowded sidewalk, a figure slouching in the shadows of an alleyway – was it really him or a specter? Lurid pulp magazines and sensationalist paperbacks overwhelmed the newsstands. Mediums conjured up his spirit and passed on his alleged words to the world. Mysteries were made where none existed before: "Dean: the unsolved questions," "James Dean's Hidden Heartbreak," "Read his words from the Beyond," and "$50,000 Reward to find Jimmy Dean!" Most curious of all was the account of a truck driver on highway 41, who claimed that three months to the day after the crash, as he was heading toward Paso Robles, a blurred streak raced past him and out of sight, followed by the unmistakable sounds of a terrible crash. As he continued on his way he found no trace of such an incident, and later, when he stopped at a roadside diner for a strong coffee, one of the other truckers told him that Jimmy's ghost would often cruise the highway between dusk and dawn.

Every reference Jimmy had made to death was dredged up and made to seem significant. His past friendship with Vampira suddenly seemed significant, and the actress claimed that she was able to conjure him up at séances, and that he also communicated with her via her radio. It seemed as if every person with whom he had had the most cursory acquaintance was clamoring to tell their story in exchange for financial returns. Another aspect of the manifestation of the growing cult was the arrival of lookalikes. So many aspiring young actors took on his style and appearance that casting directors soon became wearied. Everywhere high schools, drugstore counters, gas stations, and pool halls seemed populated by youths in blue jeans and red windbreakers, slouching and affecting the mannerisms of their hero. Jimmy's friend Nick Adams, who also appeared in *Rebel Without a Cause* became so obsessed by his own resemblance to him, exacerbated by being asked to dub extra lines in *Giant* as his voice double, that he sought police protection to guard his house and his

JIMMY'S GHOUL FRIEND: Maila Nurmi became famous as Vampira, horror-show hostess. She was a Googie's acquaintance.

▲ **SELLING THE LIFESTYLE:** Manufacturers, especially of blue jeans, established Jimmy as their style icon.

▼ **DEAN TO MUSIC:** Some of Jimmy's taped bongo-drum sessions found their way on to vinyl LPs.

collection of Dean memorabilia. He tried desperately, as so many other young actors, to fill Jimmy's shoes, and eventually created the part of Johnny Yuma, the lead in the television series *The Rebel*. He died from a drugs overdose in 1968.

There were also many musical tributes, often performed by country and blues singers. Phonograph records on 78 and 45rpm, vinyl LPs, and sheet music flooded the stores. The cult following was not confined to the United States. Teenagers around the world were affecting the uniform of blue jeans and red windbreaker, and the distinctive Dean hairstyle. Inevitably, as with other popular icons, an industry emerged to produce all kinds of objects featuring Jimmy's image: miniature busts, key rings, decorated mugs and drinking glasses, buttons, pins, masks, tee-shirts, copies of the red *Rebel* windbreaker, posters, calendars, pencils, lighters, plates, and much else. The bust sculpted by Kenneth Kendall was reproduced in both stone and bronze.

The wrecked Porsche, at the request of the California highways department was shunted around schools and country fairs, and exhibited as a warning to drive carefully, while its still-serviceable parts were cannibalized for use in other cars. One of Jimmy's racing competitors at Bakersfield, Dr. William Eschrich, paid $1,000 for the engine. Souvenir hunters continually chipped away at the aluminum skin. Finally the remains disappeared without trace.

> "James Dean's death had a profound effect on me. The instant I heard about it, I vomited. I don't know why."
>
> MONTGOMERY CLIFT, SERIOUSLY INJURED IN A CAR ACCIDENT EIGHT MONTHS LATER

There were those who found the future was so unappealing following Jimmy's death that they felt they had to take their own lives in order to join him. Several young women committed suicide in 1955, and there were more attempts on subsequent anniversaries. Ill-judged reenactments of the "chickie run" and even of the crash itself were to claim more lives. Some of the morbid cult-followers believed that Jimmy's death was self-inflicted, although there was no sustainable logic in such a hypothesis, especially with his new contract, which would have made him one of Hollywood's wealthiest stars, and the absurdity that he should choose to drive into another car when he had so many more efficient means of auto-destruction at his disposal.

Honors followed. He received a Golden Globe, Modern Screen's Special Achievement Silver Cup, and a Photoplay Gold Medal. For his performance as Cal Trask in *East of Eden*, Jimmy received an Academy Award nomination for Best Actor, the first time that such posthumous recognition had been bestowed. He did not go on to win. The Oscar for 1955 went to Ernest Borgnine for his portrayal of the leading character in *Marty*, under Delbert Mann's direction. The columnist Hedda Hopper, incensed, spoke for thousands of fans in demanding that a special honorary Oscar be awarded to Jimmy the following year, a request that the Academy quickly declined on the grounds that it would set a difficult precedent.

▼ **MACABRE EXPLOITATION:** In the name of improving road safety, Jimmy's wrecked Porsche went on public exhibition. The propaganda was probably nullified by sensation seekers.

A New Industry

James Dean's posthumous eminence represented a public need for someone to stand up for the disenfranchized young of the era. Deference to politicians and power blocs had ended. An uncertain future seemed to be the new generation's legacy.

Jimmy provided a focus, the ultimate rebel who held firm and gave the adult world something to think about. Cynically or shrewdly, his name was expropriated for commercial gain, and hundreds of thousands of artifacts were produced to perpetuate his memory. The US Post Office, aware of the commercial worth, issued stamps with his image. Jimmy inevitably assumed the status not only of a totem for the young, but also that of a great American.

▲ **MAIL CALL:** First day covers of Dean postage stamps soon became collectors' desirables.

◄ **FAN APPEAL:** All over the world, Dean followers made collages of his pictures.

"I'm obsessed. I don't think there's anything wrong with it. I'm hoping to keep his memory going. It's a tribute." DAVID LOEHR

▲ **COLLECTORS' ITEMS:** Some of the vast assembly of Dean memorabilia amassed by David Loehr.

▲ **BUTTON UP:** Pins and buttons of Jimmy are ever popular, as shown in another Loehr collection.

▲ **WEST-COAST PREMIERE:** *Giant* opens in Los Angeles, more than a year after Jimmy's death. He keeps third billing..

The world premiere of *Giant* took place in New York on October 10, 1956, followed by the West Coast opening in Los Angeles on October 17. The first anniversary of Jimmy's death had just passed, but Stevens had spent almost every day in the cutting room, ensuring that the finished film satisfied him. The differences that he had with the actor on the set were entirely cast aside: "There is no part of Jimmy I don't like, no part of him that hasn't always the attraction that goes with complete naturalness."

> "Come back, Jimmy. I love you. We're waiting for you."
>
> ANONYMOUS GIRL AT THE SCREENING OF *GIANT*

Although he had third billing after Elizabeth Taylor and Rock Hudson, it was Jimmy that the public wanted to see, and the reviews were euphoric. "Dean delivers an outstanding portrayal … it's a socko performance," said *Variety*. "It is easy to see why the fact of his passing is so hard to accept by so many," said the *Hollywood Reporter*, continuing, "Stevens has directed him beautifully, taking full advantage of Dean's unusual ability to act with his whole body as much as with his voice or face." Hollis Alpert in the *Saturday Review* said: "It's Dean, Dean, Dean. It is the late James Dean as Jett Rink that the audience will be watching – and there are many who will be watching with fascination and love." *Time* said "James Dean … clearly shows for the first (and fatefully the last) time what his admirers always said he had: a streak of genius." Even the customarily unenthusiastic Bosley Crowther in *The New York Times* relented: "It is the late James Dean who makes the malignant role of the surly ranch hand who becomes an oil baron the most tangy and corrosive in the film.… This is a haunting capstone to the brief career of Mr. Dean." John McCarten in the *New Yorker* offered the slightly cynical comment that James Dean "muttering to himself, and wearing a large Stetson low on the bridge of his nose … proves that Stanislavsky is just as much at home among the cattle as he ever was off Broadway."

There followed another Academy Award nomination for his performance in *Giant*. Again he did not win. The Oscar for Best Actor of 1956 was awarded to Yul Brynner, for his role in the film of the Rodgers and Hammerstein musical *The King and I*. Nevertheless, nobody else has ever received two consecutive posthumous nominations. The consensual view is that the studio had made a mistake by putting him up as a leading rather than a supporting actor, as he is in fact on screen for less than a quarter of the running time of *Giant*. Had he been nominated in the latter category he would almost certainly have won over Anthony Quinn, who received the Oscar for his supporting role in *Lust for Life*.

The first anniversary of his death was marked in Fairmount by a special service of remembrance held around the grave, and the Park Cemetery was almost overwhelmed by a crowd some 2,000 strong that gathered to watch Reverend DeWeerd lay a wreath on behalf of fans in West Germany, and Marcus unveil an outdoor portrait of Jimmy by Robert Ormsby, with the Winslow farmhouse in the background.

A James Dean Memorial Foundation was set up in Fairmount to "encourage talent, recognize achievement, reward genius." The intention was to raise $1 million to aid young actors, and the foundation mounted a summer stock production of Thornton Wilder's *Our Town*. An office was also established in New York, leading to problems with a rival

▲ **RESTING PLACE:** Jimmy's headstone in Park Cemetery, Fairmount – a place of pilgrimage for fans wishing to pay homage to their idol.

▼ **FAREWELL:** Soon after the funeral, four girls pay their personal tribute at the flower-bedecked open grave. The headstone was later stolen and replaced – only to be stolen again.

▲ **SILENT WALKER:** An eerie nocturnal version of Dennis Stock's famous photograph is the subject of a mural on the opposite side of the Fairmount Street.

memorial fund that was intended to help indigent young people in the acting profession. There were also conflicts within the Foundation's organization, compounded when the New York office fixed a date to publicize its aims on the influential *Steve Allen Show*, unaware that Fairmount had cut a similar deal with *The Ed Sullivan Show*, a competitor on another network, in which the Winslows appeared on the same night. The Foundation collapsed after just 18 months from poor management and internal squabbling. The more modest James Dean Memorial Scholarship Trust, founded by Adeline Brookshire, his high-school drama teacher, to reward "the most promising speech and/or drama student" at Madison-Grant High School in Fairmount, still exists.

The point has been made that the Quaker religion does not allow for saints or, for that matter, the veneration of heroes, and Fairmount adjusted remarkably well to the pressures of world fame as the hometown of James Dean. No secret is made there that this was where he spent his formative years, and the Fairmount Historical Museum dedicates most of its ground-floor space to him, with permanent exhibits such as his motorcycles and school reports, which have been loaned by the family. The privately assembled collection, created by David Loehr at the James Dean Gallery, has relocated a few miles away.

Fairmount is used to influxes of visitors from around the world. Although a tourist map distributed from the museum shows the location of places important to Jimmy – the Winslow farm, Marvin Carter's motorcycle shop, the Back Creek Friends Church, the cemetery, the old High School – there are no streets, motels, restaurants, or bars named after James Dean. Fairmount, in spite of the temptation, has no intention of exploiting the name of its world-famous son. In the last days of September the Historical Museum sponsors the Remembering James Dean Festival with events such as a Grand Parade, a James Dean lookalike contest, the James Dean Run, a pre-1970 car show in which many hundreds of street-rods, customs, and antiques take part in a parade, the James Dean Rock-Lasso Contest, and screenings of his movies. As many as 30,000 people can turn up, from all over the world. For years, among the hordes of motorcyclists has been a black-leather clad devotee who lays a wreath and styles himself "Nicky Bazooka." His Triumph bears the license plate 9-30-55. He has kept his true identity to himself, but is perfectly willing to talk to the Back Creek Friends Church meeting about his idol, Jimmy.

The headstone on Jimmy's grave proved to be highly vulnerable; both to the almost indelible lipstick smears made by young women, and to the fans armed with chisels who chipped away at its fabric in order to carry off as souvenirs splintered shards or bronze letters prized from the inscription. It was stolen completely in 1983, but later turned up resting on a tree stump on a county road. It was stolen again a week later and replaced. The original stone reappeared in 1987, in Fort Wayne, Indiana, 60 miles away. The new stone was stolen again in July 1998 and recovered two days later. Today the replacement is anchored by a concealed steel rod running deep into the ground.

The death of a great Hollywood star is in itself not an unusual event. The great names of the golden age have departed: Dietrich, Gable, Cooper, Grant, Crawford, Stewart, Wayne, Fonda, Stanwyck, and, more recently, Katharine Hepburn. Most were allowed to conclude, or wind down their careers, and go quietly after years of retirement. Death in harness is rather more rare. Marilyn Monroe and Elvis Presley are often categorized with Jimmy as great American icons who died too soon. Yet, at 35, Monroe's career was already over after her dismissal from the subsequently aborted *Something's Got to Give*. Presley was bloated and spent, his Adonis looks destroyed by alcohol, drug, and food abuse, when he was found dead at the age of 42 at his home Graceland, in Memphis in 1977.

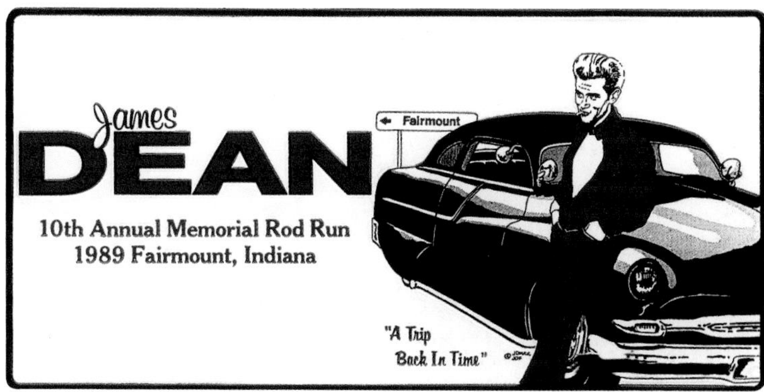

▲ **SHOW TIME:** Every year, James Dean is remembered in Fairmount with a festival that includes parades, lookalike contests, movies, and rallies of vintage cars of the 1950s.

"If a man can bridge the gap between life and death, I mean, if he can live on after he's dead, then maybe he's a great man."

JAMES DEAN

James Dean, at 24, with only one movie released at the time of his death, was still on the threshold of his achievement. Only the sudden death in 1926 of Rudolph Valentino, from peritonitis at the age of

広大なテキサスに誇りと情熱を賭けた激動の人間像！雄大なスケールで描く愛の大ロマン＝永遠の名作！
ジャイアンツ
ジェームス・ディーン●エリザベス・テーラー●ロック・ハドソン
巨匠ジョージ・スチーブンス製作・監督
原作：エドナ・ファーバー
脚色：フレッド・ギュイオル&アイバン・モファット
音楽：ディミトリ・ティオムキン
ワーナー・ブラザース映画
サントラ盤／東芝EMI（キャピトル）
FROM WARNER BROS.
GEORGE STEVENS' PRODUCTION
GIANT

31, had a similar impact, as at the time he was still in the process of consolidating his reputation as "the screen's greatest lover," and while his career may have reached a plateau it certainly had not started a descent. But James Dean's appeal, with only three features forming the canon of his film work, has persisted for the last half-century without much sign of diminishing.

James Dean was immediately regarded as a symbolic figure who epitomized the new mood of his generation. His early death gave him a kind of martyrdom that presaged his elevation to secular sainthood. A famous image from *Giant* had him clasping a rifle across his back with outstretched arms as if in imitation of the crucifixion. In many of his followers there arose a feeling of spirituality and a belief in his immortality. He was the phrase that became a song title for Bob Dylan, "Forever Young." He never had time to fail. His followers were spared the transition of their idol into dull middle age, the fate of so many others among Hollywood's great romantic heroes. The memory would be that of the young man sealed for ever in the first excited flush of adulthood, even though by a strange ironic chance, when he died he had the cut-back hairline and exposed temples created by the Warner makeup department for his appearance in *Giant* as the middle-aged Jett Rink.

In his three films he plays respectively a son unable to win the love of his father, a son who cannot achieve a basis of understanding with his parents, and an outsider who cannot penetrate a holy circle even when he has earned the material qualifications. In each role he is a loner, a misfit, at odds with the conventional perception of things. He is also a committed romantic, the hard outer shell no more than a thin veneer that covers his conflicted emotional torments. As a great romantic hero, he is in the mold of Rick, as played by Humphrey Bogart in *Casablanca*,

▲ **STAMP OF APPROVAL:** In March 1996, the US Postal Service issued this stamp, based on one of the "torn-sweater" photographs by Roy Schatt. Up to 400 million were issued.

◀ **AROUND THE WORLD:** Posters for *Giant*, from Japan and Italy.

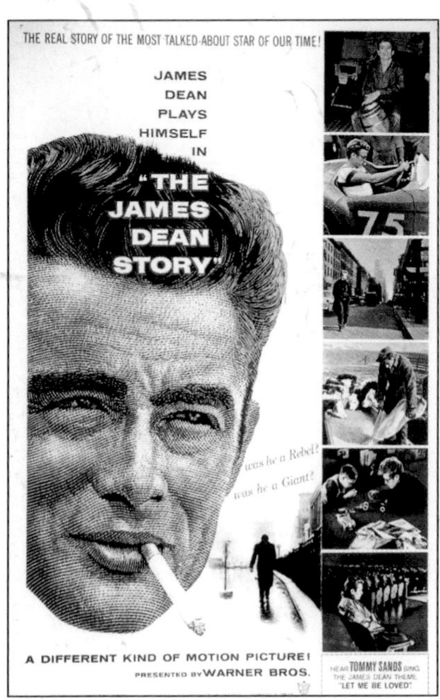

▲ **HOLLYWOOD TRIBUTE:** Two years after the crash, this documentary of Jimmy's brief life was released, featuring interviews with many of his associates. The young Robert Altman was co-director.

► **PENSIVE:** A Roy Schatt photograph of Jimmy in New York captures the introspection and moodiness that often set him apart.

especially in his second film, *Rebel Without a Cause*, where his caring sensibilities attract the love of two of his contemporaries.

It is his performance in *Rebel* that defines the seminal image. The 1950s cliché "crazy mixed-up kid" was coined in the 1950s to describe the part he was playing, the stereotype for countless copycats. The genre of youth kicking over the traces is as old as the feature film itself. In the 1920s and 1930s a cycle of such films, in which young people went to the bad on bootleg booze, drugs, and promiscuity, predominated until the Production Code Administration, headed by the Catholic zealot Joe Breen, forced Hollywood producers to go after more uplifting material. James Dean redefined the persona of the disaffected, misunderstood teenager, too easily perceived by an adult world as a sociopath, whose feelings and innate moral senses are ignored. The character Brando played in *The Wild One* is older, and his redeeming qualities are rather harder to discern, while the knife-wielding delinquents in *Blackboard Jungle* are symptomatic of their disadvantaged backgrounds. Jim Stark, however much he is torn apart by his dysfunctional parents, is really seeking love and acceptance in a white, middle-class world. To those adolescents from similar environments he was, almost inevitably, likely to become a folk hero because he crystallized their own hang-ups, and externalized their inner feelings of dissatisfaction and alienation.

James Dean achieved his symbolic position through the magnetic power he projected on screen. As an actor he was able to combine defiant bravado and tortured self-doubt – the tough shell and the sensitive interior. His handsome, slightly asymmetrical features, the gently hooded blue eyes and soft, pouting mouth, even his distinctive brushed-up hairstyle, sent countless hearts fluttering, and even if he would not cause much of a stir on the street, when he was in front of the camera a mysterious dynamic emerged. He was the possessor of a much-coveted gift in actors, the ability to command attention on the screen even when he was the secondary interest, simply in the act of being. He was continually producing the unexpected flourishes that would give excitement to his performances, such as the odd little hand movement Jett Rink employs as a salutary wave, or the way Jim Stark bobs his head over a wooden fence when he meets Judy on the way to school. A handful of great stars had this transcending presence, and they left a priceless legacy to the cinema. Even with only three movies, all made in his early twenties, James Dean is entitled to membership of that select company. Which leads inevitably to the question, how would Jimmy have developed had he lived? Would he have sustained his position or soon faded, given the considerable instabilities in his temperament? How would his portrayal of the boxer Rocky Graziano in *Somebody Up There Likes Me* have compared with Paul Newman's? Would his career path have

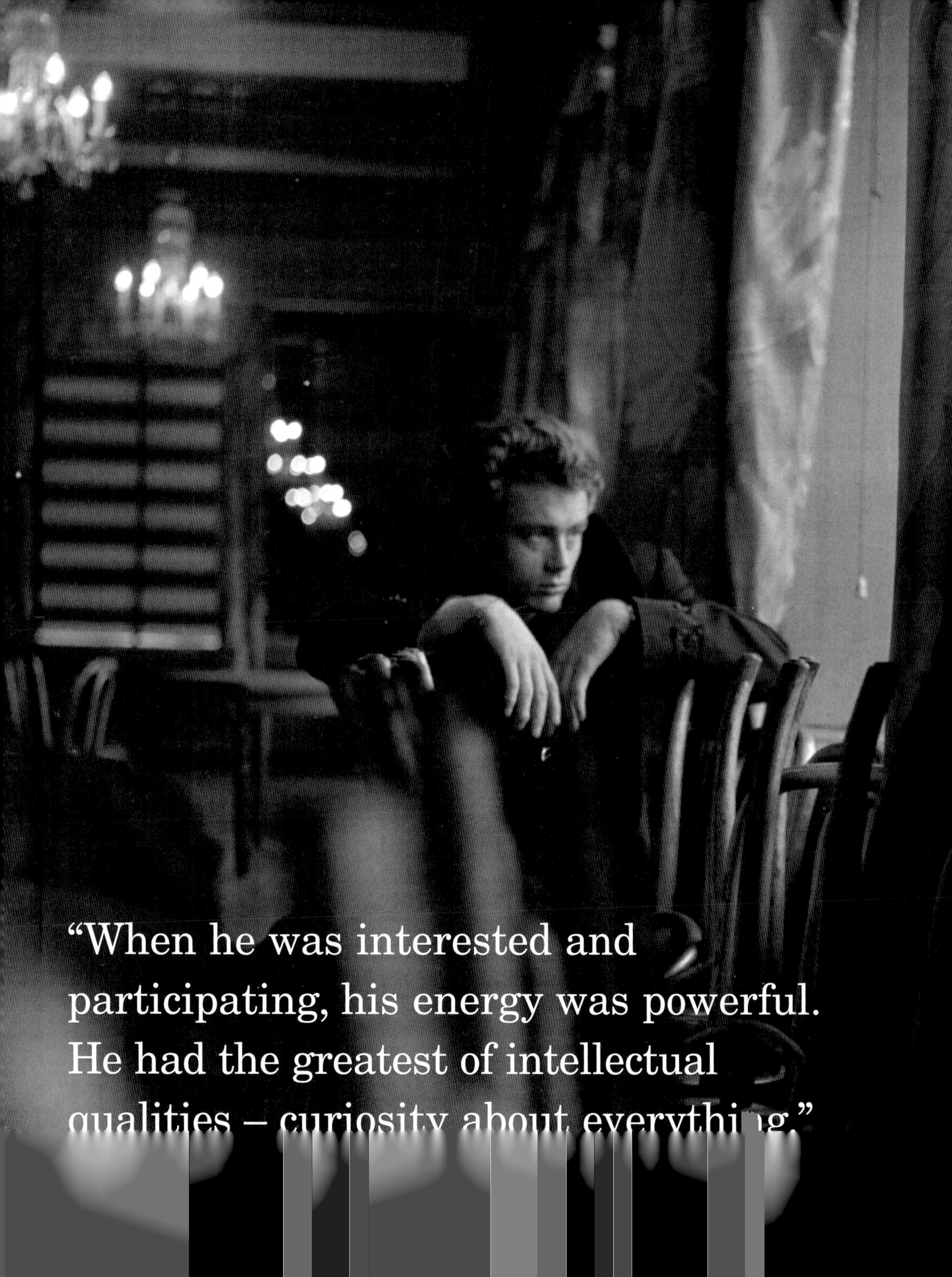

"When he was interested and participating, his energy was powerful. He had the greatest of intellectual qualities – curiosity about everything."

declined after its jet-propelled early ascent, leaving him burned out by 30? As if in anticipation that acting might one day become less important, he had been discussing the formation of a production company in partnership with Nicholas Ray, which he hoped would lead to a chance of directing.

Jimmy has managed to inspire many actors who followed him. Those who have made a point of standing out from the pack, and show their noncompliance with conforming attitudes, are usually flattered to find themselves compared with James Dean. Steve McQueen, Jack Nicholson, Clint Eastwood, Martin Sheen, Robert De Niro, Nicolas Cage, Sean Penn, and Johnny Depp, are a few among the many who have been so regarded. Cage dropped out of high school to study acting. Many years later he told students at the University of

▼ **RE-RELEASE:** A British poster of the 1970s for a reissue. The "AA" certification precluded teenagers under 18 seeing it unaccompanied.

California Santa Cruz: "I became an actor when I saw James Dean in *East of Eden*. It was the breakdown scene with his father. It was so emotional and heartbreaking that I knew right then and there what I wanted to do. I wanted to act." When Cage won his Academy Award for *Leaving Las Vegas* (1995) he made a point of putting James Dean first on his list of people to thank.

Martin Sheen's early success was as the youthful psychopath who takes his teenage girlfriend on a rural killing spree in Terrence Malick's debut feature *Badlands* (1973), which was based on the notorious exploits of a real-life teen couple. The girl, played by Sissy Spacek, is attracted to Sheen's character because he combs his hair like James Dean, and she is so besotted that she willingly goes off with him after acquiescing in the slaughter of her parents. In reality, the executed killer Charlie Starkweather was also obsessed by Jimmy. Sheen's own view is adulatory and unequivocal. "James Dean and Elvis were the spokesmen for an entire generation," he told *People* magazine in 1980, when at the 25th anniversary of Jimmy's death he went to Fairmount to participate in the memorial service and to

> "Actually, the person I related to was James Dean. I grew up with the Dean thing. *Rebel Without a Cause* had a very powerful effect on me." AL PACINO

unveil some commemorative plaques. He continued: "When I was in acting school in New York years ago, there was a saying that if Marlon Brando changed the way people acted, then James Dean changed the way people lived. He was the greatest actor who ever lived. He was simply a genius."

Actors often overstate, but it is not hard to understand Sheen's opinion. Jimmy's performances did have an ability to move people and touch their lives. His appeal is – and continues to be – startlingly universal, striking sympathetic chords both with the assertive and the vulnerable, the gregarious and the lonely, the self-confident and the insecure, and, for that matter, heterosexual and gay. The gay community regards him as their own, often completely exclusively, claiming that his affairs with women were merely public-relations creations. Yet the actor Martin Landau, who was a close friend in New York, explicitly denies any suggestion of homosexuality. "When we were together, we were two guys together, looking at girls, hitting on girls."

The belief that he was a homosexual is a persistent myth. The truth is that he was a great experimenter, and that he avidly and almost greedily soaked up all the experiences that life could offer. It is something to do with the nature of acting. A dedicated actor feels the necessity to cast in many directions in order to find qualities to refine the craft. Actors must assume mantles in order to play their parts. It is as though they must briefly become someone else, and this is particularly true of Method-trained actors. The perfect understanding of a character, the total immersion in a part, calls for a high degree of empathy to penetrate to the core, to strip away the layers in the Stanislavsky sense. There are accounts of Jimmy going out of his way to talk to a street bum for an hour or more, as he tried to explore his condition, to reach an understanding of how someone could fall into that predicament.

This examination of human characteristics does quite naturally embrace sexuality and its variations, and Jimmy would have pursued them in much the same way that he went after other experiences,

> "Because Dean died young and hard, he is not just another actor who outlived his myth and became ordinary in stale roles. He is the symbol of misunderstood youth." PAULINE KAEL

with a voracious appetite. He had always, from childhood, been insatiably curious, but he also had a habit of hurling himself into new enthusiasms as though life depended on them, and then quite suddenly casting them aside in order to turn to something else. He made a point of closely studying people almost as an exercise. Many of his relationships were conducted on a similar basis.

There were a number of serious heterosexual relationships in which the discussion of marriage, the desirable state given the mores of the 1950s, had arisen – those with Dizzy Sheridan, Pier Angeli, and Barbara Glenn among them. He had a raft of girlfriends with whom he had pleasant relationships at least for a while, among them Beverly Wills, Arlene Sachs, Betsy Palmer, April Channing, Christine White, Lili Kardell, and Ursula Andress. His Hollywood dates included Katy Jurado, Pat Hardy, Marilyn Morrison, and Leslie Caron. He was only 24 when he died, an age by which very few people would have met and married their life's partners. He was still in the throes of his emotional development, but given his youth, there was

▲ **WALL ART:** In the Los Angeles area, many murals featuring Jimmy can be found. This one is on the wall of an auto body repair shop on Santa Monica Boulevard.

"Without Jimmy Dean the Beatles would never have existed."

JOHN LENNON

nothing exceptional in that. To have gone through a number of relationships of varying seriousness is completely normal by 24, when adult life still has the adventurous quality of a voyage of discovery. The brief same-sex interlude was all part of the process, but the likely outcome is that Jimmy, having experimented and having used one such relationship as a ruthless means to a career boost, was unlikely to continue in that direction, but would have eventually found a satisfying female love. There would have been few limitations on his range of choice, for a hot Hollywood star, idolized by millions, would have been constantly beating off admirers. It is true, too, that he had many male friends in his circle, both straight and gay, and because he was an actor, a contact profession, the range would be far broader than in a more enclosed, less outgoing business.

The beauty of James Dean's place as an icon is the measure of identification. For his own and successive generations his appeal has a universality that can often seem conflicted. The beholder can find in him exactly what they want to see, be it a rebel, a victim, a bad boy, an angel. Some will esteem his plain, Indiana farm-boy background, and his roots in the solid, decent values of conservative America. Others will regard him as the perpetual delinquent, the nonconformist who defies authority to be his own man. He projected such a range of feelings and sensitivities that it transcended the period in which he lived, and offers a timeless validity. Had he lived, he would have been very happy with the tolerant aspirations of the hippie movement in the 1960s, when love and peace became cultural buzzwords. The hippies, unlike the bleak, pessimistic, and introspective beatniks of the 1950s, looked outwards and believed that the world really could be turned in a new direction. He was not merely a proto-hippie, he also had an all-embracing tolerance of humankind that was much less common in the 1950s. Many of his close friends were black, but their color mattered little to him, it was their companionship that counted. Many others were Jewish, including Barbara Glenn and Dizzy Sheridan. He always had a soft spot for those he felt were getting a raw social deal, and his concern for social losers was one of his most endearing characteristics. He inspired musicians as well as actors, and such American rock heroes as Bob Dylan, Lou Reed, and Bruce Springsteen have been motivated by his memory.

"James Dean was the damaged but beautiful soul of our time." ANDY WARHOL

Jimmy had so many facets that he could appear simultaneously to be both safe and dangerous, yet he was well aware of the ambiguous faces he could present to the world. Like Hamlet, he was constantly "on," putting on an act to conceal his uncertainty. The mercurial habits, the eager enthusiasms that were rapidly discarded, the susceptibility to advice from others, are recurring patterns. Because he was always an actor, anxious to absorb new experiences, he would follow the suggestions of Brookshire, Whitmore, Owen, Harding, Kazan, Ray, and scores of others who temporarily fulfilled guru status, even when a moment's reflection would have shown how inappropriate some of them were, such as joining Sigma Nu. He also strived to achieve aims, but having done so immediately lost interest. His struggle to get into the Actors Studio and rapid relinquishing of his involvement is an example.

Much of his moodiness and sulking was the consequence of his attitudinizing, of trying to give an impression of the mood that was currently

◀ **THE PARTING:** Mercedes McCambridge said "You could feel the loneliness beating out of him." It separated and formed him, and although he went his way, his strength still endures.

taking his fancy. Bill Bast recalls how infuriating he could be when he was putting on one of his acts. He would tell him it was a totally unnecessary waste of effort because he was not going to buy it, and urged Jimmy to cut it out and be himself. The negative qualities that Jimmy possessed went far beyond simply having a short temper and sloppy dress sense. There were his fickle interests both in friends and pursuits, his sulks and petulance, his contempt for conventional manners such as keeping feet off the furniture, his ruthless pursuit of whatever he desired regardless of the fallout, his disloyalty, his rudeness, his lack of respect for distinguished veterans in the same game such as Raymond Massey or George Stevens, his recklessness, his boozing and chain-smoking, and his generally hell-bent, self-absorbed attitude to life which would eventually kill him, just as Hamlet, by failing to behave as a normal person but allowing his fancies to possess him, is the engine of his own destruction.

In order to invent the cult hero that he was to become, Jimmy needed to nurture his grievances, his dissatisfaction. Some critics found that exactly why Jim Stark in *Rebel Without a Cause* was so angry was hard to fathom, since his situation was hardly one of deprivation. It was much the same with Jimmy, and it seems that the decision to kick against the social conventions was entirely his, not forced on him in any way. That he turned out to be a perverse proto-hippie, yet also "the Abraham Lincoln of adolescents" in the happy phrase of his biographer David Dalton, has made him an enduring icon.

The abiding sadness is that he was undoubtedly destined to be a very great actor, and could have enriched the movie-going experience incalculably in the last 50 years, had he not met his tragic end at Cholame in September 1955.

Once, on being asked by a reporter what it was that he respected above all else, James Dean had replied: "That's easy. Death. It's the only thing left to respect. It's the one inevitable, undeniable truth. Everything else can be questioned. But death is truth. In it lies the only nobility for man, and beyond it, the only hope."

▲ **IN THE MOOD:** Roy Schatt's pictures at a New York television rehearsal show Jimmy's characteristic incabability of sitting in a chair the normal way.

“You’ve got to live fast;
death comes early” JAMES DEAN

Timeline
by Kip Brown

1930–38

July 26, 1930
23-year-old veterans administration dental technician Winton Dean marries 19-year-old drugstore clerk Mildred Wilson at Grant County Courthouse in downtown Marion, Indiana.

February 8, 1931
2.00am: James Byron Dean is born at Seven Gables Apartments in Marion, Indiana.

September 1936
Winton, Mildred, and Jimmy Dean move to Santa Monica, California after Winton is transferred to the West Los Angeles Veterans' Administration Center, aka the Sawtelle "Old Soldiers Home." The family settles into a house at 1215-A 26th Street.

February 8, 1938
Jimmy's 7th birthday. Enters McKinley Elementary School in Santa Monica.

1940

July 14
Mildred Dean dies of cancer of the uterus at the Dean family home (1422 23rd Street) in Santa Monica, California.

July 16
Returns to Fairmount, Indiana with grandmother, Emma Dean, and casket bearing the remains of his mother. Trip is made via train (*The Challenger*). It has been decided to let Jimmy temporarily live with his relatives, the Winslows – Aunt Ortense, Uncle Marcus, and cousin Joan – at their farm on the Fairmount–Jonesboro border.

July 20
Mildred Dean is buried at Grant Memorial Park in Marion, Indiana.

August 22
The Fairmount News reports on the addition of Miss Adeline Mart Nall to the staff at Fairmount High School as instructor of English, French, and Speech.

September 3
Enters 4th grade at Fairmount West Ward.

1943–48

November 2, 1943
Jimmy's cousin, Marcus "Markie" Dean Winslow Jr., is born in Marion, Indiana.

August 27, 1945
Begins freshman year at Fairmount High School.

February 8, 1946
Jimmy turns 15. Soon receives his first motorcycle, a Czech-made C/Z.

March 28, 1947
Appears in Fairmount High School play *Mooncalf Mugford.*

October 16, 1947
Appears in Fairmount High School Junior class play *Our Hearts Were Young and Gay.*

February 12, 1948
Appears in Fairmount High School play *The Monkey's Paw.*

August 30, 1948
Begins senior year at Fairmount High School. Writes brief autobiographical study for new school principal, Roland DuBois, which he entitles "My Case Study."

October 29, 1948
Appears as Frankenstein's monster in Fairmount High School Halloween Carnival play *Goon with the Wind.*

1949

February 8
Celebrates 18th birthday.

February 9
Appears in Fairmount High production of *An Apple from Coles County.*

February 13
Jimmy and classmate Barbara Leach compete in the Grant County Lions Club's "Voice of Youth Forum" debate in Marion, the topic whether or not "The United States President should be elected by a direct vote of the people." Today's debate is broadcast live over local radio station WBAT-AM.

February 14
Registers for the Draft in Marion, as required by the Selective Service Act of 1948.

April 6
Appears in Fairmount High class play *You Can't Take It With You.*

April 8
Takes 1st place at National Forensic League's Dramatic Declamation Contest in Peru, Indiana with his performance/recitation of Charles Dickens' *A Madman's Manuscript.*

April 9
Declared state winner of Dramatic Declamation Contest in Peru, thus making him eligible to enter the National Forensic League's National Speaking Tourney in Longmont, Colorado.

April 29 & 30
Performs *A Madman's Manuscript* at the National Forensic League Tournament Nationals in Longmont, Colorado. Finishes 6th in the semifinal round, thus eliminating him from the finals.

May 7–12
Fairmount High senior class trip to Washington, D.C.

May 16
Graduates from Fairmount High School, ranked 20th out of 49 in his class.

May 31
Leaves Fairmount for Chicago where he boards a bus bound for Santa Monica. Moves in with his father and stepmother Ethel at their home in neighboring Venice.

June 2
The Fairmount News reports, "James Dean was honored at farewell party Monday night."

August 11
Appears under stage name Byron James in Santa Monica Theater Guild musical production *Romance of Scarlet Gulch.*

September 12
Begins classes at Santa Monica College, where he has enrolled as a Physical Education major.

1950

April 28
Appears in Santa Monica City College Theater Guild's traditional May Day production of old-fashioned melodrama *She Was Only a Farmer's Daughter.*

July 4
Arrives in Fairmount with father Winton for two-week visit with family and friends. They will be joined later by Jimmy's stepmother, Ethel, who is away in Iowa visiting relatives.

Summer
Works as counselor at summer camp in Glendora, California.

September 18
Enters UCLA in Westwood, where he has enrolled as a Theater Arts major. Pledges Sigma Nu fraternity on Gayley Avenue.

November 28
Final dress rehearsal for UCLA stage production of Shakespeare's *Macbeth*, in which Jimmy portrays Malcolm. Meets Bill Bast for the first time.

November 29
Macbeth opens at UCLA's Royce Hall (thru December 2). Soon signs with his first agent, Isabel Draesemer.

1951

January
Drops out of both UCLA and Sigma Nu. Moves with Bill Bast into an apartment in Santa Monica. Appears in Pepsi-Cola commercial spot.

March
Begins attending informal acting workshop in Brentwood, led by actor James Whitmore.

March 25
Appears as John the Beloved in Easter TV drama *Hill Number One.* Gains first fan club as a result, the Immaculate Heart James Dean Appreciation Society.

April
Gets short-lived job as uniformed usher at CBS Radio in Hollywood. Through Bill Bast meets actress Beverly Wills, daughter of comedic actress Joan Davis, and a featured player in the hit CBS radio comedy, *Junior Miss.*

April 28
Undergoes required Armed Forces physical exam.

June
Gets job parking cars in lot near CBS, Ted's Auto Park. Here he

meets 35-year-old advertising executive/radio producer Rogers Brackett. Jimmy moves from Ted Avery's Hollywood apartment into Brackett's West Hollywood digs, the Sunset Plaza Hotel and Apartments.

July 28
Makes first of four appearances in CBS radio adventure-drama series *Alias Jane Doe*, directed by Brackett.

August 11
Films bit part for 20th Century Fox war film, *Fixed Bayonets!*

September 29
Films bit part for Jerry Lewis/Dean Martin film comedy, *Sailor Beware.*

October 8
Filming starts on Universal comedy, *Has Anybody Seen My Gal?* Jimmy will film bit part in coming days.

October 10
Leaves Los Angeles with Brackett via train bound for Chicago, Illinois.

October 15
Travels from Chicago to Fairmount for a five-day surprise visit.

October 20
Travels with former mentor, Rev. James DeWeerd, from Fairmount to Chicago. Jimmy will eventually travel on to New York

October 29
Appears in minor role in Bigelow-Sanford Film Theater production of *T.K.O.*

November 14
US Selective Service issues 20-year-old Jimmy an IVF deferment ("unfit for military service"), exact reason unknown.

November 20
Gala public premiere of *Fixed Bayonets!* in New York City.

1952

January 27
Appears in Columbia Television Workshop production of *Into the Valley.*

January 31
Sailor Beware premieres in New York City.

February 8
Celebrates 21st birthday. Meets future agent, Jane Deacy.

February 20
Appears in episode of CBS-TV's *The Web* entitled "Sleeping Dogs."

March 3
Appears in episode of CBS-TV's *Studio One* entitled "Ten Thousand Horses Singing."

March 17
Appears in episode of CBS-TV's *Lux Video Theater* entitled "The Foggy, Foggy Dew."

May
Auditions with Christine White for New York's famed Actors Studio.

May 11
Appears in episode of radio program *Theater Guild on the Air* entitled "Prologue to Glory."

May 26
Appears in episode of CBS-TV's *Studio One* entitled "Abraham Lincoln."

June 22
Appears in episode of NBC-TV's *Hallmark Hall of Fame* entitled "The Forgotten Children."

June 25
Has Anybody Seen My Gal? opens in Hollywood and Los Angeles.

July
Writes Marcus and Ortense Winslow back in Fairmount, proudly informing them of his acceptance into New York's famed Actors Studio.

August
Participates in dramatic reading of Franz Kafka's *The Metamorphosis*, at the Village Theater in New York City.

October 9
Hitchhikes from New York to Fairmount with friends Liz "Dizzy" Sheridan and Bill Bast. Awaits word on possible audition for *See the Jaguar.*

October 20
Begins rehearsals for *See the Jaguar.*

November 13
See the Jaguar opens out-of-town tryouts in Hartford, Connecticut.

November 18
See the Jaguar opens out-of-town tryouts in Philadelphia, Pennsylvania.

November 24
Warner Bros. announces purchase of screen rights to John Steinbeck's latest novel, *East of Eden.*

December 3
Debuts on Broadway in *See the Jaguar.* The play closes on its first Saturday night – December 6.

1953

January 15
Appears on NBC-TV's *Kate Smith Hour* in dramatic segment "The Hound of Heaven."

January 29
Appears in episode of NBC-TV's *Treasury Men in Action* entitled "The Case of the Watchful Dog."

February 8
Appears in episode of CBS-TV's *You Are There!* entitled "The Killing of Jesse James."

April 14
Appears in episode of CBS-TV's *Danger* entitled "No Room."

April 16
Appears in episode of NBC-TV's *Treasury Men in Action* entitled "The Case of the Sawed-Off Shotgun."

May 1
Appears in episode of ABC-TV's *Tales of Tomorrow* entitled "The Evil Within."

May 10
Appears in Actors Studio experimental production of *End as a Man.* Performances also run May 17 and June 11.

June 16
Has unbilled role as a scarecrow's mirror image in stage production of *The Scarecrow*, at the Theatre de Lys in New York City.

July 17
Appears in episode of NBC-TV's *Campbell Soundstage* entitled "Something for an Empty Briefcase."

August 17
Appears in episode of CBS-TV's *Studio One Summer Theater* entitled "Sentence of Death."

August 25
Appears in episode of CBS-TV's *Danger* in "Death is My Neighbor."

September 11
Appears in episode of NBC-TV's *The Big Story* entitled "Rex Newman."

October 4
Appears in episode of CBS-TV's *Omnibus* entitled "Glory in the Flower."

October 14
Appears in episode of NBC-TV's *Kraft Television Theater* entitled "Keep Our Honor Bright."

October 16
Appears in episode of NBC-TV's *Campbell Soundstage* entitled "Life Sentence."

November
Auditions for Broadway play *The Immoralist.*

November 11
Appears in episode of NBC-TV's *Kraft Television Theater* entitled "A Long Time Till Dawn."

November 17
Appears in episode of NBC-TV's *Armstrong's Circle Theater* entitled "The Bells of Cockaigne."

November 23
Appears in episode of NBC-TV's *Robert Montgomery Presents* entitled "Harvest."

November 26
Arrives in Fairmount, Indiana for Thanksgiving holiday.

December 15 & 16
Screen-tests for Warner Bros.' upcoming war film, *Battle Cry.*

December 18
Rehearsals for *The Immoralist* get underway at the Ziegeld Theater in New York City.

January 11
The Immoralist opens out-of-town tryouts in Philadelphia, Pennsylvania.

1954

February 1
The Immoralist opens week-long series of public previews.

February 5
East of Eden director Elia Kazan cables Warner Bros. chief Jack Warner: "Found new boy that I am most enthusiastic about...."

February 8
Opens on Broadway in *The Immoralist*. Submits two-week notice.

February 12
Rehearses for off-Broadway play *Women of Trachis*, a translation of Sophocles' *Trachiniae* by Ezra Pound, at Cherry Lane Theater in New York City. Meets future *East of Eden/Rebel Without a Cause* composer Leonard Rosenman, who has been asked to compose some incidental music for the production.

February 14
Spends day off from *The Immoralist* by appearing with Eli Wallach, Anne Jackson, and Joseph Sullivan in one-night only performance of *Woman of Trachis*, at the New School for Social Research in New York City.

February 16
Screen tests for role of Cal in *East of Eden*, in New York City.

February 20
Jimmy's possible final two performances in *The Immoralist*. Daniel Blum's Theatre World soon selects Dean as one of their most "Promising Personalities" of the 1953–1954 theater season.

February 22
Eden director Elia Kazan cables Warner Bros. chief Jack Warner touting Jimmy as "the boy for Cal."

March 1
Warner Bros. (New York) cables Jack Warner, "Kazan advises definitely using Jimmy Dean for role Cal."

March 6
The New York Times reports, "Immoralist Star Signed by Kazan for Eden."

March 30
Appears in episode of CBS-TV's *Danger* – "The Little Woman."

April 7
Signs nine-picture deal with Warner Bros.

April 8
Jimmy and Elia Kazan fly from New York to Los Angeles to begin prepping for *Eden*. Temporarily moves in with his father and stepmother at their home at South Bundy Drive in West Los Angeles.

April 10
Heads to desert town of Borrego Springs, California with pal Bill Bast, with orders from Kazan to get a tan and gain weight. A week later, Jimmy travels to San Francisco to continue his *Eden* preparation with Monty Roberts.

April 26
Writes girlfriend Barbara Glenn back in New York City. Signs letter "Jim (Brando Clift) Dean."

April 30
Warner Bros. pays Jimmy $700 advance against his *East of Eden* salary.

Early May
Purchases red MG-TD sportscar and palomino horse ("Cisco") with part of his $700 advance from Warner Bros.

May 17
Final *East of Eden* script is submitted.

May 27
Eden filming starts in Mendocino, California (thru June 1).

June 3
Eden filming starts in Salinas, California (thru June 10).

June 12
Eden filming moves to Warner Bros. Studios in Burbank, California.

June 14
Pier Angeli's first day of filming on *The Silver Chalice* at Warner Bros.

June 19
Pier Angeli's 22nd birthday. Jimmy gifts the actress with matching gold necklace and bracelet.

June 28
Daily Variety columnist Army Archerd reports Pier Angeli as a "regular visitor to see James Dean."

August 9
Final day of filming on *Eden*.

August 10
Attends 15th anniversary Jubilee Premiere re-release of *Gone With the Wind* in Hollywood with Pier Angeli.

September 5
Appears in episode of NBC-TV's *Philco Television Playhouse* entitled "Run Like a Thief."

September 22
Attends Hollywood premiere of film *Sabrina* with actress Terry Moore.

September 23
Meets Maila "Vampira" Nurmi for the first time at Sunset Boulevard coffee shop, Googie's.

September 24
Daily Variety columnist Army Archerd reports Jimmy and Pier "pfft" as a couple.

September 29
Makes last public appearance with Pier Angeli at the star-studded Hollywood premiere of Warner Bros.' *A Star Is Born*, at the Pantages Theater.

October 4
Pier Angeli and singer Vic Damone announce their engagement.

October 7
Warner Bros. notifies Jimmy of its intent to extend his contract starting December 20 to cover his next film, *Rebel Without a Cause*.

November 6
The Los Angeles Times reports Jimmy as under consideration for role in MGM's *The Cobweb*. Deal is eventually scuttled after MGM and Warner Bros. fail to come to terms regarding Jimmy's loanout.

November 7
The Los Angeles Times publishes columnist Philip K. Scheur's recent interview with Jimmy.

November 9
Appears live from New York in episode of CBS-TV's *Danger* entitled "Padlocks." Returns to Los Angeles following broadcast.

November 14
Appears with future *Rebel Without a Cause* co-star Natalie Wood in tonight's episode of CBS-TV's *General Electric Theater* entitled "I'm a Fool."

November 24
Pier Angeli marries Vic Damone at St. Timothy's Roman Catholic Church in Rancho Park, California. Jimmy waits across the street on his motorcycle, then later guns his engine as the newlyweds emerge.

December 4
Elia Kazan screens *Eden* for Jimmy and others, at Warner Bros.

December 6
Eden is sneak-previewed in Huntington Park, California.

December 8
Eden is sneak-previewed in Encino, California.

December 12
Co-stars with future US president Ronald Reagan in episode of CBS-TV's *General Electric Theater* entitled "The Dark, Dark Hour" aka "Out of the Night."

Late December
Returns to New York City from Los Angeles.

December 29
Poses for "Torn Sweater" series of photographs at photographer-friend Roy Schatt's New York studio.

1955

January 4
Appears in episode of ABC-TV's *U.S. Steel Hour* entitled "The Thief." *Daily Variety* and *Hollywood Reporter* both announce *Rebel Without a Cause* as Jimmy's next film.

Mid January
Returns to Los Angeles from New York. Soon moves into garage-apartment on Sunset Plaza Drive.

January 22
Singer Toni Lee (Scott) introduces Jimmy to artist Kenneth Kendall at latter's studio on Melrose Avenue.

February
Purchases white Porsche 356 Super Speedster.

February 8
Celebrates 24th birthday in New York City. It's during this visit to the Big Apple, in particular Times Square and its surrounding environs, that photographer Dennis Stock will take the most iconic images of the actor.

February 12
Attends Fairmount High School's semi-formal Sweetheart Ball with photographer Dennis Stock. There, he obligingly signs autographs and sits in with the local band on bongos. Stock will photograph Dean over the next few days at various Fairmount locales, including the actor's future burial site, Park Cemetery.

February 17
Flies from Indianapolis to New York City.

March 5
Flies from New York City to Los Angeles.

March 7
Life magazine profiles Jimmy ("Moody New Star: Hoosier James Dean Excites Hollywood").

March 9
Jimmy is a no-show at the star-studded celebrity benefit preview of *East of Eden* at Astor Theater in New York City. Honorary usherettes include Marilyn Monroe, Marlene Dietrich, Terry Moore, and Eva Marie Saint.

March 10
Eden opens to the public at the Astor Theater in New York City. A clip from the film is shown on tonight's *Lux Video Theater*. Jimmy appears prior to tonight's drama, "The Life of Emile Zola," in a brief filmed segment.

March 13
The New York Times publishes Howard Thompson's recent interview with Jimmy ("Another Dean Hits the Big Leagues").

March 16
Eden opens in Los Angeles.

March 23
Shoots black and white screen-tests for *Rebel Without a Cause*, first with Natalie Wood and Sal Mineo, then with finalists for the juvenile delinquent roles, including Corey Allen, Frank Mazzola, Beverly Long, Jack Grinnage, Steffi Sidney, Dennis Hopper, Tom Bernard, and Nick Adams.

March 26 & 27
Competes in his first official automobile race, the Palm Springs Road Races.

March 27
Syndicated newspaper columnist Hedda Hopper profiles Jimmy.

March 30
Filming starts on *Rebel Without a Cause* at Griffith Observatory.

April 2
Warner Bros. extends Jimmy's contract to cover *Giant*. *Rebel* filming switches from black and white to color.

April 16
Rebel filming moves to abandoned mansion previously utilized in 1950 film classic *Sunset Boulevard*.

May 1
Competes in Bakersfield National Sports Car Races.

May 6
Appears in episode of CBS-TV's *Schlitz Playhouse of Stars* entitled "The Unlighted Road."

May 14
Louella Parsons reports Jimmy as under consideration for the role of retired boxer Rocky Graziano in MGM's *Somebody Up There Likes Me*.

May 18
Attends press luncheon announcing start of production on *Giant*.

May 19
Giant starts shooting minus Jimmy, who's still in *Rebel*, at Warner Bros. in Burbank.

May 26
Last day of filming on *Rebel Without a Cause*.

May 29
Competes in Santa Barbara Road Races. A blown piston forces Jimmy to withdraw early from the race – his last.

May 31
Giant filming moves to Charlottesville, Virginia. Jimmy remains in Los Angeles.

June 6
Joins *Giant* cast and crew in Marfa, Texas.

July 9
First Unit filming on *Giant* completed in Marfa.

July 11
Giant shooting returns to Warner Bros. in Burbank.

July 23
Moves from garage-apartment on Sunset Plaza to log cabin-style home in San Fernando Valley suburb of Sherman Oaks, California. Jimmy's move comes on a day that he's supposed to be at work on the set of *Giant*, which doesn't go down too well with the film's director, George Stevens.

July 28
Films interview segment with actor Gig Young for future airing in an upcoming episode of Warner Bros. new television program, *Warner Bros. Presents*. Topics discussed include Jimmy's racing career and highway safety.

August 1
Signs one-year lease on home in Sherman Oaks, California. *Hollywood Reporter* columnist Mike Connolly will interview Jimmy here in the coming days. That interview will appear in the December 1955 issue of *Modern Screen* magazine.

August 14
Attends Frank Sinatra-hosted party at Villa Capri Restaurant in Hollywood with Ursula Andress.

August 29
Attends black-tie Thalians benefit at Sunset Strip nightclub Ciro's with Ursula Andress.

September 4
Attends Santa Barbara Road Races to watch good friend Lew Bracker compete.

September 10
Wraps filming on his "Last Supper" scene.

September 17
Jimmy's last day of filming on *Giant*. Later, he and Ursula Andress attend preview screening of *Rebel Without a Cause* in Westwood.

September 22
Daily Variety reports, "Jimmy Dean's new speedwagon cost $6,900.00." Said "speedwagon" is a brand new Porsche 550 Spyder, purchased recently from Competition Motors in Hollywood.

September 25
Attends party tossed in his honor by his agent, Jane Deacy, at West Hollywood hotel, the Chateau Marmont. Guests include Jimmy's aunt, Ortense Winslow, and uncles, Marcus Winslow and Charles Nolan Dean, who are in town visiting their famous nephew.

September 30
Dies in car crash en route to weekend races in Salinas.

October 4
Body flown back to Indiana.

October 8
Funeral services conducted at Friends Church in Fairmount, Indiana, followed by interment at nearby Park Cemetery.

October 11
A jury rules Jimmy's death accidental at official coroner's inquest in Paso Robles, California.

October 13
Giant wraps up production.

October 26
Rebel Without a Cause opens sans premiere at the Astor Theater in New York City.

November 9
Rebel Without a Cause opens in Los Angeles.

1956

October 10
Giant world premieres at the Roxy Theater in New York City.

October 17
Hollywood invitational premiere of *Giant* at Grauman's Chinese Theater.

Stage and Television Appearances

Stage Appearances

DATE	PLAY	VENUE
December 3, 1952	*See the Jaguar*	Cort Theater
May 10, 1953	*End as a Man*	Actors Studio
June 16, 1953	*The Scarecrow*	Theatre de Lys
June 23, 1953	*The Fell Swoop*	Palm Garden
February 8, 1954	*The Immoralist*	Royale Theater (Broadway)
February 14, 1954	*Women of Trachis*	New School of Social Research

Television Appearances

DATE	SERIES	EPISODE
December 13, 1950		Pepsi-Cola Commercial
March 25, 1951	*Family Theater*	"Hill Number One"
October 29, 1951	*Bigelow Theater*	"T.K.O."
January 27, 1952	*CBS Television Workshop*	"Into the Valley"
February 1952	*The Trouble with Father*	"Jackie Knows it All"
February 20, 1952	*The Web*	"Sleeping Dogs"
March 3, 1952	*Studio One*	"Ten Thousand Horses Singing"
March 17, 1952	*Lux Video Theater*	"The Foggy, Foggy Dew"
May 21, 1952	*Theater Guild on the Air*	"Prologue to Glory"
May 26, 1952	*Studio One*	"Abraham Lincoln"
June 22, 1952	*Hallmark Hall of Fame*	"The Forgotten Children"
January 15, 1953	*The Kate Smith Hour*	"The Hound of Heaven"
January 29, 1953	*Treasury Men in Action*	"The Case of the Watchful Dog"
February 8, 1953	*You Are There!*	"The Killing of Jesse James"
April 14, 1953	*Danger*	"No Room"
April 16, 1953	*Treasury Men in Action*	"The Case of the Sawed-Off Shotgun"
May 1, 1953	*Tales of Tomorrow*	"The Evil Within"
July 17, 1953	*Campbell Soundstage*	"Something for an Empty Briefcase"
August 17, 1953	*Studio One Summer Theater*	"Sentence of Death"
August 25, 1953	*Danger*	"Death is My Neighbor"
September 11, 1953	*The Big Story*	"Rex Newman"
October 4, 1953	*Omnibus*	"Glory in the Flower"
October 14, 1953	*Kraft Television Theater*	"Keep Our Honor Bright"
October 16, 1953	*Campbell Soundstage*	"Life Sentence"
November 11, 1955	*Kraft Television Theater*	"A Long Time Till Dawn"
November 17, 1953	*Armstrong's Circle Theater*	"The Bells of Cockaigne"

November 23, 1953	*Robert Montgomery Presents*	"Harvest"
March 30, 1954	*Danger*	"The Little Woman"
September 5, 1954	*Philco Television Playhouse*	"Run Like a Thief"
November 9, 1954	*Danger*	"Padlocks"
November 14, 1954	*General Electric Theater*	"I'm a Fool"
December 12, 1954	*General Electric Theater*	"The Dark, Dark Hour"
January 4, 1955	*U.S. Steel Hour*	"The Thief"
May 6, 1955	*Schlitz Playhouse of Stars*	"The Unlighted Road"

▲ **MAKING A PICASSO:** Jimmy clowns for photographer Roy Schatt on the set of *The Thief*; Diana Lynn looks unamused.

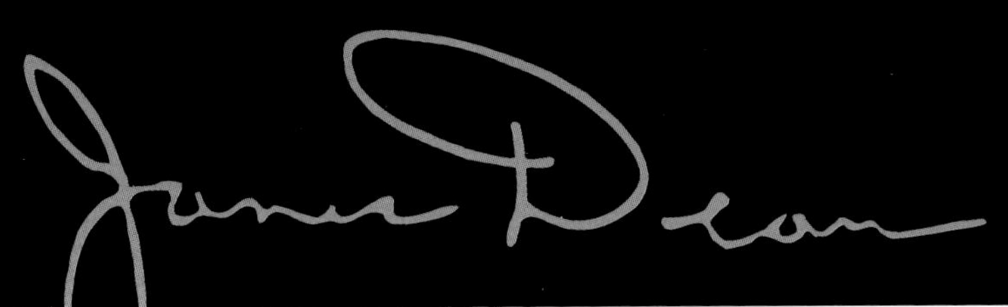

Filmographies

Fixed Bayonets! (1951)

Director: Samuel Fuller
Producer: Jules Buck
Cast: Richard Baseheart, Gene Evans, Michael O'Shea, Richard Hylton, Crag Hill, Skip Homeier (James Dean played uncredited bit part as a GI)

92 minutes, black and white
Twentieth Century Fox

Sailor Beware (1952)

Director: Hal Walker
Producer: Hal Wallis
Cast: Dean Martin, Jerry Lewis, Corinne Calvet, Marion Marshall, Robert Strauss, Leif Erickson (James Dean played an uncredited bit part as a boxing second)

108 minutes, black and white
Paramount

Has Anybody Seen My Gal (1952)

Director: Douglas Sirk
Producer: Ted Richmond
Cast: Piper Laurie, Rock Hudson, Charles Coburn, Gigi Perreau, Lynn Bari, Larry Gates, William Reynolds, Skip Homeier (James Dean played uncredited bit part as a young man at a soda fountain)

88 minutes, Technicolor
Universal-International

Warner Bros. have embarked on an ambitious programme to commemorate the 50th anniversary of James Dean's death and first film, and are producing a feature-length documentary, *James Dean Forever Young*, in conjunction with the world digital premiere of their three films, *East of Eden*, *Rebel Without a Cause* and *Giant*. Further information can be obtained from Warner Bros. via their website at **www.warnervision.com**

East of Eden (1955)

Producer and director: Elia Kazan
Screenwriter: Paul Osborn, based on the novel by John Steinbeck
Cinematographer: Ted McCord
Editor: Owen Marks
Art director: James Basevi
Costumes: Anna Hill Johnstone
Composer: Leonard Rosenman

Cast
Julie Harris: ABRA
James Dean: CAL TRASK
Raymond Massey: ADAM TRASK
Burl Ives: SAM THE SHERIFF
Richard Davalos: ARON TRASK
Jo Van Fleet: KATE
Albert Dekker: WILL HAMILTON
Lois Smith: ANNE
Harold Gordon: GUSTAV ALBRECHT
Nick Dennis: RANTANI

115 minutes, WarnerColor
CinemaScope

Premiere: March 9, 1955
(Astor, New York)

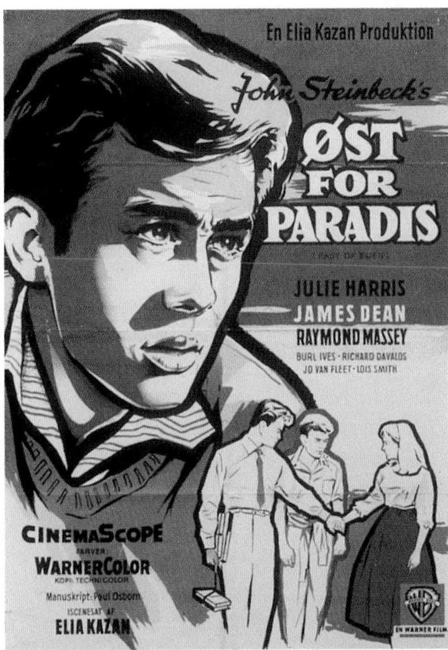

Rebel Without a Cause (1955)

Director: Nicholas Ray
Producer: David Weisbart
Screenwriters: Stewart Stern, Irving Shulman, Nicholas Ray
Cinematographer: Ernest Haller
Editor: William Ziegler
Production design: Malcolm C. Bert
Costumes: Moss Mabry
Composer: Leonard Rosenman

Cast
James Dean: JIM STARK
Natalie Wood: JUDY
Sal Mineo: PLATO
Jim Backus: FRANK STARK
Ann Doran: MRS. STARK
Corey Allen: BUZZ
William Hopper: JUDY'S FATHER
Rochelle Hudson: JUDY'S MOTHER
Dennis Hopper: GOON
Edward Platt: RAY FREMICK
Steffi Sidney: MIL
Marietta Canty: PLATO'S NURSE
Beverly Long: HELEN
Frank Mazzola: CRUNCH
Jack Simmons: COOKIE
Nick Adams: CHICK
Jack Grinnage: MOOSE

111 minutes, WarnerColor
CinemaScope

Premiere: October 27, 1955
(Astor, New York)

Giant (1956)

Producer and Director: George Stevens
Producer: Henry Ginsberg
Writers: Fred Guiol, Ivan Moffat, based on the novel by Edna Ferber
Cinematographer: William C. Mellor
Editor: William Hornbeck
Production design: Boris Leven
Costumes: Marjorie Best, Moss Mabry (for Elizabeth Taylor)
Composer: Dmitri Tiomkin

Cast
Elizabeth Taylor: LESLIE LYNNTON BENEDICT
Rock Hudson: JORDAN 'BICK' BENEDICT
James Dean: JETT RINK
Carroll Baker: LUZ BENEDICT II
Jane Withers: VASHTI SNYTHE
Chill Wills: UNCLE BAWLEY BENEDICT
Mercedes McCambridge: LUZ BENEDICT
Dennis Hopper: JORDAN BENEDICT III
Sal Mineo: ANGEL OBREGON II
Rod Taylor: SIR DAVID KARFREY
Judith Evelyn: MRS. NANCY LYNNTON
Earl Holliman: BOB DACE
Robert Nichols: PINKY SNYTHE
Paul Fix: DR. HORACE LYNNTON
Alexander Scourby: OLD POLO
Fran Bennett: JUDY BENEDICT
Charles Watts: SENATOR WHITESIDE
Elsa Cárdenas: JUANA BENEDICT
Carolyn Craig: LACEY LYNNTON
Monte Hale: BALE CLINCH
Sheb Wooley: GABE TARGET
Mary Ann Edwards: ADARENE CLINCH
Victor Millan: ANGEL OBREGON
Micky Simpson: SARGE
Pilar Del Rey: MRS. OBREGON
Maurice Jara: DR. GUERRA
Noreen Nash: LONA LANE
Ray Whitley: WATTS
Napoleon Whiting: JEFFERSON

201 minutes, WarnerColor

Premiere: November 10, 1956 (New York)

Bibliography

Adams, Leith and Burns, Keith (eds.), *James Dean: Behind the Scene*, Birch Lane Press, New York 1990
Alexander, Paul, *Boulevard of Broken Dreams: The Life, Times, and Legend of James Dean*, Plume, New York, 1997
Andrew, Geoff, *The Films of Nicholas Ray*, BFI Publishing, London, 2004
Arens, Axel, *James Dean: Photographs*, W.W. Norton, New York, 1992
Backus, Jim, *Rocks on the Roof*, Putnam's, New York, 1958
Baker, Carol, *Baby Doll*, Dell, New York, 1985
Bast, William, *James Dean: Biography*, Ballantine Books, New York, 1956
Beath, Warren Newton, *The Death of James Dean*, Grove Press, New York, 1986
Brando, Marlon, *Songs My Mother Taught Me*, Random House, New York, 1994
Ciment, Michel, *Kazan on Kazan*, Viking Press, New York, 1974
Cunningham, Terry, *The Timeless James Dean*, Stagedoor Publishing, London, 2004
Dalton, David & Cayen, Ron, *James Dean: American Icon*, St Martin's Press, 1984
Dalton, David, *James Dean: The Mutant King*, Straight Arrow, San Francisco, 1974
Ferber, Edna, *Giant*, Doubleday, New York, 1952
Gilmore, John, *Live Fast – Die Young: My Life with James Dean*, Thunder's Mouth Press, New York, 1997
Guinness, Alec, *Blessings in Disguise*, Alfred A. Knopf, New York, 1986
Herndon, Venable, *James Dean: A Short Life*, Doubleday, New York, 1974
Holley, Val, *James Dean, the Biography*, St.Martin's Press, New York, 1995
Hoskyns, Barney, *James Dean, Shooting Star*, Doubleday, New York, 1989
Howlett, John, *James Dean: A Biography*, Plexus Publishing, London, 1975
Hyams, Joe, *Little Boy Lost*, Arrow, New York, 1992
Jacobs, Timothy, *James Dean*, Arlington, London, 1991
Kazan, Elia, *A Life*, Alfred A. Knopf, New York, 1988
Kreidi, John Francis, *Nicholas Ray*, Twayne, New York, 1977
Levene, Bruce, *James Dean in Mendocimo: The Filming of "East of Eden"*, Pacific Transcriptions, Mendocino, 1994
Lindner, Robert, *Rebel Without a Cause*, Grove Press, New York, 1944
Martinetti, Ronald, *The James Dean Story*, Pinnacle Books, New York, 1975
McCambridge, Mercedes, *Mercedes McCambridge: The Quality of Mercy*, Times Books, New York, 1981
Moore, Leonard J., *Citizen Klammen: The Ku Klux Klan in Indiana, 1921–1928*, University of North Carolina Press, Chapel Hill, 1991
Olesky, Walter G., *James Dean*, Lucent Books, San Diego, 2001
Riese, Randall, *The Unabridged James Dean: His Life and Legacy from A to Z*, Contemporary Books, Chicago, 1991
Roth, Beaulah and Sanford, *James Dean*, Pomegranate, Corte Madera, CA, 1983
Schatt, Roy, *James Dean: A Portrait*, Delilah, New York, 1982
Spoto, Donald, *Rebel: The Life and Legend of James Dean*, HarperCollins, New York, 1996
Sheridan, Liz, *Dizzy & Jimmy My Life with James Dean*, Regan Books, New York, 2000
Steinbeck, John, *East of Eden*, New York, Viking Press, 1952
Stern, Phil, *Phil Stern's Hollywood: Photographs 1940–1979*, Alfred A. Knopf, New York, 1993
St. Michael, Mick, *James Dean in His Own Words*, Omnibus, London, 1989
Stock, Dennis, *James Dean Revisited*, Chronicle Books, San Francisco, 1987
Tanitch, Robert, *The Unknown James Dean*, Batsford, London, 1997
Tynan, Kenneth, *Bull Fever*, Atheneum, New York, 1966
Wakefield, Dan, *New York in the Fifties*, Houghton, Boston, 1992
Wilk, Max (ed.), *The Golden Age of Television*, Delacorte, New York, 1976
Zinnemann, Fred, *A Life in the Movies*, Scribner's, New York, 1992

Index

Numbers in italics refer to illustrations

Actors Studio, 73, 78, 88, 104, 129, 137, *139*, 175, 219
Adams, Nick, 68, 175, 195, 201-2
Adler, Stella, 123
Algonquin Hotel, New York, 79
Alias Jane Doe, 76
Allen, Corey, 153, 158, 161
All That Heaven Allows, 171
American Federation of Television and Radio Actors (AFTRA), 71
Amick, Dr. James, 24
Anderson, Judith, 183
Anderson, Sherwood: "I'm a Fool", 126
Andress, Ursula, 126, *129*, 129, 182, *183*, 184, 186, 216
Andrew, Geoff, 148
Angeli, Pier, 117, *118*, *119*, 119, 120, 123, 183, 216
Apocalypse Now, 65
Armstrong Circle Theater, 94
Army Medical Corps, 32
Arthur, Robert Alan: *A Man is Ten Feet Tall*, 87
Avery, Ray, 61
Avery, Ted, 74, 76
Axe of God, The, 72
Ayers, Lemuel, 90, 93

Back Creek, 25, 30
Back Creek Friends Church, 30, 36, 208, 209
Backus, Jim, 151, 155, *156*, 200
Badlands, 215
Baker, "Cannon Ball", 47
Baker, Carroll, 175, 175, 194
Bakersfield, 187, 202
Barris, George, 186
Bars, 36
Barton, James, 87
Bast, William (Bill), 68, 71, 73, 74, 77, 89, 90, 93, 220
Battle Cry, 100
Battleground, 73
"Bazooka, Nicky", 209
Beat the Clock, 80, 86
Bellah, James, 67, 68, 73
Benedek, Lazio, 116
Benny, Jack, 34
Berlin, Irving, 79
Billy the Kid, 183
Blackboard Jungle, 116, 200, 212
Blackwell's Corner, 12
Bob & Carol & Ted & Alice, 154
Boetticher, Budd, 77
Bogart, Humphrey, 120, 133, 211
Boomerang!, 103
Booth, John Wilkes, 51
Borgnine, Ernest, 87, 203
Borrego Springs, 110
Bosustow, Stephen, 151
Bracker, Lew, 183, 195
Brackett, Rodgers, 76, 77, 78, 79, 81, 87, 92
Brady Gang, 23
Brando, Marlon, 64, 65, 65, 79, 80, 81, 89, 100, 102, 103, 104, 116, *116*, *122*, 122, 123, 126, 129, 131, 147, 149, 200, 212, 215
Breen, Joe, 212
Breen Office, 106
Brentwood School, Santa Monica, 27
Bridge on the River Kwai, The, 11
Broadway, 64, 65, 73, 79, 87, 92, 94, 95, 104
Brooks, Richard, 200
Brookshire, Adeline, 34, 34, 36-7, 38-9, 41, 42, 48, 51, 61, 62, *64*, 78, 90, 208, 219
Brynner, Yul, 206-7
Burbank studio, 15, 100, 113, 182, 194

Cage, Nicolas, 214-15
Cagney, Jeanne, 73
California, 19, 20, 27, 57, 59, 112, 141
see also names of places
Campbell Soundstage, 94
Cardénas, Elsa, 168
Caron, Leslie, 216
Carter, Marvin, 44, 208
Casablanca, 211
Case, Frank, 79
CBS, 71, 74, 86, 89, 94, 109
Challenger, The (train), 29
Channing, April, 216
Chapman, John, 92-3
Charlottesville, 172
Chayefsky, Paddy: *Marty*, 87
Chicago, 23, 41, 53, 78, 79, 87
Cholame, car crash at, 11-15, *198*, 198-9, 220
CinemaScope, 73, 106, 151, 173
Clayton, Dick, 78, 110, 129, 134, 183, 195
Cleopatra, 171
Clift, Montgomery, *79*, 79-80, 89, 166, 174, 202
Climenhaga, Joel, 67-8
Coburn, Charles, 77
Cobweb, The, 126
Command Decision, 73
Competition Motors, 11, 183, 186
Conrad, Barnaby: *Matador*, 88
Cooke, Alistair, 94
Corn is Green, The, 183
Crawford, Cheryl, 88
Cromwell's Pharmacy/ Drugstore, New York, *80*, 81, 94, 137
Crowther, Bosley, 131, 200, 206
Crumpacker, Sanger, 61, 62
Culver City police department, 147
Custer, Robert, 77

Daily Variety, 200
Dalton, David, 220
Damone, Vic, 120
D'Amore, Patsy, 10
Danger, 94, 109, 126
Davalos, Richard, *105*, 106, *107*, 110, 115, 129
Davis, Jim, 33
Davis, Marion, 26
Davis, Sammy, Jr., 182
Day, Doris, 171
Deacy, Jane, 78, 88, 90, 93, 109, 110, 126, 183
Dean, Cal, 141
Dean, Charles, *24*, *29*, 52, 183
Dean, Emma, *27*, *28*, 28, *29*, 34, 52, 141, 183
Dean, Ethel, *45*, 47, 57, 62, 83, 110, 195
Dean (née Wilson), Mildred, 19, *20*, 20, *24*, 24, 25, 27-8, 29
Dean, Winton, 19, *20*, 20, *24*, 24, 25, 27, 28, 30, *31*, 32, *45*, 47, 51-2, 57-8, 59, 62, 67, 83, 90, 109-10, 183, 195
De Niro, Robert, 214
Denver Zephyr (train), 41
Depp, Johnny, 214
Derek, John, 129
Desirée, 123
Detroit, 23
DeWeerd, Reverend James, 46-7, 51, 61, 64, 77, 78-9, 195, 196, 207
Dickens, Charles: *The Pickwick Papers*, 41
Dillinger, John, 23
Dior, Christian, 44
Doan, Reverend Zeno, 24
Dr No, 129
Doran, Ann, 151, 200
Douglas, Kirk, 117, 120
Draesemer, Isabel, 68, 78
Dreiser, Theodore, 23
An American Tragedy, 79, 166
DuBois, Roland, 19, 20
Duffield, Brainard: *Mooncalf Mugford*, 37
Dunham, Katherine, 94, 137
Durant, Will, 66
Dylan, Bob, 211, 219

Earlham College, 51
East of Eden, 102, 103, 106, 109, 112-15, 117, 119, 120, 123, 125, 129, 131, 133-4, 138, 141, 143, 151, 186, 195, 199, 203, 215, 231
Eastwood, Clint, 214
Edge of the City, 87
Ed Sullivan Show, The, 207
Erickson, Leif, 73
Eschrich, Dr. William, 202
Eshleman, Richard: *The Axe of God*, 72

Fairbanks, Jerry, 68, 72-3
Fairmount:
description of, 33
JD's early years in, 24-5, 27, 30-53
JD's return visits to, 78, 89, 90, 139-41
JD's funeral held in, 195-6
memorial activities, 207-9, 215
brief mentions, 23, 134
Fairmount Friends Church, *194*, 195, *197*
Fairmount High School:
JD attends plays at, 34
JD's schooldays at, 19-20, 36-52
Fairmount Historical Museum, 20, 33, 44, 139, 208, 209
Fairmount News, The, 41, 43, 53, 58, 195
Family Theater Presents, 72-3
Famous Artists, 110
Feist, Byron, 24
Ferber, Edna, 149, 165, 181, *181*, 195

Fisher, Eddie, 120
Fixed Bayonets!, 76, 231
Foote, Cone, and Belding, 76, 78
Ford, Constance, 92, 93
Ford, Glenn, 200
Ford's Theatre, Washington, 49, 51
Foreman, Carl, 64
Forest Lawn Cemetery, Glendale, 59
Franklin, Sidney, 77
Fuller, Samuel, 76

Galey, F. Stanton, 49
Garcia, Lucy, 177
Garner, Jerry, 43
General Electric Theater, 126
Gentleman's Agreement, 103
Ghost and Mrs Muir, The, 154
Giant, 10, 15, 59, 149, 162, 165-83, 186, 194, 195, 200, 206, 207, 211, 233
Gide, André, 94
Gielgud, John, 65, 89
Ginsberg, Henry, 15, 195
Glendora, 62, 66
Glenn, Barbara, *89*, 94, 95, 110, 117, 129, 216, 219
Godfather, The, 65
Goetz, Ruth and Augustus, 94
Googie's coffee shop, 110, 112, 134, 149, 151
Goon with the Wind, 38
Gordon, Michael, 92
Grant Memorial Park Cemetery, 29
Graziano, Rocky, 183, 212
Grinnage, Jack, 161
Group Theater, 88, 103
Guinness, Alec, 10-11
Gunga Din, 166
Gunn, Billy, 89
Gypsy, 154

Haley, Bill, 200
Hallmark Hall of Fame, 87
Hallmark Playhouse, 76
Hamlet, 60
Happy Land, 154
Harding, Bill, 66, 219
Harding, Major, 66
Hardy, Pat, 216
Harris, Julie, 106, *107*, 110, *113*, 114, *122*, 123, *123*, 124, 125
Hart, Moss, & Kaufmann, George S.: *You Can't Take It With You*, 38-9
Harvey, Reverend Xen, 195-6
Has Anybody Seen My Gal, 77, 231
Hawks, Howard, 79
Head, Hearts, Hands, and Health organization (4-H), 44, 46
Hearst, William Randolph, 26
Hector's cafeteria, New York, 80
Hemingway, Ernest, 77
  Death in the Afternoon, 193
Hepburn, Audrey, 120
Hickman, Bill, 11, 15, 183, 186
Hill Number One, 73
Hixon, Dianne, 59, 61
Hoffman, Dustin, 88
Holden, William, 120
Hollister, 116
Hollywood, 64, 65, 73, 76, 109, 110, 129, 133, 149, 212
Hollywood Reporter, The, 129, 200, 206
"Hoosiers", 23

Hoover, J. Edgar, 23
Hope, Bob, 34
Hopper, Dennis, 161, 167
Hopper, Hedda, 44, 73, 203
Horn and Hardart, 80
Houseman, John, 148
House Un-American Activities Committee, 64, 103
Hudson, Rock, 77, 149, 165, 169, *171*, 171, 173, 174, 176, 177, 181, 206
Hunter, Otie V., 11
Hussey, Ruth, 73
Hutton, Barbara, 12

Immaculate Heart School, 73
Immoralist, The, 94-5, 100, 102, 109
In a Lonely Place, 147, 148
Indiana:
  description of, 23
  JD's family background and early years in, 19-25, 28-53
  see also Fairmount; Indianapolis; Marion
Indiana University, 62
Indianapolis, 23, 78-9
Indianapolis 500 (Indy 500) motor-racing event, 23, 46, 162
Inge, William: *Picnic*, 104
Inside Daisy Clover, 154
I Remember Mama, 81
Iroquois Hotel, New York, 79, 93

Jackson, Anne, 109
Jackson, Cyril, 94, 137
Jacobs, W.W.: *The Monkey's Paw*, 38
James Dean Gallery, 208
James Dean Memorial Foundation, 207-8
James Dean Memorial Scholarship Trust, 208
Jerry's Bar, New York, 80-1, 87, 137
Johnny Guitar, 147, 148
Johnson, Georgann, 128
Jonesboro, 24
Jourdan, Louis, 94, 95
Junior Miss, 74
Jurado, Katy, 216

Kardell, Lili, 126, 216
Karloff, Boris, 38
Kaufman, George S., & Hart, Moss: *You Can't Take It With You*, 38-9
Kazan, Elia, 64, 65, 73, 79, 88, 95, 102, 103, *103*, 104, 106, 109-10, 114, 115, 120, *122*, 122, 123, 125, 129, 131, 148, 153, 154, 219
Kendall, Kenneth, 151, 202
Kennedy, Arthur, 92, 93
Kerr, Walter F., 92, 95
Keystone Kops, 26
Kinescope, 93-4
King and I, The, 207
Kitt, Eartha, 94, 137, *138*
Knock on Any Door, 148
Korean War, 51, 76-7
Kraft Television Theater, 87, 94
Ku Klux Klan, 23

Ladd, Alan, 166
Ladykillers, The, 11
Lake Arrowhead, 59
Landau, Martin, *86*, 88, *89*, *96*, 215
Lassie Come Home, 171
Leach, Barbara, 39
Leaving Las Vegas, 215
Left-Handed Gun, The, 183
Leigh, Vivien, 79

Leslie, Joan, 73
Leven, Boris, 165
Levy, Ralph, 81
Lewis, Jeanetta, 68, 74
Lewis, Jerry, 77, 78
Life, 133, 136, 143, 155
Lincoln, Abraham, 49, 51
Lindner, Dr. Robert, 147
Lockhart, Gene, 73
Loehr, David, 205, 208
Long, Beverly, 68, 161
Longmont, 41, 42
Lorca, Arlene (Sacha), 94
Los Angles, 26, 53, 110, 171, 206
Los Angeles Examiner, 131
Los Angeles Times, 60
Louis Shurr Agency, 88
Lover Come Back, 171
Lucci, Jerry, 80
Luce, Henry, 136
Lukas, Paul, 129
Lumet, Sidney, 87
Lust for Life, 207
Lux Video Theatre, 87

Macbeth, 67-8
McCambridge, Mercedes, 167, *168*
McCarten, John, 206
McCarthy, Glenn, 165, 167
McCarthy, Jim, 42
McCullough, Clyde, 89
McDowall, Roddy, 73
McKinley Elementary School, Santa Monica, 27
McPherson, Elizabeth ("Bette"), 48, 49, 58-9
McQueen, Steve, 214
MacRae, Gordon, 102
Madison-Grant High School, 208
Madman's Manuscript, A, 41
Magnificent Obsession, 171
Magnum, 133
Malick, Terrence, 215
Mama, 81
Mangan, Dick, 62
Manhattan Melodrama, 23
Mann, Daniel, 95
Mann, Delbert, 203
Manners, Dorothy, 131
Marfa, 165, 176-7, 181, 182
Marion, 20, 23, 24, 28, 29, 33, 64
Marion College of Dance and Theatrical Arts, 25
Marion High School, 39
Martin, Dean, 77
Martin Kane, Private Eye, 86
Marty, 87, 203
Massey, Raymond, 113, 115, 125, 125, 129, 220
Mead, Margaret, 66
Mellor, William, 173, 176
Men, The, 64, 65
Men are Like Streetcars, 78
Mendocino, 112, 113
Meredith, Burgess, 126
Method, the, 65, 79, 80, 88-9, 166, 216
  see also Stanislavsky technique
Methodists, 24, 46
Mexicali, 77
MGM, 116, 126, 183, 200
Michigan, 23
Mighty Joe Young, 120
Mili, Gjon, 133
Miller, Henry: *Tropic of Cancer*, 72
Miller, Jeanette, 186

Miller Playhouse Theatre Guild, 58
Mineo, Sal, 151, 156, 158, *161*, 161, 200
Minnelli, Vincenti, 126
Miracle on 34th Street, 154
Moffitt, Jack, 129, 200
Monkey's Paw, The, 38
Monroe, Marilyn, 20, 209
Mooncalf Mugford, 37
Moore, Terry, 120, *120*
Moretti, Maria, 199
Morrison, Marilyn, 216
Morrow, Vic, 200

Nash, N. Richard: *See the Jaguar*, 92-3
National Forensic League, 39, 41, 53
National Safety Council, 184
National Velvet, 171
NBC, 88, 94
Newman, John Henry, 51
Newman, Paul, 104, *104*, 106, 117, 183, 212
New York:
  JD decides to go to, 73, 78
  JD in, 79-95, 100, 126, 136-8
  premiere of *East of Eden*, 129
  premiere of *Giant*, 206
  premiere of *Rebel Without a Cause*, 199
  brief mentions, 64, 65, 134, 147, 207
New York Daily Mirror, 129
New York Daily News, 92-3
New Yorker, 206
New York Herald Tribune, 92
New York Post, 93
New York Times, 131, 200, 206
Nicholson, Jack, 214
No Sad Songs for Me, 154
Nose, India, 32
Nurmi, Maila (Vampira), 110, 112, 201, *201*

Oklahoma!, 102
Olivier, Laurence, 65, 89
Omnibus, 94
On the Waterfront, 65, 102, 103
Ophelios, 61
Ormsby, Robert, 207
Orr, William, 100
Osborn, Paul, 102
Our Hearts Were Young and Gay, 37-8
Our Town, 207
Owen, Gene Nielson, 59-60, 61, 62, 67, 219

Pacino, Al, 215
Page, Geraldine, 88, 94, 137
Palmer, Betsy, 94, 216
Palm Springs, 155, 187
Panavision, 173
Panic in the Streets, 103
Parade magazine, 149
Paramount, 79
Park Cemetery, Fairmount, 141, *141*, 196, 207, *207*
Parker, Louis N., 38
Pasadena, 61
Paso Robles, 12, 15, 196
Peacock, Myron, 32
Penn, Arthur, 183
Penn, Sean, 214
People magazine, 215
Pepsi-Cola commercial, 68, 71, 78
Peyton, Father Patrick, 73
Philadelphia, 92
Philco TV Playhouse, 126
Picnic, 104
Pierangeli, Mrs., 120
Pillow Talk, 171
Pinky, 103
Place in the Sun, A, 79, 80, 166, 171, 174
Platt, Ed, 158
Poe, Edgar Allan: *Telltale Heart*, 60
Poitier, Sidney, 200
Pound, Ezra: *Women of Trachis*, 109
Presley, Elvis, 20, 209

Quakers, 24, 30, 32, 208
Quality Street, 166
Quinn, Anthony, 207
Quinn, Frank, 129

Rainmaker, The, 137
Ray, Nicholas, 133, 147, 148, *148*, 153, 155, *155*, 158, 161, 162, 199, 214, 219
Rebel, The, 202
Rebel Without a Cause, 58, 68, 126, 141, 147, 149, 151-62, 175, 176, 184, 199-200, 201, 211-12, 215, 220, 232
Red River, 79
Reed, Lou, 219
Rehearsal Club, 83
Reseda, 62
Reventlow, Lance, 12
Reynolds, Debbie, 120
Richardson, Ralph, 65
Riley, James Whitcomb, 23
Robe, The, 73
"Rock Around the Clock", 116, 200
Rockwell, Norman, 33
Rodgers and Hammerstein, 79, 102, 207
Romance of Scarlet Gulch, 58
Romeo and Juliet, 147
Romeo's, New York, 80
Roosevelt, President, 32
Rose, Billy, 94, 95
Rose, Reginald: *Twelve Angry Men*, 87
Rosenman, Leonard, *86*, 94, 109, 125, 200
Ross, Harold, 79
Roth, Beulah, 186
Roth, Sanford, 11, 15, 186
Royalton Hotel, New York, 93

Sabrina, 120
Sachs, Arlene, 216
Sailor Beware, 77, 78, 110, 231
Saint-Exupéry, Antoine de: *The Little Prince*, 77-8, 87
St Louis World's Fair, 33
Salinas, 11, 113, 186
San Bernardino National Forest, 59
San Fernando Valley, 26
San Luis Obispo County, 196, 198
Santa Barbara, 68, 162, 183, 187
Santa Monica, 26, 26, 27, 30, 57, 66, 71
Santa Monica City College:
  JD as student at, 52, 57-62
Santa Monica Mountains, 26, 194
Santa Monica Theater Guild, 62
Sardi's, New York, 95
Sartre, Jean-Paul, 129
Saturday Evening Post, The, 33
Saturday Review, 206
Schatt, Roy, 94, 96, 136, 212
Scott, George C., 88
Scott, Toni Lee, 149, 151
Screen Actors Guild (SAG), 71
Searchers, The, 154
See the Jaguar, 92-3
Seinfeld, 93
Selective Service System (SSS), 47, 77
Send Me No Flowers, 171
Sennett, Mack, 26
Shakespeare, William, 60
Shane, 166
Shearer, Lloyd, 149
Sheen, Martin, 214, 215
Sheldon, James, 81, 88
Sheridan, Elizabeth (Dizzy), 83, 86, 87, 88, 89, 90, 92, 93, 216, 219
Sheridan, Frank, 86
Sheridan, Mrs., 87
She Was Only a Farmer's Daughter, 61-2
Shulman, Irving, 147
Shumlin, Herman, 95
Sidney, Steffi, 161
Sigma Nu, 66, 68, 71, 219
Silver Chalice, The, 106, 117, 119
Simmons, Jack, 112, 156, 195
Sirk, Douglas, 77, 171
Skinner, Cornelia Otis, and Kimbrough, Emily: *Our Hearts Were Young and Gay*, 37-8
Somebody Up There Likes Me, 106, 183, 212
Something's Got to Give, 209
Sophocles: *Trachiniae*, 109
Spacek, Sissy, 215
Splendor in the Grass, 154
Spotlight, 67
Springsteen, Bruce, 219
Stanislavsky tecnique, 64, 88, 216
  see also Method, the
Starkweather, Charlie, 215
Stars over Hollywood, 76
Steiger, Rod, 87
Steinbeck, John, *102*, 102, 104, 129
Stern, Stewart, 147, 156
Steve Allen Show, 207
Stevens, George, 79, 149, 162, 165, 166, 166, 171, 173, 176, 181, 182, 186, 194, 200, 206, 220
Stock, Dennis, 133-45, 145, 155, 195, 196
Strasberg, Lee, 73, 88
Streetcar Named Desire, A, 64, 65, 79, 102, 103
Studio One, 86-7, 94
Sunset Boulevard, 156
Swing Time, 166

Tarkington, Booth, 23
Taylor, Elizabeth, 79, 149, *164*, 165, 166, 169, *170*, 171, *173*, 173-4, 177, 182, 183, 186, 194, 195, 206
Teahouse of the August Moon, The, 126
Texas, 165 *see also* Marfa
There's One Born Every Minute, 171
They Live by Night, 147, 148
Tijuana, 68, 77
Time, 129, 206
Toomey, Regis, 73
Tomorrow is Forever, 154
Tree Grows in Brooklyn, A, 148
Truman, President Harry S., 49
Turnupseed, Donald, 12, 14, 196, 197, 198-9
Twelve Angry Men, 87
Twentieth Century Limited (train), 79

UCLA, 52, 58, 62, 66, 67, 72, 73, 74, 77
Undercover Man, 73
Uris, Leon, 100, 147
US Post Office, 204
US Steel Hour, 94

Valentino, Rudolph, 209
Vampira (Maila Nurmi), 110, 112, 201, *201*
Van Fleet, Jo, *112*, 113, 129

Van Patten, Dick, 81
Variety, 206
Villa Capri restaurant, 10, 182
Viva Zapata!, 102, 103
Voice of America, 148
"Voice of Youth", 39
Vonnegut, Kurt, 23

Wagner, Robert, 154
Wallace, Lew, 23
Wallach, Eli, 108, 109
Warhol, Andy, 192, 219
Warner, Jack, 102, 129, 151
Warner Brothers, 11, 15, 79, 100, 109, 110, 115, 126, 147, 149, 158, 165, 183, 194, 199, 200
Washington, school visit to 47, 49, 51
Watts, Richard, Jr., 93, 95
Weaver, Paul, 43
Web, The, 86
Welles, Orson, 79
West Los Angeles Veterans' Administration Center, 27
West Side Story, 154
West Ward Elementary School, 32
Weutherich, Rolf, 11, 14, 14, 15, 186, 199
White, Christine, 88, 93, 216
Whitmore, James, 73, 78, 219
Wilder, Alec, 79, 92
Wilder, Billy, 120, 156
Wilder, Thornton: *Our Town*, 207
Wilding, Michael, 165
Wild One, The, 116, 212
Williams, Emlyn: *The Corn is Green*, 183
Williams, Tennessee, 92
A Steetcar Named Desire, 64, 65, 79, 103
Wills, Beverly, 74, 216
Wills, Chill, 176
Winslow, Ansel, 30
Winslow, Ida, 30
Winslow, Joan (later Joan Peacock), 25, 27, 28, 30, 32, 52, 195
Winslow, Joseph, 30
Winslow, Levi, 30
Winslow, Marcus, 25, 28, 30, 30, 32, 43, 44, 51, 52, 90, 141, 183, 195, 196, 207
Winslow, Marcus, Jr. ("Markie"), 28, 32, 50, 52, 90, 110, 141, 142, 143, 183
Winslow (née Dean), Ortense, 20, 22, 24, *25*, 25, 28, *30*, 30, 32, 34, 51, 90, 141, 183, 195
Winslow, Walker, 30
Winslow farm, 18-19, 25, 30, 30, 32, 208
Withers, Jane, 177, 177
Women's Christian Temperance Union (WCTU), 32, 34, 36
Wood, Natalie, 126, 131, 146, 151, *154*, 154, 155, *156*, 156, 158, 161, 200
Worth Evans Ranch, 165
Wright, Frank Lloyd, 148
Written on the Wind, 171

You Can't Take It With You, 38-9
Young, Gig, 15, 184
Young and Rubicam advertising agency, 81

Zinnemann, Fred, 64, 65, 102

Picture credits

The images collected for this book have been predominantly sourced by the archivist David Loehr through his unique collection, together with many family photographs provided by the James Dean Estate.
The nature of photography within the Hollywood studio system was that many publicity stills were released for free editorial use with the associated photographic credits not provided. We acknowledge the pioneering photography of Sid Avery, Floyd McCarty, Richard Miller, Roy Schatt, Sanford Roth, Dennis Stock and Frank Worth, and we would be pleased to rectify any omissions or inaccuracies in future editions.

American Legends: Ky Dy 217

© AmericanPostcardArt.com 2004: 23, 26(b)

© The Andy Warhol Foundation for the Visual Arts, Inc./ARS, NY and DACS, London 2004: 192

TM 2004 James Dean by CMG Worldwide, Inc. www.JamesDean.com: 5, 6-7, 11, 12(t), 12(b), 16, 17, 18, 20, 21, 21(inset), 22, 24(t), 24(m), 24(b), 25, 26(t), 27(t), 27(b), 28, 29(t), 29(b), 29(r), 30(t), 31, 32, 35, 36, 37(b), 40, 42, 45, 50, 51, 52, 53, 54, 55, 56, 58, 59, 60, 63, 69, 70, 80, 81, 83, 84, 85, 86, 89(t), 90, 91, 92, 95, 96(t), 96(b), 97, 108, 119, 126, 127, 151, 152(inset), 169, 173, 182, 183, 185(b), 186, 188(inset), 191, 194, 196, 197, 198, 213, 220, 221, 223, 230, 240

The Kobal Collection: 65 John Engstead, 79, 115 Warner Bros, 116(l) MGM, 116(r) Columbia, 125 Warner Bros, 156(b) Warner Bros, 158 Warner Bros, 176 Warner Bros

The David Loehr Collection: 1, 8, 9, 10, 33, 34(t), 34(b), 37(t), 38, 39, 41, 43, 44 Nelva Jean Thomas, 47, 48, 64, 66, 67, 72, 74, 75, 76, 77, 78, 82, 89(b), 93, 94, 98, 99, 101, 102(b), 103 Warner Bros, 104 Warner Bros, 105 Warner Bros, 107 Warner Bros, 110, 111 Warner Bros, 112-113 Warner Bros, 113(b) Warner Bros, 114 Warner Bros, 117 Warner Bros, 118 Warner Bros, 118(inset) Warner Bros, 120, 121 Warner Bros, 122 Warner Bros, 123 Warner Bros, 124 Warner Bros, 128, 129, 130(l), 130(r), 130-131, 145(t), 146 Warner Bros, 148(l) Warner Bros, 148(b) Warner Bros, 149 Warner Bros, 150 Warner Bros, 152 Warner Bros, 153(l) Warner Bros, 153(r) Warner Bros, 154 Warner Bros, 155 Warner Bros, 156(t) Warner Bros, 157 Warner Bros, 159 Warner Bros, 160 Warner Bros, 161(t) Warner Bros, 161(b) Warner Bros, 163 Warner Bros, 164 Warner Bros, 166(b) Warner Bros, 167 Warner Bros, 168 Warner Bros, 170 Warner Bros, 174 Warner Bros, 175(t) Warner Bros, 175(b) Warner Bros, 177 Warner Bros, 180 Warner Bros, 181 Warner Bros, 187, 188 Warner Bros, 189, 199, 200, 201, 202(t), 202(b), 203, 204, 205(t), 205(bl), 205(br), 206 Warner Bros, 207(t), 207(b), 209, 210, 211(t) courtesy of the US Postal office, 211(b), 212, 214, 222, 231(t), 231(m), 231(b), 232(t), 232(b), 233(l), 233(r)

MPTV.net: 2-3 Bob Willoughby, 112 Floyd McCarty, 166(t) Sid Avery, 172 Sid Avery, 178-179 Richard Miller

© 1987 Oscar for Jimmy, Inc./Seita Ohnishi; photo by Sanford Roth: 14, 15(t), 15(b), 184, 185(t), 218, 228

George Perry: 13(t), 13(b), 30(b), 208

© Dennis Stock/Magnum Photos: 132, 135, 136, 137, 138, 139, 140, 141, 142, 143(t), 143(b), 144

Topham Picturepoint: 102(t)

Robert Middleton: 145(b)

Photo by Aaron Levin/Courtesy of Steve Yeager: 190

The author would like to thank the following people:

Without the co-operation, encouragement, and sustained support of Marcus Winslow Jr and the James Dean Estate this book would not have happened. He disclosed to us written materials and photographs that have never before been seen outside the family, and devoted many hours to discussing his cousin, who to him was like a favorite brother. Gratitude is also due to his sister, Joan Winslow Peacock.

At CMG in Indianapolis Mark Roesler, Jamie Maslanka, Dominic Lizama, Chris Dixon, and Cris Piquinela opened many doors, provided a wealth of photographs from their Legends Archives, and generally oiled the progress of the book. The reader can find more information on the official James Dean web site at www.jamesdean.com.

In Fairmount David Loehr not only fulfilled the role of archivist with extraordinary skill, opening up his outstanding and unparalleled collection of James Dean photographs, publications, and memorabilia which were to be the principal visual source, but also arranged interviews with citizens of Fairmount who knew James Dean, particularly his high-school team mate and later pall-bearer Bob Pulley, and Mildred Carter, widow of Marvin Carter, owner of the Indian Motorcycle shop at Back Creek. Gratitude is also due to the Fairmount Historical Museum, with its unique collection of Deaniana, much of it lent by the Winslow family, the Back Creek Friends Church, and the Park Cemetery. The new James Dean Gallery in Marion, Indiana which opened in May 2004 is the main repository of David Loehr's expanding collection. Trace Poulson provided stills photography. More information about the gallery can be found at www.jamesdeangallery.com.

Gratitude is also due to Warner Bros. in Burbank, California for their participation and support of the book, and in particular to Brian Jamieson at Warner Home Video has provided boundless enthusiasm and constant assistance in the project, as has Brian's remarkable assistant Marcella Mparmeris. Leith Adams, the Warner archivist, Julie Heath, Director of Clip Licensing at Warners, and Randi Hokett of the Warner Bros. collection at the University of Southern California organized the scrutiny of James Dean materials held by the archive.

Kip Brown, creator of the James Dean Timeline, has devoted many years to discovering fresh information about James Dean, and his awareness is unrivalled. He acted as an admirable, efficient, and all-knowing editorial consultant. William ("Bill") Bast who probably knew Jimmy better than anyone still alive was an eloquent, helpful informant.

Dennis Stock in London and Connecticut devoted considerable time to discussing his friendship with Jimmy, and not only gave his permission to reproduce his extraordinary photographs, but freely advised on the manner in which the should be used. Fran Morales his agent at Magnum most efficiently dealt with the paperwork.

Both Lisa Dubisz at MPTV and Dave Kent at The Kobal Collection have been generously supportive of the project.

Seita Ohnishi very kindly provided the important photographs by Sandford Roth, and I appreciate the help given by his attorney Yuji Mitani.

My gratitude as ever is due to my very dear friends Dr Norman Friedmann and Dr Irene Kassorla of Beverly Hills, whose exceptional wisdom, constant support, and generous hospitality helped this project to achieve fruition.

For Palazzo Editions, Colin Webb, the mainspring of Palazzo, conceived and enabled the book to be produced, devolving his unique experience and expertise from four decades of visual publishing, and was ably assisted by Georgina Wills. That ultimately publishing is a family business is shown by the assistance of Victoria Webb in basic research and general editorial assistance, and by my son Matthew who, although born in the 1970s, has a remarkable affinity with the James Dean era, and applied a discerning eye to the process of picture selection. Sonya Newland displayed outstanding patience, thoroughness, diplomacy, and taste to the onerous job of editing and coordinating the book. On the production side my thanks are due to David Costa and his gifted design team of Sian Rance and Nadine Levy at Wherefore Art? who were responsible for the layout of the book. Susanne Hodgart contributed her outstanding knowledge of photographic resources, and at Dorling Kindersley Stephanie Jackson, Adele Hayward, Peter Luff, and Dawn Henderson gave their professional skill and dedication to the book.

Lastly, my wife Frances, with customary serenity and tolerance provided her unflinching devotion throughout the research, writing, and editing of the book, putting up without complaint my midnight working and constant travels to Indiana, Los Angeles, New York, and other places that were part of the life of James Dean.

London October 2004